Men and Money

Books by Paul Ferris

Reporting
The City
The Church of England
The Doctors
The Nameless: abortion in Britain today

Novels
A Changed Man
Then We Fall
A Family Affair
The Destroyer
The Dam

Paul Ferris

Men and Money

Financial Europe today

Hutchinson of London

HUTCHINSON & CO (*Publishers*) LTD
178–202 Great Portland Street, London W1

London Melbourne Sydney
Auckland Bombay Toronto
Johannesburg New York

First Published 1968

*This book has been set in Times,
printed in Great Britain on Antique Wove paper
by Balding & Mansell Ltd,
of London and Wisbech, and bound by
Wm. Brendon & Son Ltd, of Tiptree, Essex.*

9 0898401 0

Contents

Financial reporting is full of phrases like 'pounds were weak' and 'dollars were in demand.' These mean what they say, but the technicalities involved can be confusing. For a brief account of international money—what 'pounds' and 'dollars' mean when they are used as currencies between countries—see Chapter 11.

Where a sum of money is expressed in any currency but its own, it has usually been translated into U.S. dollars, which have become the international standard of comparison. To turn dollars into pounds, divide by 2·4; or divide by 12, then multiply by 5. To turn pounds into dollars, divide by 5, then multiply by 12.

A billion is one thousand million.

1 *Public Relations*

Once upon a time, when the world was comparatively young and finance seemed an elegant affair, men talked about money as they talked about their health—discreetly and with due regard for the proprieties. Making money might mean cutting competitors' throats, running banks and manipulating markets might demand hearts of stone and brains of ice, but the world where these things happened was essentially a private one, inhabited by a handful of people who operated their mysterious machinery in the belief that to be secretive was as indispensable as to be honest. The idea lingers everywhere; even the United States has large companies (Mars, Hughes Tool, the Reader's Digest Association) which have managed to stay in private hands, and use to the full the licence this gives them to withhold information.

In Europe the old order is more powerful. It's melting but it survives in many places. This is a book about the money-men of Europe, who have been steadily shuffling into the public gaze since the end of the second world war, and whose features are beginning to grow familiar as the financial sections of newspapers and business-type documentaries on television examine the mysteries that turn out to be not so mysterious after all.

The money-men often don't know what to make of it, beyond a vague idea that they are expected to say things to chaps with notebooks. In Amsterdam I went to see a man at the private bank of Pierson, Heldring & Pierson. This is an old-style partnership with unlimited liability. The nearest to a name-plate on the street was the monogram 'PHP' in frosted glass, and the banker said that they published no figures and solicited no deposits from the public. There was no such thing as an advertisement for Piersons; there wasn't even one of those shiny booklets with an embossed crest on the cover, containing an innocuous history of the firm up to a safe point in the past such as 1939, which some private banks now publish as a concession to the times. The banker remarked that when they and Chase Manhattan took a share in a Dutch bank, the Nederlandsche Credietbank—Piersons being involved to smoothe the deal and make the American move more acceptable to Dutch public opinion—the publicity was greater than they would have liked. Chase took 17½ per cent. of the Credietbank and Piersons took 7½ per cent., though my informant didn't say so. They had felt it was 'important not to be mentioned', but in the end it was inescapable. It was a pity. Why, then, I asked, in view of this dread of publicity, was he talking to me? 'I'm not telling you any secrets, am I?' he said. I suggested they would hardly be telling any secrets in advertisements, either. He gazed at the solemn dark furniture and changed the subject.

Much of the new willingness to talk is based on the sound principle that a polite interview need reveal nothing of importance. But the processes of publicity are insidious and soon roll back the frontiers of reticence. Once reporters and cameramen begin to trail in and out of banking parlours and finance ministries, 'no comment' becomes an inadequate response. Information-mindedness is catching. When I first went to the Bank of England, in 1959, I couldn't even discover the title of the person who saw me, and he made a point of saying that his intention in seeing me was to choke me off. The City, sure of its position as the best if not quite the biggest financial centre in the world, tucked away among shadowy lanes and gaunt architecture, had little time for commentators from outside. But things have changed—post-war buildings have appeared and so have post-war attitudes. In 1964 a B.B.C. television unit was making some films about the City, and met the expected difficulties in entering the Bank of England. Someone suggested writing to the then Governor of the Bank, the third Earl of Cromer, who had been (and now is again) a managing director of Baring Brothers, the merchant bankers. The

City's merchant bankers have been the most successful group of corporate money-men in Europe in the last twenty years, and it is no coincidence that some of them were being generous with information and gossip well before the other institutions. Their antennae picked up changes in the climate—the climate of business and the climate of public opinion.

Lord Cromer was written to and replied cordially, and before long the cameras were inside the Bank, he and other executives were being interviewed under the chandeliers, and the unit was allowed into the vaults to film rooms full of gold bars and packaged banknotes (accompanied, just in case, by a squad of Bank officials, in the ratio of two officials for each television man). Lord Cromer's cooperation torpedoed the old guard of nameless Bank officials who clung to the good old days, one of whom was heard muttering furiously under his breath as he watched the unit at work.

Changes at the Bank go beyond gestures to journalists. In 1959 the Bank's regular reports were meagre and much complained of by economists and politicians, who used to point out how much better a job they made of it at other central banks, such as the Bundesbank in Germany and the Federal Reserve in the United States. Today the Bank of England has mended its ways, and its quarterly reports are nothing to be ashamed of.

The next stage in publicity among bankers is more eye-catching, and is beginning throughout Europe, with Britain in the lead. A passive willingness to give information is being overtaken by an active desire to hand it out, in the good cause of making money. Banks whose advertising used to be confined to a slab of annual report on the same page as the stock market prices, set in the same tiny type, now hire advertising agents to prove how human and successful they are. What they want are the public's deposits. Money is increasingly in the hands of the non-rich, and at the same time it is being increasingly competed for by hire-purchase and other finance companies, building societies, savings banks and giro (or postal cheque) schemes. Pierson, Heldring & Pierson may have been able to resist the temptation, but banks that don't fall over themselves to get deposits are going to be an eccentric minority within a very few years. Mr Peters, partner in Conrad Hinrich Donner, merchant bankers in Hamburg with more than 170 years of trade-financing behind them, said simply that 'before the war, if someone had come in here with ten thousand Deutsche marks, my father would have told him to take it round to the Deutsche Bank. After the war, if anyone brought *five* thousand, he'd have said "Thank you very much."'

Among the liveliest exponent of the new methods is Hambros, the London merchant bank, which hired a public relations firm in the 1950s, and has graduated to relaxed appearances by directors on television, and Press conferences that are an entertainment in themselves. As reported by *The Times*, this is the chairman, Mr. Jocelyn Olaf Hambro, born 1919 (Eton, Trinity College, Cambridge, and the Coldstream Guards), answering a question about their interests in Greece: 'We've got a company which squeezes lemons jointly with Schweppes. It makes Bitter Lemon. The peasants are still bringing their lemons in and they're still being squeezed—the lemons, not the peasants.'

Hambros use a slightly different tone when soliciting money, as in a Press advertisement for Hambro Abbey Trust, a unit trust (in the U.S., a mutual fund), where the headline, 'Would *you* pit your investment wits against Hambro's team?' ran across the top of a photograph showing six stern-faced men, with an unsmiling Jocelyn Hambro in the middle, seated around a table—the Investment Panel, about to do its stuff on the Abbey Trust portfolio. The advertisement, which invited purchases down to a minimum of £100, was crammed with phrases like 'years of accumulated skill and expertise' and 'string of international contacts'. A later series of Hambro ads, aimed at earthy industrialists, featured sports like boxing and wrestling—'When the crunch comes', shouted the headline. There are still diehards who resent this big-drum approach in the City, but Hambros can point to a balance sheet total of more than £300 million, compared with less than £200 million a few years ago.

The most prominent new publicists are the deposit banks, known in Britain as clearing banks, which in ten years have completely changed their mood and approach to the public. Once lofty marble halls where a man with a hole in his sock would not only have felt uneasy but would have been *meant* to feel uneasy, they have been trying feverishly to make themselves more homely and approachable. They have unbent with fun pictures and jolly booklets. The District Bank has used Twiggy, the model, in its ads. The Westminster has been issuing cheques in pink, yellow, blue and green. Lloyds hoisted an illuminated cheque in Piccadilly Circus, being endlessly made out in neon writing to A. N. Other for £10. Before it merged with the Westminster, the National Provincial ('where people still manage to be people') had a daring ad. headlined 'What do you do with a bank manager who spends two evenings a week on the fiddle?' This featured the manager of a Soho branch who 'often spends a couple of evenings a week, not just playing a violin but making one', and suggested that to open an account with such an interesting man was 'no kind of ordeal whatsoever'. When the National Provincial's new head office in the City, a 30-storey tower, was opened by the Lord Mayor of London, the curtains were drawn in such a way as to display 'NP' on the outside in letters twelve storeys deep.

British banks still have a long way to go before they shake off their stern marble past, and their wildest fun-ventures fail to match such extremes of advertising as the flamboyant campaign staged in 1966 by the newly founded International City Bank & Trust Co. of New Orleans. This used what the bank called 'the basics of marketing', and went off with such a bang that it collected more than $23 million in deposits on opening day. For months before, nineteen lunches and receptions had been held for architects, estate agents, dentists, accountants and other professional groups. On the last five nights of the count-down there were black-tie receptions for groups who, as the marketing vice-president puts it, 'do not ordinarily receive invitations to such functions. These included barbers, taxicab drivers, labour unions, etc.' On opening day they had a brass band and a parade of vintage cars. Officials took taxis and gave $10 to every driver who mentioned the bank, and as the year went on, ads. exhorted 'Hurry! Bring Money!' Deposits passed $100 million by the end of 1966, and an ad. raved 'We Made It! Thanks, and a Happy New Year from New Orleans' Newest 100 Million Dollar Bank. (You've made it possible)'—though a year later deposits had fallen somewhat, and I.C.B. was an $84 million bank.

If the clearing banks would find this more than they could swallow, their advertising is still far ahead of that in most European countries. The Dutch, close to British practice in many ways, have some cheerful bank advertisements, and so do the Belgians. At the head office of the

Banque de Bruxelles, an ornate building behind a courtyard of swept gravel, they were displaying a poster of a happy young man with a bright orange face and a badge in his lapel inscribed 'Monsieur B. de B.', announcing that there were 7,000 like him in the 700 (since risen to 800) branches of the bank. An executive said that a few years previously he had suggested that the bank's advertisements make something of the fact that 'B.B.' for Banque de Bruxelles also stood for Brigitte Bardot; unfortunately his colleagues wouldn't have it, and now that the climate was improving, he supposed that Brigitte Bardot was getting a bit unfashionable.

The French, their big banks hungry for deposits, are moving rapidly towards improved public relations. The élite of smaller, snobbier banks is having to change. No less an institution than the Paris branch of the Rothschilds has reorganised itself, made some of its shares available to the public (while keeping the bank under family control), and announced that with its new name of Banque Rothschild it means to compete for deposits. A *New York Times* headline, condescending or possibly sarcastic, read: 'Rothschilds to do Business with the Common Man', and Baron Guy de Rothschild, head of the French branch of the many-rooted family, came straight to the point when asked at a Press conference why it was happening. 'We need money', he said.

Bankers in Italy, where the popular attitude to money-systems is comparatively backward, have barely begun on the road that will lead them eventually to brass bands and lit-up cheques. They can still be heard to say quaintly that 'we would not rely on a bank that advertised itself.' In Germany the banks have been curiously slow to hit the public with advertising, given the intense competition for deposits and the general sophistication of the system. At the Deutsche Bank, the largest there, I interviewed officials at one of these courteous but intimidatingly formal sessions around a shiny board-room table that Germans like to organise, and heard them say that while they naturally wanted to attract people's money, they used advertisements sparingly. They and their competitors clubbed together on television to put the case for banks in general as opposed to the powerful publicly-owned savings banks and giro system; the policy of the Deutsche Bank itself was 'not to advertise at all, except our balance sheet.' If they did more, they explained, then their competitors would do the same, and who could tell where it would all end? 'We would soon be down to the standard of cigarette advertising', they said. 'It may seem a little bit old-fashioned, but we haven't done so badly.'

It sounded an honest if unfashionable philosophy for the times, but it didn't last long after that. A manager at the Dresdner Bank, the Deutsche Bank's chief rival, described what happened a few months later. The Dresdner, traditionally more aggressive, had decided to improve its service to investors (German banks do the work of stockbrokers), and employees had been given special courses on how to deal with over-the-counter inquiries. A campaign to publicise the new approach was due to begin on a Monday, but at the end of the previous week, the Deutsche Bank got in first with an investor-directed campaign of its own. This infuriated them at the Dresdner, and also caused alarm, because the Deutsche Bank was advertising a more specific scheme for investment linked with life insurance. Some Dresdner executives wanted to do the same, and there were violent arguments before the non-specific faction won.

The Dresdner manager added that many people in his bank were unhappy at this open warfare, with its full-page newspaper ads. and magazine interviews, an uneasiness that was no doubt matched inside the Deutsche Bank, where speculation as to where it might all end had been given something to feed on. It is the kind of thing that will happen more and more over the next decade as a bank's anxiety to befriend the public forces competitors to go one better.

Much the same principle is at work among European industrial companies, whose reluctance to give financial information is steadily decreasing as the need to be nice to shareholders increases. Shares in U.S. companies are attracting European investors (with dozens of U.S. stockbrokers looking for business on the Continent), and the difference between standards of disclosure has become embarrassingly obvious. Europe's industries make only modest use of stock exchange borrowing by American standards. Bank loans and Government aid often take the place of an issue of securities to which the public and the institutions (insurance companies and the like) will subscribe. It isn't that Europeans save less, but that a lot of the money disappears into commercial and savings banks, or is channelled to the Government, and reaches the companies indirectly.

As companies are coming to need more investment—to expand, compete and pay higher wages—their appetite for new capital is growing uncomfortably fast. The need to attract investors' money is greater than ever before.

Years of bland company reports, in which the most interesting feature might be the chairman's comments on the political situation, are now beginning to catch up with the companies. Dr Claudio Segré,[1] the Italian economist who was a Common Market official before becoming a private banker in Paris, said in a speech that European companies' 'traditional reluctance to disclose information that would make it possible to appraise correctly their asset value and their profitability appears to have been a double-edged weapon, now that they have to convince the market that their prospects are not so bad after all.' When the Italian Stock Exchange was enjoying a boom a few years ago, an American investor asked his Italian adviser for a list of companies that gave the least information about themselves, so that he could make some speculative investments; his cynical theory was that Italian firms never gave information worth having unless they were in trouble and desperate to attract money, so that the less they said, the better were their prospects.

Dr Segré, who has had plenty of experience of the way European managements think, told me while he was still at E.E.C. headquarters in Brussels that 'every reform of company law includes or will include measures for higher standards of information, but these still aren't high enough. This is especially true in Italy, where it's bound up with the tax situation: companies have felt all along that disclosing more information could bring additional tax burdens. On the other hand, there's the pressure to move away from the family-owned type of concern, into more outward-looking organisations—pressure from international competition, pressure from American subsidiaries in Europe. All this is moving slowly—in some cases it's moving fast—but the changes will meet a lot of resistance all along.'

Big German, Dutch and Swedish companies are probably the most forthcoming in Europe, apart from the British, who are well ahead—

[1] Dr Segré was chairman of a group that produced an exhaustive E.E.C. report in 1966 on 'The Development of a European Capital Market'—the Segré Report.

though the general level is still lower than it is in the United States, where the Securities and Exchange Commission lays down standards of disclosure that make most European chairmen feel naked even to contemplate. But any shortcomings in countries like Britain and the Netherlands are trivial beside the reticence that's common elsewhere in Europe. They are reticent about profits and reticent about losses. The French have some prize examples of impenetrability, including Michelin & Cie, the big tyre and rubber manufacturers—still a suspicious family partnership, which 'admits' to an annual turnover of about $12 million, a ridiculously low figure. In Switzerland, where the country is too small to sustain large companies unless they do much of their business through foreign subsidiaries, prospectuses and annual reports suffer especially from lack of 'consolidation'—figures for the subsidiaries are not included with those for the parent company. 'If you believe their figures,' said a stockbroker from Geneva, 'they earn so little that they couldn't afford to have the annual report printed'.

A manager at a Dutch investment trust was leafing through the remains of the two-foot pile of solid information that arrives in the post every morning; it was a lot but it wasn't enough. He cited the case of 'very good Swiss-international companies' with the most respectable names, which fail to give a true picture of their worldwide operations. 'Swiss companies are very bad in this respect,' he said. 'The daughter companies outside Switzerland may be three or four times as big as the mother company, but their earnings don't get published. It is horrible for an Englishman, eh?' 'Shareholders' meetings in Switzerland are like being in church', said a Zurich banker. 'Nobody says anything.'

Another investment-trust manager voiced the kind of fear that thrives among investors when company secrecy is the rule; and especially in a place like Europe, where two world wars have trampled up and down, bringing savage inflation and mistrust of paper assets. 'We often see shares in a second-class company begin to rise a few weeks before a company reports', he said, 'and we know that people in that company, probably the managing directors, are aware of what the report will say, and that they are buying shares to sell later at a profit.'

Investors who live in the dark can hardly be blamed if they grow cynical about the market. But it is a type of cynicism that companies in need of capital can't afford to encourage. Egged on by government legislation that is hardening into an effective weapon in many countries, companies are beginning to show themselves to an interested public—joining the general shuffle towards the centre of the stage, where the light is better.

2 *Twenty-five Institutions*

The countries that carry real financial weight in Europe are Britain, Switzerland and the Common Market group—Germany, France, Italy, Holland, Belgium and Luxembourg. The backbone of their systems, separate and fiercely competitive yet interlocked by a common interest in their raw material, money, are the banks.

Auburn's *Comparative Banking* lists more than 400 'principal banks' in the eight countries. If all banks, banking cooperatives and little credit institutions are included, the total soars into thousands: Switzerland alone has more than 400; Germany has nearly 12,000. Of the world's 100 largest banks, ranked in terms of deposits by the *American Banker* magazine, twenty-nine are in the United States, forty-three in Western Europe. In addition, Europe, and in particular London, has been invaded by American and Japanese bankers, anxious to share in the Eurodollar market, which deals in dollars owned outside the U.S. by banks and businessmen.

Governments own some banks in some of the eight countries, and may have further control over the economy through the use of State credit institutions or holding companies that snatch up the public's money from under the bankers' noses, and lend it out again as the Government thinks best. Each country has its stock exchange, working with varying degrees of success against widespread popular suspicion of investment (the result of too many inflations and monetary disasters in the past) and the wiles of governments that want to raise the money and hand it out themselves.

But there are too many banks, markets, dealers, brokers, lenders, borrowers, investors and advisers to be summarised with much hope of combining detail with coherence. The following table lists twenty-five important financial institutions in Europe, including banks, investment trusts and State organisations. It isn't comprehensive and it isn't a list of the biggest or necessarily the best, but it gives some idea of what there is at the top.

Britain

BANK OF ENGLAND
Oldest central bank in the world. Nationalised 1946. Highly efficient technically, and successfully nurtures its august image outside Britain despite vicissitudes of sterling.

LONDON STOCK EXCHANGE
Second largest in the world (after New York), handling securities worth £100 billion, with a turnover of £38 billion a year (1967 figures). 3,300 stockbrokers, fast amalgamating into fewer, bigger firms. No direct Government control or supervision.

BARCLAYS/LLOYDS/MARTINS
New group of clearing (deposit) banks, formed by merger (subject to approval by Monopolies Commission) in 1968. Total deposits of more than £5,500 million make it easily world's largest bank outside United States, where three banks are larger.

S. G. WARBURG & CO.
Merchant bank, founded after second world war by German Jewish emigré from Hamburg banking family, S. G. (Now Sir Siegmund) Warburg. Imaginative, adventurous, rich. One of the leaders in organising long-term Eurodollar loans. Controlled by Warburg's Mercury Securities, with interests in insurance, metals, advertising.

BANK OF LONDON AND SOUTH AMERICA
One of British 'overseas' banks, based in London but oriented towards one area of the world—in this case, Latin America, where it is

politically as well as financially important. Most of its business is done in foreign currencies, and especially U.S. dollars; thanks to its chairman, Sir George Bolton, it was one of the first banks to see the possibilities in Eurodollar trading. In many ways it's a 'dollar bank' —perhaps the shape of things to come in the City.

Germany

BUNDESBANK
The most independent of Europe's central banks, a reaction against its manipulation by the Nazis. Germany's prosperity and strong foreign-exchange position help to give it authority. Dr. Otmar Emminger, in charge of overseas affairs, is a key figure in attempts to keep world money in good order.

DEUTSCHE BANK
Largest in the country. Well down the world league (around 25th) but predominant in Germany because it's a 'department store' bank, running investment trusts and (with other banks) controlling the stock market. Big holdings of industrial shares. Growing international business. Driving force after war, Dr. Hermann Abs, is now benevolent wise-uncle figure among Europe's bankers.

France

BANQUE NATIONALE DE PARIS
State-owned. Created in 1966 by a forced marriage between two of the deposit banks nationalised in 1945, arranged by then Finance Minister, M. Debré. Biggest bank on the Continent. Mainly domestic business.

BANQUE DE PARIS ET DES PAYS-BAS
The leading *banque d'affaires*, with interests throughout French industry, from cars to champagne. Branches all over Europe, subsidiaries in London and New York, investments worldwide. Man behind it is Jean Reyre, career economist and banker, now elderly but still firmly in control.

SERVICE DES CHÈQUES POSTAUX
The world's largest 'giro' system for making payments by postal transfer, without the use of cheques. Run by the State through 20,000 post offices.

CAISSE DES DÉPÔTS ET CONSIGNATIONS
A public institution with enormous deposits, mainly from savings banks (both State- and privately-owned), which it lends to the Government or puts into public works. With deposits of about $18 billion, growing all the time, it handles more funds than the 'Big three' French banks put together.

Italy

I.R.I.-ISTITUTO PER LA RICOSTRUZIONE INDUSTRIALE
The State holding company, set up in 1933, which controls hundreds of firms and most of the banking system. This gives the Government more direct influence over business than anywhere else in Western Europe. But I.R.I. and the private sector seem to co-exist quite happily.

CASSA DI RISPARMIO DELLE PROVINCIE LOMBARDE
One of the largest of Europe's many savings banks, which tend to be trusted by small savers more than the commercial banks. Deposits of more than $4 billion. A lot of the money goes into housing mortgages and Government bonds. Also does ordinary commercial business, and has a foreign department.

THE VATICAN
Assets unknown, but Italy's Finance Minister has estimated domestic shareholdings at $160 million. Worldwide shares might be worth ten times as much. Has its own bank and financial administration.

Belgium

SOCIÉTÉ GÉNÉRALE DE BELGIQUE
Holding company with large interests throughout Belgian industry. Linked with the leading bank, the Société Générale de Banque.

Badly hit when the Congolese nationalised their copper industry, seizing assets of Société Générale associates.

KREDIETBANK

Ranks third in the country, but is strong in Flemish areas, now becoming more powerful, largely as result of foreign investment around Antwerp. Subsidiary in Luxembourg, Kredietbank S.A. Luxembourgeoise, leads in finding ways of using the country and its convenient tax laws to organise international loans.

BANQUE EUROPÉENNE DE CRÉDIT À MOYEN TERME

One of several international banks formed recently to make medium-term (3–8 years) loans to European companies, using money borrowed in Eurodollar market. Head office in Brussels because it's a convenient centre. Eight banks in six countries participate: Société Générale de Banque (Belgium), Amsterdam-Rotterdam Bank (Netherlands), Banca Commerciale Italiana (Italy), Deutsche Bank (Germany), Crédit Lyonnais and Société Générale (France), Midland Bank and Samuel Montagu (Britain). Idea came from Louis Franck—nephew of a former Governor of Belgium's national bank—who is chairman of Montagu Trust, London merchant-banking and insurance group which is one-third owned by the Midland.

Luxembourg

ADELA INVESTMENT CO.

One of many investment companies registered in the Grand Duchy, where taxes are low and attracting foreign finance companies is a major industry. Adela, with its head office in Luxembourg and its operations office in Peru, invests in Latin America on behalf of a group of about 140 well-heeled shareholders who are all banks, industrial companies and finance houses.

Netherlands

ROBECO

An investment trust, based in Rotterdam but investing shareholders' money throughout the world, mainly in Europe and North America.

Associated trusts called Rolinco and Utilico. The largest international investment trust owned in Europe, with funds in all three worth $630 million.

Switzerland

UNION BANK OF SWITZERLAND
SWISS BANK CORPORATION
SWISS CREDIT BANK

The three leading banks, all of them showing only modest deposits by world standards, but important because of their role in taking money from firms and individuals in Europe and elsewhere, and lending it out again in the money markets of other countries. They also manage extensive portfolios of foreign shares for an international clientele.

THE PRIVATE BANKERS OF GENEVA, BASLE AND ZURICH

Although these are all separate firms, coming together now and then to form syndicates, they occupy a single place in most people's view of the financial hierarchy. Not more than fifteen or twenty are of much importance. Most of them are virtually investment bankers—almost glorified stockbrokers.

BANK FOR INTERNATIONAL SETTLEMENTS

Established in 1930 and based in Basle as a convenient centre, the B.I.S. has developed into a sort of central bank for the central bankers of Europe, with the U.S. attending but not actually joining. Invaluable as a talking-shop and meeting-place.

INVESTORS OVERSEAS SERVICE

A billion-dollar empire operated from Geneva by an American financial impresario, Bernard Cornfeld. I.O.S., controlled by a Panama company, is basically a mutual fund (in Britain, a unit trust) that invests in other mutual funds in the U.S. Thousands of salesmen sell door-to-door on the Continent—opening up an entirely new investment market under the noses of Europe's own money-men.

3 *The New Europe*

Nowhere on earth has so many sophisticated money-systems crowded side by side as Europe. But Europe dreams of a time when the differences will melt away. As the Common Market takes shape, the idea (if not the reality) of rigidly defined financial sovereignty is already becoming blurred. Business in general takes a more international view. It's fashionable to talk about 'the European company', with a legal framework acceptable to all the Common Market countries. There is no such thing at present, which makes things easier for the American corporations that have invaded Europe, since they can plan their strategy on a broader scale than their local competitors. But European industry is slowly forming larger units in search of wider markets. In the same way, and often for the same reason, money markets and money institutions are regrouping and coalescing. Not since the last century when new banks opened up in response to the industrial revolution has there been so much financial scurrying about, and there can never have been so many loud declarations by the bankers that today their eyes are fixed on world horizons.

The old band of crafty, aggressive banks with famous names always has been outward looking; these are the British merchant banks and the Continental *banques d'affaires*, which both correspond roughly to the American investment banks, except that the *banques d'affaires* own large shareholdings in industry. But Rothschilds, Lazards and the rest are small by modern standards. The deposit banks have the money, and now they are trying to energise themselves and be big and international, like the Americans. In addition, they hope that by being big they will be better able to compete for the public's money inside their own countries. There's a lot of competing to be done. On the Continent, Government agencies handle a high proportion of the man-in-the-street's money, either through savings banks or the dreaded post office giro.[1] One of the first signs that the British Post Office was becoming more commercial minded was the introduction of a giro in 1968, to the dismay of the banks, who immediately concocted a version of their own.

The result of these pressures has been to produce mergers and alliances among the deposit banks that are important for business but dull to observe, since it's difficult for anyone to make an ordinary commercial deposit bank sound like anything but a stony institution, full of clerks and pieces of paper, about as exciting as a filing cabinet. The typical senior deposit banker is a greyer figure than the typical executive from a merchant bank in London, a *banque d'affaires* in Paris or a private bank in Frankfurt. A deposit banker would argue that it's too much of a generalisation, but the other takes more risks, knows more people, does more travelling, is less concerned with routine, mixes more with industrialists and politicians, and is likely to be richer.

I was with a financial editor when the merger proposal between three British clearing banks, Barclays, Lloyds and Martins, was announced in 1968. He groaned at the thought of having to write columns about it, though in terms of cash and sheer size it was the biggest event for years in British banking. The proposal came soon after two other leading banks, Westminster and National Provincial, had merged to form the National Westminster. Other domestic mergers have been taking place throughout the Common Market.

[1] The first giro was in Austria, in 1883. Accounts are held centrally, and money is moved from one to another, as instructed by the customer, who fills in a form and posts it. Normally no interest is paid, and so the customer aims at a rapid turnover of money. The French, Germans, Swiss and Dutch are the Continent's most enthusiastic giro-users, with the Italians learning fast, and bankers expend much energy trying to tempt people to use either ordinary bank account s or their own giros. Because it manages the whole operation from within the same organisation, a post office giro has an advantage over competing systems run by an assortment of banks.

Internationally, alliances broke out all over Europe in 1967 in the form of merry friendships and tentative embraces that didn't quite seem to fit the character of the sober fellows who run the deposit banks. But this made them all the more significant: if the deposit banks were moving, anything might happen. No figure in finance is more determinedly international than the European banker who has just helped to father some grand institution with offices in six capital cities, and a title like 'International European Bank for Medium Term Commercial Credit'. The significance of 'medium-term credit' is that this is the period—from about three to eight years—not covered by the long- and short-term lending already in progress in the international money market, the Eurodollar market, which has been developing over the past ten years.

A stake in this Euro-market, with clients throughout European industry, was the chief object of these banking alliances. None of them were mergers and few involved anything so specific as an exchange of shares. The usual form was for a group of banks to form a company that could operate across frontiers, passing business from hand to hand. Among the resounding titles were the Société Financière Européenne, the International Commercial Bank, the Banque Européenne de Crédit à Moyen Terme and the Compagnie Internationale de Crédit à Moyen Terme. Large banks and some smaller ones from Britain and all the Common Market countries were involved; so were U.S. banks, including the Bank of America, American Express and Bankers Trust of New York.

Although they had positive objectives, these alliances suggested undercurrents of fear. They were part of a nervous response to the coming of bigness—the worldwide corporation with its sharp-eyed treasurer, always on the look-out for money at a fraction per cent. cheaper; the worldwide bank, able to shunt money and quote rates in many countries as part of a single operation. When people talk about banks and companies on this scale, they are usually thinking of the Americans. European bankers are always thinking of Americans. At Rome's Banca Nazionale del Lavoro, which is in a group with the Bank of America, a foreign manager looked over his spectacles and said, 'What are the origins of our Société Financière Européenne? The origins are that American firms come to Europe, and if we are not careful they crush us because they are so big. The new company will attempt to fight this situation. I don't mean *fight*, I mean *counter* it.'

Bankers were careful not to make their new alliances sound too powerful, in case it upset the balance of their existing relationships in other countries. The combination of rivalry and cooperation has always been one of the peculiarities of banking. Money-systems involve millions of transactions for millions of customers, who keep moving themselves and their goods from one country to another. The endless international merry-go-round of documents and phone calls works on confidence and survives only because banks, unlike people, can be trusted to transfer credit when they say they will. To keep it going there must be trustworthy bankers all over the place. A bank in Munich may suddenly need a bank in Valparaiso; a query on a document that arrives in New York may have to be answered by someone reliable in Vienna. Since no bank can be everywhere, loose associations have developed for mutual aid; we look after your clients in Britain, you look after ours in Italy: we push a bit of business your way in Australia and you do the same for us in Mexico.

This web of contacts is coming to look less appropriate, as financial competition increases across frontiers. But it is still important. London has about ten groups of 'overseas' banks, such as Barclays D.C.O. and the Australia and New Zealand Bank, with a chain of branches, mainly but not entirely in the Commonwealth. There are 4,500 of them in dozens of countries, relics of the days when Britain had an empire. But in all Western Europe outside Britain, London banks have only about fifty branches, many of them in holiday resorts and provincial towns. The system of 'correspondent' banks, or old pals, prevails among the clearing banks. The Midland, which has always been particularly keen on correspondents, has 1,200 of them, and the others have several thousand more. Even as expansionist a bank as Chase Manhattan says it wants to go on working with correspondents as well as enlarging its branch network and buying its way into local banks; altogether it uses 1,700 correspondents outside the U.S.

All this means that bankers feel they must describe any new international alliance in terms that don't tread on people's toes. I found bankers in Europe anxious to point out that their new creations couldn't possibly upset anyone; occasionally they said openly that they were afraid of losing business if they offended their old pals, usually they managed to imply that it was more a question of etiquette than profits. Professor Alberto Ferrari, general manager of the Banca Nazionale del Lavoro, said it was important not to think that by associating with Barclays of London, the Dresdner of Dusseldorf and the other partners in Société Financière Européenne, they were in any way prejudicing their excellent relations with everyone else. 'Our idea', he said, 'is to set up a child that will walk on its own. Our idea is not to set up a club.' The same phrase came from Mr Helmut Haeusgen, a managing director of the Dresdner Bank: 'There is no intention of setting up an exclusive club. We set it up for special purposes. It doesn't mean that we will not go into other fields with other banks.' There was, he said, 'complete polygamy in international business. International banks are not faithful or anything like that.' The result, he seemed to conclude hopefully, was that one could have the best of both worlds, competing but still being friends.

Some people doubt whether the two techniques can be reconciled so easily; others doubt whether, in any case, there is much point in these new alliances except perhaps as psychological rallying-points. 'I believe they have charming meetings', said a London merchant banker sarcastically. 'These new groups are like liners with outboard motors', said another. Both were expressing the contempt that men from foreign-oriented banks sometimes feel for the domestic deposit bank that is groping for broader activities.

Deposit banks will rarely admit that they can get out of their depth when they leave domestic for foreign business; 'international' has become a magic word, as indispensable to the fashionable banker as his plane tickets and Telex bookings to Hilton hotels, and I met only one deposit banker who was willing to question, openly and vigorously, the assumption that everyone was beginning to look outward and think European. He was a German, a senior figure at one of the largest banks, and he thought that in Germany they were looking inward and thinking German. He said he knew he was a heretic to think like that, and added that his remarks must not be attributed to him—he made it sound as though his fellow directors would stop him planehopping around Europe with his awful heresies, and sentence him to be a branch manager in Bavaria.

The truth about banks in Europe, he said, was that their profits, their past and everything about them emphasised that they were domestic institutions. Their heart was in the fight for their own country's deposits and in financing their own country's industry. 'The more I see of it,' he said, 'the more I think that international business is a sideline.' It was certainly true of German banks. He brushed aside Dr. Hermann Abs of the Deutsche Bank as an exception. A more usual state of affairs was the man who thought that by travelling for a few weeks each year in Africa and Asia, he had joined the new breed of world bankers.

He saw nothing wrong in being domestic-minded, but he objected to the pretence that it was otherwise. 'In our banks', he said, 'the overseas people never have a leading role, or they do domestic things in addition, as I do. In my own bank, the powerful people are the old traditional people, those who look after domestic credit and the Stock Exchange. That's the side where a man can make a career. There are many branches for him to manage. But on the international side it is more restricted, and in the end, you are always the second man. What is the quality of the people who are available? When I hear about these new multi-national institutions, I say, Tell me who you are appointing to work in them and I will tell you whether I am impressed. So far I am not impressed.'

Many deposit bankers would say he was living in the past, wallowing in the mentality that has trapped the big banker inside his own country, and left the richer international pickings to the more agile *banques d'affaires*. The filing-cabinet men are changing, seeking new partners and new alignments as part of the biggest financial upheaval, apart from wars and the 1930s crisis, this century. It has taken them a long time, but they are entitled to say they are on the move at last.

Common Market

A new generation of financial instruments and institutions is taking shape on supra-national lines. Formal financial unity within the Common Market is still far away; committees look at the multiplicity of individual markets and systems, report sadly on the lack of progress towards unity, and are succeded by more committees that do the same. But no bureaucrat invented financial Europe and it's unlikely that the bureaucrats will redesign it, at least by themselves. The coming together of financial Europe will be a stealthier process. When economic union finally arrives, it won't be a neat administrative invention; it will consist of people who want to buy, sell, borrow and lend as advantageously as possible, and they will use whatever suits them, in the Common Market or outside it.

The Common Market itself was set up in 1958 under the Treaty of Rome, with the object of integrating the economic resources of five major countries—Germany, France, Italy, Holland and Belgium—and a minor one, Luxembourg. Luxembourg is politically negligible and financially unimportant apart from its role as a tax haven (it doesn't even have a central bank), but it is tied to Belgium, with which it has a Customs union, and it fits easily enough into the structure.

The E.E.C. countries in general have prospered in the last twenty years, partly by their own efforts, partly thanks to the $12,800 million of U.S. Marshall Aid immediately after 1945, and U.S. industrial investment later on. At the end of 1966, $7,587 million was directly invested in the Common Market in the shape of factories, oil refineries, trading and financial companies, and so on; more than two-thirds of this has been invested since 1960.[2] Annual income per head within the E.E.C. is $1,260; this compares with $2,208 in Sweden (the highest in Europe), $1,446 in Britain, and $2,867 in the U.S.

There is plenty of competition among the Six, encouraged, on the whole, by the E.E.C.'s planners. Germany's influence may have been decisive here—both in France and Italy the Government controls the economy more directly and obviously, using a whole apparatus of credit institutes and State-owned banks, but neither country prospered as Germany, with its emphasis on free-enterprise, did in the early and mid 1950s. In creating the framework for a united Europe, the E.E.C.'s achievements so far include a Customs union which allows industrial goods to move freely between the Six without Customs duty being charged, and a common agricultural policy

[2] Total U.S. direct investment in Europe is $16,200 million, about the same as in Canada, and roughly three-tenths of the world total. Britain has more than any other European country, with $5,652 million; 44 per cent of this was invested before 1960.

which is centrally financed, though the details are not yet settled to everyone's liking. These are the most obvious results. Somewhere in the future there may be financial unity, but it's a long way off. Although 'the eventual abolition of tax frontiers' is one of the goals, the day when everyone's income tax within the Common Market is harmonised (a favourite word at E.E.C. headquarters in Brussels) is probably as distant as the day when the Six will use a common currency. Indirect taxation will come first, and a uniform type of sales-turnover tax, an 'added value tax',[3] should have been introduced into all countries in the Six by 1970, though to begin with the rates will be different.

The members of the Common Market, whose populations total more than 180 million, have their own monetary policies; they make their own budgets, adjust their own interest rates, and squeeze or unsqueeze the national economy as it suits them best: not without considering their neighbours, but without considering them first. In a true common market, capital will move freely, stock exchanges will work as one, taxation will be the same, and governments will co-ordinate their financial policies. Asked, in 1967, about the prospects for this kind of unity in the next few years, M. Robert Marjolin, then Vice President of the Commission, the E.E.C.'s chief executive body, would say only that 'I hope we shall make progress,' adding that by 1970 'we shall achieve a greater degree of coordination but there will still be six economic units working closely together.'

Nations, like people, care more about money than they care about almost anything else. 'When you get to monetary policy', said a sage American banker, who is delighted with European disunity because it makes his job easier, 'you really begin hitting the nerve-ends of policy. You get into the hard core of resistance to change. This is the point where countries draw back.'

A further complication is that Britain, now officially hell-bent on entering the Common Market[4] if its members in general and France

[3] Called 'TVA' on the Continent, this is a complicated tax on consumption of goods and services. It applies a levy to the 'added value' which (for instance) accrues to raw materials when they are turned into manufactured goods and sold.

[4] Also interested in membership are a group of European countries that, with Britain, form the European Free Trade Association. E.F.T.A., set up in 1960,

in particular will admit her, is in poor economic health. The problems of sterling—due partly to the ailing British economy, partly to the pound's peculiar status and duties, as described in Chapter 11—might become the problems of the E.E.C. London has the best financial machinery in Europe, but it also has the weakest currency. The pound has to be supported by loans from abroad, helped by expensively high interest rates that attract foreign money to London, and protected by an elaborate system of exchange control that the Bank of England operates on behalf of the Treasury with many private sighs and groans.

Exchange control aims to conserve a country's reserves of gold and foreign currency (a mild variety was practised in England as long ago as 1299, according to Lord Cromer). British firms are allowed to buy as much foreign exchange as they like in order to pay for imports, but not to build factories overseas; every application is scrutinised and many refused.

E.E.C. countries have only mild exchange controls, though they can be quickly reimposed when there's a national crisis, as in the case of France in 1968. Their industries can expand more easily in other countries. Their citizens can spend what they like when they go abroad, in contrast to the British, who are allowed £50 a year for pleasure, a constant reminder of straitened circumstances.

Eurodollars, Eurobonds

Financial Europe is still a collection of fragments, and the planners are patient men who are still finding out how the pieces should fit. Conscious planning isn't the only force at work. The American industrialists and bankers who have come to Europe are imposing a unity of their own, since it suits them, and seems only natural, to regard it as one place and not many. In particular, the dollar has provided Europe with the means to operate both a money market

comprises Britain, Sweden, Norway, Denmark, Switzerland, Austria and Portugal, with Finland as an associate. It has comparatively modest ambitions to reduce trade barriers, with no political intentions. A small permanent secretariat co-ordinates it from Geneva. E.F.T.A.'s population of 100 million is not much more than half that of the E.E.C., but its foreign trade—i.e. with places outside the group—approaches that of the Six. Annual income per head within E.F.T.A. averages $1,408, $150 more than in the Common Market.

(short-term borrowing and lending by banks) and a capital market (long-term money-raising by industry and governments) that serve every country at once. The E.E.C. is still dreaming about this. It has no common currency in which to run a money market, and each country's stock exchanges attend to capital-raising in a more or less parochial way.

Largely by accident, dollars in the hands of banks, corporations and individuals outside the U.S. have come to serve as a kind of common currency. These are the so-called Eurodollars, used throughout the world but linked especially with Europe because its financial skills are the best outside America, and its appetite for money is never satisfied.

There is no physical 'Eurodollar', and the Eurodollar market consists of the interplay of borrowing and lending between banks, industrial corporations and wealthy private investors. No central bank or authority controls it. The dealing is concentrated in London, whose merchant bankers were quick to snap up the business in the early days, but involves every money centre in Europe, and many throughout the world.

A Eurodollar, a word the purists hated at first, is a claim for a dollar, in the hands of someone outside the United States who doesn't want to transfer the money to America. The market began in the 1950s when American regulations fixed a maximum rate of interest that could be paid on dollars owned by non-Americans who deposited them back in the U.S. Dollar-owners complained that they wanted a better rate, and the idea evolved of lending them out to someone who would pay more.

The dollar was already the world's chief trading currency; the pound was in decline, and had just been given another push in the wrong direction by the Suez crisis of 1956. Because of America's spending overseas, billions of dollars were owned throughout the world, forming a pool of credit whose usefulness was only gradually realised. Plenty of pounds were in circulation, too, but they were not popular. The dollar was trusted (though later it came under suspicion, and many turned to gold). Eurodollars helped to fill the gap caused by sterling's decline from grace. According to Sir George Bolton of the Bank of London and South America, it was 'a conscious effort by a number of us to create a money market from the bits and pieces that were floating about. But it wasn't the act of a cabal: it was more a sort of osmosis.'

The Eurodollar market just grew, until now everyone is in it, Russians and Greeks, Italians and Irishmen. Some say it consists of as much as $20 billion, but no one can be sure because the same million dollars may pass through four or five hands before it reaches the ultimate borrower who changes it into his own currency.

Eurodollars whiz round the world, as invisible as air, in the form of credit transfers arranged by telephone and confirmed by Telex. They are continually being changed into and out of a score of national currencies, to meet the needs of borrowers and lenders in the countries involved. Without anyone having tried to devise the system, they have come to provide the basis for the world's first large-scale international money market. No group of economists and financial theorists would ever have sat down and agreed on such a system (the intransigent French no doubt would have found political objections to using dollars), and bankers like to point to it as an example of what free enterprise and the profit motive can achieve when capitalists are left to work things out for themselves. The same is true of a later development, the Eurobond market, through which governments and industrial companies (many of them subsidiaries of American firms) borrow money over longer periods by issuing bonds that are subscribed to in Eurodollars.

Both Eurodollars and Eurobonds are supra-national, in the sense that they owe their origin and existence to a world of 'international finance' whose whole is greater than its national parts. Sometimes the Eurobond borrower is an abstraction—neither country, city nor company. The European Coal and Steel Community, a unified market for coal and steel that was run by a 'High Authority' as part of the Common Market—it was set up in 1952 as the first piece of positive integration among the Six—has borrowed tens of millions of dollars against issues of Eurobonds.

When the borrower is something more recognisable, like the City of Copenhagen or Mobil Oil, it still isn't quite what it would be in other circumstances. The usual method of issuing the bonds is via a holding company set up in the accommodating little land of Luxembourg, which allows interest on the bonds to be paid net, instead of lopping off a 'withholding tax' at source, as most countries do. Withholding taxes are imposed by States, and the Eurobond market is Stateless. This suits the investors, who want to lay hands on the full amount of interest, so that even if they eventually pay tax, they have had the use of the money for that much longer. In practice, it's likely that many Eurobond investors never pay any tax on their interest; the securities are bearer bonds, not registered, and the owners are untraceable by tax authorities. From the start, one constant in the Eurobond market has been that interest must be paid net, and another has been the atmosphere of secrecy that surrounds the identity of investors. No bank in the business doubts that tax is being fiddled on an enormous scale.

The situation thrives on the evasion of national authority. Each bank, bond and investor is subject to some sort of surveillance by someone, somewhere, but the market as a whole occupies a dimension of its own. It may not be exactly what people mean when they talk about European integration; it is undeniably helping to plant the idea in people's minds that Europe is one place, not a collection of many. The words 'Eurodollar' and 'Eurobond' caught on because they *sounded* right.

Everywhere at Once

Someone once suggested that the ideal headquarters for a capitalist would be in a permanently airborne aircraft or satellite; this has yet to come, but in the meantime, the technique of being in many places at once, without ever being anywhere inconvenient, is lovingly cultivated.

One example can stand for many: the Alexander Hamilton Fund, an investment trust launched in 1967. An investment fund or trust collects money in exchange for shares in itself, then puts the money into a range of securities, so spreading the risk for the original investor. Many European trusts take advantage of a growing appetite for overseas investment among Europeans, who have a particularly soft spot for North American securities. The trusts usually offer shares denominated in dollars, and are sponsored by a constellation of banks.

Alexander Hamilton was the idea of the Bank of London and South America. This is a British bank that was rejuvenated by Sir George Bolton, a former Bank of England man, who became chairman in 1957, and turned Bolsa into one of the most active overseas banks in the City. It does most of its business in dollars, not sterling, and Bolton, an eloquent and entertaining man with an unconventional look that doesn't quite fit the City, was among the first to exploit the infant Eurodollar market. Ten per cent of Bolsa's capital is owned by an American bank, the Mellon National Bank of Pittsburgh. Bolsa has an interest in S. G. Warburg, the Frankfurt merchant bankers who are connected with Warburgs of London. It is a member of Intercontinental Banking Services, a permanent City consortium set up to handle overseas business in dollars as well as sterling. Bolton told me once that his work with international monetary organisations after the second world war had made him 'more and more conscious of the isolation of the average Briton from the basic realities of life,' and his reshaping of Bolsa is part of his attack on this isolationism.

The object of the Alexander Hamilton Fund was to invest its shareholders' money principally in U.S. securities, with the aim of long-term capital gain. Bolsa set it up in conjunction with the Bank of Scotland, a French bank and a Swedish bank. The French one was Banque Worms, a *banque d'affaires*, part of a 120-year-old industrial group that began by importing British coal into France, and now owns, among other things, a third of the French oil-tanker fleet. Earlier in 1967, Bolsa and the Bank of Scotland jointly invested $6 million in Banque Worms, for which they each obtained 10 per cent of the French bank, as well as some directorships; it edged the British banks into Europe and it edged the French bank out of France; the newspaper cuttings spoke of 'growing international links,' and everyone was happy. The fourth bank, the Svenska Handelsbanken, is the largest in Sweden, where overseas investment trusts are becoming popular.

Between them, the banks arranged to 'procure subscribers' for 990,000 of the million shares being offered, for which the banks would pay the fund $10 a share. The shares would then be sold to the subscribers at slightly more than $10 each; the offer-price was $10 30 cents, a margin, that, applied to 990,000 shares, would come to $297,000. Underwriting the issue of shares helps to keep banks above the poverty-line. However, the discount wouldn't all have stayed with the four sponsors. Some of it would have been passed on to the fifteen banks and stockbrokers known as the placing group. These were the ones who would actually place the shares with the buyers. Among them were four French banks, two in the Netherlands, one in Luxembourg, one in Denmark, and three firms of London stockbrokers, all brought in as reliable friends who would place shares with their clients, and receive a modest helping of gravy in return. When bankers talk about 'good contacts', one of the kinds of contact that's uppermost in their minds is the sort that leads to underwriting. Also among the fifteen were Bolsa and the other three sponsors, reappearing as members of the placing group.

The investment fund itself was established as a holding company in Luxembourg, where it would meet few taxes, and could pay dividends on its shares free of withholding tax. Its secretary and general manager were in Luxembourg, its auditors next door in Brussels. But the daily management of the fund wasn't to be handled in Europe, but in New York. And the investment advice appeared to be coming from the Bahamas. The reason for this is slightly involved, but logical enough.

The fund was set up to put European money into North American stock markets. The sponsors wanted the benefit of American expertise, and so Bolsa planned the fund in conjunction with the Bank of New York. This was founded in 1784 and is the oldest American bank to keep its original name. When Bolsa and the Bank of New York were talking on their Telex machines, they used to refer to 'the proposed Luxembourg investment trust', until someone lost patience with this unwieldy phrase, and, looking round for a label, called it the 'Alexander Hamilton', after the man who founded the bank in 1784. The name stuck, and when the fund was formed, it was officially adopted; it was felt to be highly respectable, since Hamilton had been First Secretary to the U.S. Treasury, and his face still appears on $10 bills.

The Bank of New York specialises in investment advice. It also provided the chairman of the Alexander Hamilton board and three of the other nine directors. But its services were not to be sold direct to the Luxembourg company. Yet another company was established, with the name of Alexander Hamilton Services; this was the one in the Bahamas, the group of holiday islands in the Caribbean within the Commonwealth but self-governing in matters of internal finance.

Like Luxembourg, it is a low-tax area that sets out to attract holding companies. The point of Alexander Hamilton Services was to provide a convenient clearing-house in agreeable conditions. It set up an Investment Advisory Committee, with members from the Bank of New York, some of the sponsors, and other financial institutions. It was then in a position to collect the fees for advice paid by Alexander Hamilton in Luxembourg; pay little or no tax on them; and pass the money on to (a) the members of the advisory committee and (b) the Bank of New York, which was handling the day-to-day running of the fund. Eventually, if the Bahamas company wished, it could retain some of the untaxed money that was coming in, and use it for other developments.

There's nothing unusual about the Alexander Hamilton arrangement; its almost metaphysical air is a commonplace among financial operators. It was an investment trust sponsored by banks in three European countries (Britain, France and Sweden), placing its shares with the help of institutions in three more (Denmark, Holland, Luxembourg), getting its investment advice and daily management in New York, and setting up companies in Luxembourg and the Bahamas because countries like these have little political or fiscal flavour of their own: they are a sort of no-man's-land where a company can operate internationally, without being tied down by different sets of laws in different countries.

The amount of money being paid to the services company in the Bahamas, destined for the advisory committee and the Bank of New York, wasn't large—one-half per cent. each year of the value of the assets, which were $10 million to begin with. This would mean an annual fee of $50,000. Later it would be higher, as more shares were issued[5] and their value rose, but the immediate, direct return to the Bank of New York would be modest, since the advisory committee would take half the $50,000.

What sharpened the Bank of New York's interest in Alexander Hamilton was that the bank had never gone outside its own city. By 1967 it wanted to climb on the bandwagon and move into Europe, and to have its name linked with those of leading European banks

[5] A further issue of a million shares, early in 1968, was supported by more or less the same group of banks and brokers, plus a few more from Scandinavia, Germany and Italy.

would help to smoothe the way. 'Get your name on to a large number of investment advisers' desks', said a man at Bolsa, 'and you will find yourself getting a large amount of business.' Alexander Hamilton was launched in August 1967. Two months later the Bank of New York opened its London office, with a flourish that included a large dignified advertisement showing a large dignified front door, and sober-suited men arriving with brief cases. Alexander Hamilton had helped to pave the way.

It's becoming harder to take a purely national view of finance. From stockbrokers to tax lawyers, the trend is towards internationalism. But it would be foolish to exaggerate the extent to which the money-men are joining forces. The conservative Swiss still sit behind their mountains; the deceptively amiable British still know in their bones that there is nowhere like the City of London; both are intensely individualistic about money. The six countries of the Common Market are still six distinct entities when it comes to banking and investment, each with its own reserves of gold and foreign currencies, its own economic theories. Standards of living are widely different.[6] The scene is full of idiosyncracies and the gossip of old neighbours. Paris (they say in London) is infatuated with the desire to become the financial hub of Europe; Luxembourg (they say in Paris) should not be allowed to continue as a tax-haven; German bankers work too hard at creating the illusion that they are working hard; the Italians all dodge their taxes; the Dutch are more to be trusted than most—the things they say about one another suggest what an assorted lot they are, and how much needs to happen to financial Europe.

6 Italy's is the lowest, Luxembourg's the highest, according to a 1967 study by the E.E.C.'s Commission. Some contrasts in the ownership of consumer goods: *Car*, 48 per cent of wage-earners' households in France, 20 per cent in Italy. *Telephone*, 6 per cent in France, 9 per cent in Germany, 40 per cent in Luxembourg. *Refrigerator*, 36 per cent in Belgium, 68 per cent in Germany. *Television set*, 27 per cent in Luxembourg, 55 per cent in Italy, 57 per cent in Netherlands.

4 *Inside The Six*

(i) **Italy:** Balances of Power

Bankers speculate where the financial centre of Europe might or should be in the future, but no one, not even the Italians, thinks it could be anywhere in Italy. London commands the most practical arguments; Paris has the desire but not the capacity; Brussels has the bureaucrats if not the financiers; Frankfurt glows with centuries of financial acumen, but wars have disrupted its machinery; Zurich sits near the middle of the web, banker to the world yet oddly parochial in its attitudes. But the Italians are newcomers to the big financial league. Both Rome and Milan, the chief financial cities, are away from the centre of Europe, and not only in a geographical sense.

Eight hundred years ago the Italians were the world's first international bankers. Even before this the money-changers or *bancherii* of Genoa were taking deposits and making loans. Throughout the Middle Ages, bankers from Lombardy and Florence, in north and central Italy, were operating in other countries, though their loans to foreign States were often made for political rather than economic reasons, and they had faded from the scene by the time the outlines of modern Europe were emerging in the sixteenth century—when America had been discovered, and Europe had turned away from the Mediterranean. The oldest banks still in existence in any country were founded then. The Banco di Napoli, founded 1539, calls itself 'the oldest bank in the world' in its advertising, but the Monte dei Paschi di Siena claims to beat that by sixty-seven years and to have been founded in 1472. Both have hundreds of branches in Italy, and the Bank of Naples has overseas branches, including offices in New York and Buenos Aires. Other old banks are in Sicily and Turin.

They are far from moribund, but because for centuries—until the unification of Italy in 1861—they belonged to individual cities and districts, and were never part of a trading empire, they have remained local banks at heart. Banks reflect a country's political importance; the private bankers of a little country like Holland still have an international flavour because of their long association with trade, wealth and power. Italy was cut off from the main stream of economic Europe, and only since 1945 has it really begun to catch up with its neighbours.

A financial system with a long gentle history that has had to adapt itself drastically in the last fifty years might be expected to look rather misshapen. It certainly has some odd aspects. though the Italians are entitled to point out that it has seen them through their post-war 'economic miracle', and that, like the City of London, it doesn't matter if it's peculiar as long as it works.

It is not an easy system for outsiders to understand, if only because the Italians are secretive about money and accustomed to keeping details from prying officials and tax-collectors. In Rome, the past has a hold on everything, including finance. The first bank you see at Leonardo da Vinci airport is the Banco di Santo Spirito, the Bank of the Holy Ghost, founded by Pope Paul V in 1605 and still popularly supposed to be controlled by the Vatican. Perhaps it is, though officially it belongs to the State. But in Italy there is often a feeling that shadowy circles of power are interlocked with those that are visible and official. Italian bankers seem to enjoy giving this impression, though it may be just an affectation, like the City man's air of amateurism.

The Bank of the Holy Ghost has total deposits of about $700 million, as much as a modest-sized bank in a large American city would expect to have. It has more than 200 branches, including the only branches at both the Rome airports. The man who saw me at the head office was not sure why this should be, nor why it was that people thought the Vatican controlled it, which it didn't. It was founded by a Pope and was located inside Vatican City till a hundred years ago; the Papal edict of 1605 hung in the hallway, more than a square yard of parchment, beautifully inscribed. Until 1967 a nobleman whose family has long-standing Vatican connections, Marchese Giovanni Sacchetti, was chairman, but he retired and was replaced by a man from Autostrade, the State-controlled road-building group.

In the basement were the archives, fat ledgers stacked on metal shelves in a bare room. Formerly the bank had been in a palace; now it occupied new premises, and the temperature in the basement was regulated so that the documents would keep for another few centuries. Some of the ledgers were two feet thick ('That must have been a good year for business', said the guide), and the oldest was dated 1606. There were letters about funds and merchandise; the writing was still more black than brown; they didn't look real.

I had been told that the Bank of the Holy Ghost was regularly used by the Vatican for channelling funds overseas, but the bank itself preferred not to talk about it. It probably is so used, and the Vatican probably does influence the management through 'friends' on the board. It retains a symbolic shareholding, at most 0·04 per cent of the total, leaving 99·96 per cent in the hands of the ubiquitous Istituto per la Ricostruzione Industriale, I.R.I., the State holding company which straddles Italian finance and industry.

With I.R.I., one shifts abruptly from the world of old parchment and the eternally uncommunicative Vatican to the modern mysteries of State intervention. Directly or indirectly, the State owns a larger slice of industry and commerce than in any other West European country. The situation stems from the early 1930s, when Italy's banking system, which was still comparatively young, collapsed under the financial crisis that was roaring through Europe in the wake of the Wall Street crash. Banks were heavily involved with industries, holding large blocks of shares (as multi-purpose banks still do in some countries, notably Germany), and they were jointly facing ruin when Mussolini's government stepped in and created I.R.I., the Institute for Industrial Reconstruction, as the centrepiece of the salvage operation. It was an accountant's nightmare, with banks owned by industries and the same industries apparently owned by the banks, and it took years to unravel.

I.R.I. emerged owning, besides 99·96 per cent. of the Banco di Santo Spirito, most of the shares in three of the country's four chief banks: Credito Italiano, the Banca Commerciale Italiana and the

Banco di Roma, all of them dating from the end of the nineteenth century (the fourth, the Banca Nazionale del Lavoro, was already directly owned by the State). The banks themselves were no longer allowed to own shares in industry, but I.R.I. was encouraged to do so. Over the years it solidified into a giant undertaking. Aiming to break even rather than make a profit, I.R.I. directly controls more than half Italy's steel output through Finsider, the telephone and telecommunication system through STET, much shipbuilding and engineering through Fincantieri and Finmeccanica, the major shipping lines through Finmare, and the motorway programme through Autostrade. The national airline, Alitalia, is owned by I.R.I., and so is RAI, the radio and TV network, a publicity agency, paper mills, and a long list of firms that brings the total of majority shareholdings to several hundred. Alfa-Romeo, the automobile firm, is owned by I.R.I.; the Ministry of State Participations, to which I.R.I. is responsible, upset some people during the 1967 business recession by asking other State industries to buy Alfa-Romeo cars.

The dangers of the I.R.I. system are evident enough. It can borrow money cheaply by issuing bonds under preferential conditions, and it gets other money from the Government which is virtually interest-free. It is big and getting bigger. But it has to use much of its energy in 'social' projects, often developments in the backward South (such as the Alfa-Romeo factory at Naples), and its bigness doesn't appear to have led to sloth—on the contrary, its managements generally have a high reputation.

I.R.I. headquarters in Rome, a large block in a fashionable street, houses a sophisticated staff that includes management and marketing analysts. The corridors that I saw had the pasty walls and bleak vistas of a British Ministry in Whitehall; harsh murals of industrial scenery, showing gaudy cranes, ships and locomotives, gave the place an earnest air. An official with a card behind his desk that read, in English, 'Old bankers never die, they just lose interest,' said that I.R.I.'s policy was to grant the maximum amount of independence. The formula is pragmatic rather than doctrinaire, which is one reason why Britain's recently formed Industrial Reorganisation Corporation is so interested in it: the idea that the State can intervene without upsetting the business community is always attractive. The I.R.C. operates as a type of State merchant bank, an *entrepreneur* rather than an owner, though it may eventually develop as I.R.I. has done. The I.R.I. chairman, Dr. Guiseppe Petrilli, has described his empire as being the product of 'empirical evolution', with the State wanting neither to abdicate as 'guarantor of the public interest', nor compromise the workings of a 'market economy'.

The frequent presence of directors from private firms on the boards of I.R.I. companies helps to smoothe the relationship between Civil Servants and capitalists, who are a flamboyant breed in Italy. Among I.R.I.'s banking properties is the resourceful Mediobanca, established after the war as one of several special credit institutions which can lend money to industry for longer than the twelve months to which the commercial banks are limited by law. I.R.I. banks own half the shares, and use Mediobanca to do the lending and investing they can't handle themselves. Its directors include Giovanni Agnelli, the boss of Fiat, and Leopoldo Pirelli, of the tyre and cable group. Also on the board is another familiar figure in the Italian power game, Dr. Massimo Spada, usually referred to with a wink or a grin as 'a Vatican man'. Dr. Spada was the administrative secretary to the Vatican's bank, the Istituto per le Opere di Religione, the Institute for Religious Works, from 1929 to 1961. I wrote to ask about his Vatican connections, and he replied non-commitally to say that this name appears in the Papal Yearbook as Confidential Chamberlain of the Sword and Cloak (this seems to be the nearest translation). Dr. Spada pops up all over the place, including the board of Finsider (I.R.I.'s iron and steel company) and the boards of private holding companies like Bastogi (originally a railway company) which have widespread investments throughout Italian industry. The presence of Dr. Spada means that the Vatican has some of its money there. I.R.I. controls Finsider through a 51·5 per cent. shareholding, and one assumes that the Vatican has a good slice of the remaining 48·5 per cent.

A striking instance of I.R.I. intervention in the private sector occurred in 1964, when Olivetti, the typewriter and office-machine company, ran into financial trouble, and had to be rescued by a syndicate of major shareholders—organised by the second in command at I.R.I., Professor Bruno Visentini, a lawyer and leading man-behind-the-scenes—which included Mediobanca, the Fiats and the Pirellis. Visentini, still vice-chairman at I.R.I., became chairman of Olivetti; State and private enterprise moved forward, apparently in step.

Public and private enterprise co-operate successfully without anyone being sure of the exact balance of power between them. Alberto Cavallari, a well-known writer for the *Corriere della Sera* of Milan, suggested to me that no one can ascertain the balance that exists between public and private sectors in Italy, any more than one can ascertain the balance between Church and State. I.R.I. was a compromise between private and public ownership, full of contradictions because it had been produced by a contradictory society.

Banking is the area where State intervention is greatest, but the banks are not to be lumped together as one monolithic unit. They are sharply different; they compete for business; they make rude remarks about one another. These banks appear in a variety of packages, each with its own set of regulations. There are six 'public law banks,' four of them old regional institutions—the Banco di Napoli, the Monte dei Paschi di Siena, and their companions in Sicily and Turin. They were started with charity and good works in mind, and they still don't make a profit. The 'public law' category also includes the Banca Nazionale del Lavoro, begun in 1913 to lend money to co-operatives, which later went into ordinary commercial business and has become Italy's largest bank in terms of deposits.

The country's most active bank is probably the Banca Commerciale Italiana—which, with the Banco di Roma and the Credito Italiano, make up another category, the 'banks of national interest'. These are the ones that I.R.I. bailed out in the 1930s, and now controls without (as everyone insists) any interference, apart from appointing or approving the top management. B.C.I. has fewer deposits than Lavoro, but as a B.C.I. man remarked, 'It's only a few hundred billion lire,[1] and anyway we don't recognise the quantity of deposits as a unique criterion. We are a very active bank. We finance more trade than they do.' Banks like to be biggest. The B.C.I. man added that many Lavoro deposits came from official sources, such as Government credits for the railways or the telephone service; whereas B.C.I. deposits were true deposits from industry and the public.

Like the Credito Italiano, B.C.I. has its headquarters in Milan, a solid northern city in the industrialised region. It's the commercial

[1] Less than it sounds, since 1 lira is an almost invisible amount of money, worth only a fraction of a penny. The difference between the two banks' deposits is about a billion dollars.

and financial centre because the money is all around it; it looks a bit like Leeds. Lavoro has its head office in Rome, where priests and tourists set the atmosphere, and banks take long lunch-hours that make them raise their eyebrows in Milan. The central bank, the Bank of Italy, and I.R.I. are in Rome because the Government and Civil Service are there, but Milan has the clustering of banks and the big Stock Exchange that make a truly national financial district.

B.C.I. is the Italian bank that's best known outside its own country, partly because in the last few years it has taken a leading part in the Eurobond market, helping to float and place shares for the Luxembourg holding companies that have been set up by industrial corporations and foreign governments to tap the pool of Eurodollars. Banks that want to lead in Eurobonds must not only be able to impress the financial community with their ability to organise things better and safer than anyone else (the sort of elegant confidence trick that the London merchant banks pulled off in the early 1960s) but must actually be able to find buyers who will put up the necessary millions of dollars for the bonds. This is where B.C.I. and other Italian banks came into the picture around 1964, when Italy followed a financial crisis—caused, as they usually are, by importing more than it exported—with a financial bonanza, achieved by lowering imports and raising exports. Italians were encouraged to invest their surplus dollars in the Eurobond market, and by 1966 the money was pouring out. Even branches of banks down in Sicily were said to be selling Eurobonds over the counter. All the leading Italian banks shared in the boom, and B.C.I. used its overseas experience (it finances about a third of Italy's foreign trade), together with its capacity for placing shares, to shoulder its way into top place as an organiser of Euro-loans.

B.C.I. is still coloured by the personality of Raffaele Mattioli, who helped to rescue it in the 1930s and ran it until he retired, comparatively speaking, into a back seat. Mattioli, one of the handful of bankers whose name means something throughout Europe, is an intellectual, which is less rare among bankers on the Continent than it would be in Britain. He is also an historian and writer, and his annual reports have unnervingly flowery passages ('It is charitable to pass over in silence the increasingly ruthless and disorderly competition which our work of collecting deposits has faced').

After the 'banks of national interest' comes a group of institutions like Mediobanca and I.M.I. (Istituto Mobiliare Italiano) whose function is to lend money to industry over the longer periods forbidden to other banks since they got themselves into trouble in the 1930s. Still in the public sector, there are hundreds of co-operative banks and local credit institutes, and a range of powerful savings banks that concentrate on the small man's deposits, but go in for commercial banking as well, including trade financing. Milan has the country's and possibly Europe's largest savings bank, the Cassa di Risparmio delle Provincie Lombarde, which has deposits of more than $4 billion, more telephone lines listed than any other bank in Milan—43 against the Credito Italiano's 40—and a barrack-like headquarters with a staff of 2,000 to deal with 3,500,000 depositors. Profits go to hospitals, schools and public utilities, and the annual reports reflect an awareness of virtue—'We march on towards our lofty purpose with the utmost efficiency of which we are capable,' and so on.

A savings bank, even one as large as this, is felt by many small depositors to be friendlier or safer or somehow more natural than a commercial bank. It does much of the same business, from discounting bills to financing imports, but its roots are in the countryside, which is important in a country like Italy that hasn't finished shaking off its past. The Cassa di Risparmio of Lombardy has hundreds of branches, many of them in the middle of nowhere: important fixed points in a country that still moves slowly outside the cities.

Little banks seem better than big banks, money under the mattress sometimes seems better still. 'Many peasants keep their money in their homes,' said a Milanese banker. 'When they get slightly more sophisticated, they keep it in the post office.' He thought there were too many tiny banks scattered over Italy, but he and others pointed out that regional loyalties were strong, so that a provincial town still clings to its bank as a badge of prestige.

From small-town institutions to the polished corridors of the Banca Commerciale Italiana, the banking system is run by the authorities—either national, local or charitable. Four-fifths of the money is there, leaving little for the independent deposit banks, which aren't very important in the overall picture—though the cement millionaire, Carlo Pesenti, is hoping to change this by building up a large privately-owned bank, the Istituto Bancario Italiano. The Pesenti group includes an industrial holding company, Italmobiliare, with many ramifications in the Italian fashion. I.B.I. was formed in 1968 when Pesenti brought together eight small banks in Italy's biggest banking merger since the war. The Bank of Italy gave its blessing, and so, presumably, did the Vatican: Dr. Spada was on the board.

A Passion for Secrecy

The way its banks and many of its industries are owned sets Italy a little apart from the rest of the Common Market. It isn't outright nationalisation but it isn't free enterprise. If Mr Cavallari is right, it expresses the equivocal Italian attitude to the State. Officialdom is less easily defined than it is in Britain and the U.S.; perhaps it is less respected as well. John Gunther notes in his book 'Inside Europe Today' that Italy has 'little tradition of the good citizen . . . what counts is private opportunity, private gain,' a truth that's evidenced by the way Italians feel about taxation. This is another characteristic of financial Italy that helps to set it apart. The Italians aren't the only ones who dodge taxes and keep their monetary affairs secret, but they do it more enthusiastically than most. If there is any guilt, I didn't see it. The nearest was the stockbroker who talked energetically about swindles for half an hour, and finished up with 'Don't be too unkind to us.' He knew what outsiders might think, but he didn't think it himself. It's perfectly possible to be a good citizen in the Italian sense of the word, and at the same time to be lying about income and expenses; tax is a game rather than an obligation. It is assumed that the need to keep one's affairs to oneself is common to all those who have houses, paintings, jewellery, horses, securities, or anything else that the State can and will tax if it gets the opportunity. Middle-class families usually pay by cash and not cheque in shops and department stores because the idea of using cheques in the High Street is still comparatively new, but cash transactions are also popular because they're so anonymous.

One small by-product of the national passion for secrecy is the continuing success of 'pawnbroking banks', the Monte di Credito su Pegno, where, it's claimed, quite affluent people will bring their jewellery and fur-coats to raise money for, among other things, stock-market speculation. I was told this in Milan, at the Banca del Monte di Milano. The Monti are semi-public institutions, run on the same lines as savings banks, which began in the fifteenth century as a means of combating usury. The one in Milan was founded in 1496 by a duke, and now stands in the shadow of the Cassa di Risparmio delle Provincie Lombarde across the road, where they smiled pityingly at the suggestion that one should attach importance to the pawn-broking side of the Monte's business. But the Monte was proud of it, insisting that, whereas fifteen years ago a third of the goods were pawned because their owners were poor, nowadays it was no more than a tenth. A loan can be for as much as a couple of thousand pounds—'a more private way of raising money than a mortgage on property,' said the Monte, adding that it appealed to Italians, who 'don't want everyone to know their financial affairs.'

A banking hall with a marble floor and a faint smell of perfumed women was busy taking in jewellery, watches and cameras. The bank was anxious to dispel any lingering suspicions of seediness and embarrassment, said the guide; I could observe for myself that people behaved as casually as if it were a shop. Behind the counters, rings and watches were valued in locked cubicles, clipped into polythene packets, and sent off by conveyor belt. Handfuls of banknotes for hundreds of thousands of lire were being handed over. The poor, of course, had another entrance and a dingier hall for their candlesticks and blankets, while the man who brought in something of really substantial value, like a diamond bracelet or a piece of antique silver, would be received in a private drawing room upstairs.

Vaults and galleries extended behind the outer rooms, heavy with dust and ancient mothball smells, blocking the view in all directions with middle-class possessions that were here on loan, while their owners paid about 9 per cent annually on the cash, but usually (stressed the Monte) redeemed the goods within three months, suggesting that all they wanted was a quick bit of capital. It didn't seem quite the sophisticated money-world of glossy bank advertising, but these gloomy vistas of consumer goods had the virtue of providing funds that no one knew about. It was early summer, and the place was filling up with fur coats; they had about 8,500, some packed in boxes, the most valuable hung in containers with a little window in the side. There was a nest of sewing machines. Four hundred television sets in plastic bags stretched into the distance. Long tables were laid with multi-coloured carpets; the guide pointed to one worth £450, but didn't go so far as to say that some Milanese family was walking on the floorboards in order to have a dabble in the stock market. There was a room full of deposit boxes, behind steel bars and bullet-proof glass, where the gems ended up, looking like packets of green and white sweets; a detective padded behind us. On the way out we passed parcels of sheets coming in from second-class clients, the vanishing 10 per cent. When I said there seemed rather a lot of them for such a small percentage, the Monte replied that the figure meant value, not people: there were more people with sheets than people with emeralds, but the former supplied only a tenth as much turnover as the latter.

The Italian love of financial privacy seems to be inextricably mixed up with the taxation system: each helps to cause the other, and either may be blamed for being at the root of the trouble. In the end, Italians pay as much as most people in taxation. As a percentage of gross national product—the country's turnover—taxes and social-security contributions take between 30 and 35 per cent, the same as in Britain, and 5–10 per cent more than in the U.S., where the social-security element is low. But direct taxes make up only a small proportion of the total in Italy—a fifth, compared with half in Britain and three-fifths in the U.S. Indirect taxes keep prices high. 'It is an immoral system because it hits the whole population,' said an official at the Banca del Lavoro, who added that it would certainly become fairer to the poor, but not just yet: there was a lot of resistance from the average business man, who clung to the ramshackle tax system because 'God knows what will happen if they change it.'

There is a certain chaos about taxation everywhere. I heard a stockbroker in the Netherlands, irritated by the complexities of the British tax laws as they affected his Dutch clients, say that either the English were very naïve to suppose that anyone would conscientiously fill in so many clumsy forms, or they were liberal in interpreting their own system. 'I haven't got the time to contact clients who own British securities, and get all the answers to their ridiculous question,' he said. 'I just write a lot of nonsense and hope for the best.'

In Italy, chaos has taken over. Tax evasion and vengeful officialdom flourish side by side, two sides of the same coin. The Finance Ministry will suddenly announce with a flourish that a bunch of foreign film stars and pop singers haven't been paying their taxes, making it sound more like a publicity stunt than an attempt to enforce the law. In Sicily, riven by an earthquake in 1968, officials were reported to be stopping lorries bringing emergency supplies to make sure that the necessary taxes had been paid.

The effort that goes into collecting or not collecting taxes in Italy is prodigious because of the mutual mistrust between taxpayers and authorities. I sat for an hour or two with the head of a bank's legal department, while he tried to explain it through an interpreter. Taxes were paid at several levels—to the State, the province, the commune and so on. Income was taxed and so was wealth. Companies complained that they were always taxed at least twice, first on what they owned and then on what they earned. There could be 'presumed' and 'real' taxes on the same items—the interpreter interjected his personal case. He lived in a flat which he owned. If he had been renting the flat to someone else, he would have paid a tax on this income. Therefore the authorities taxed him a little on the rent he would have received if he weren't living in it himself. But if he actually did let the flat to a tenant who paid him real rent on which to be taxed, he would continue to pay the little tax already imposed to meet a hypothetical situation.

The basic principle was that the State taxed every manifestation of the ability to pay. If you put a card in the window of a stationer's to advertise a room to let or a car for sale, you must put a small stamp on it: you possessed something, so you must contribute something to society. The interpreter said he had heard that tax officials sometimes mingled with the crowds arriving for the opera at La Scala in Milan, so as to price the jewellery and fur coats being worn by the wives of prominent citizens, ready for the next demand. Because there were so many taxes so assiduously pursued by the State, taxpayers resisted as best they could. 'If you tell the truth,' said the lawyer, 'they won't believe you. They know you are *not* telling the truth.'

We were in a dark room lined with fifteenth century frescoes; it was rather like a chapel, which is characteristic of old Italian banks. I asked which came first, over-charging by the State or underpaying by the citizen, but the lawyer said that that was a chicken-and-an-egg question. However, it was a psychological fact that rather than pay his taxes like a good citizen, the Italian was constantly looking for ways around the law, and the State was constantly trying to fill in the gaps. The interpreter, who was English, added an aside of his own, saying, 'It's interesting how he approaches the topic. He's being very vague about it. He's not being practical.'

The bigger the taxpayer, the thicker the smoke-screen emitted by the accountants. Companies argue interminably with the tax authorities, undervaluing assets and understating earnings. Half a dozen bankers told me exactly the same, that many companies produce a series of balance sheets: an optimistic one for the bankers, a pessimistic one for the authorities, a true one to keep in the chairman's office.

'It is very common in Italy to have more than one balance sheet,' said a man at Banca Ambrosiano, one of the non-State banks. 'As a matter of fact, almost every company, big and small, has two. When a bank gives credit to clients, it never asks for the *official* balance sheet. One rings up the managing director and asks for the real figures. The fiscal inspector will not see the true balance sheet. It's a sort of market. They say "a hundred" in order to get fifty. You say "ten" in order to pay twenty. They know you are lying, and you know that they know.'

'The company figures are low and the taxes are charged at a high level,' said a man at the Banca del Lavoro. 'The two may meet in the middle, so that the amount paid by the company is near what it should be. But as long as this practice is not corrected, there is a vicious circle. Reality is being denied.' A Roman banker who used to work in the Vatican said that he didn't consider it was anything to do with conscience; it was simply the way one had to behave in a bureaucracy. Figures were very relative in Italy. 'The authorities don't believe you. They will multiply by two, so you must put in smaller amounts.'

These artful habits help to make Italian company reports among the least helpful in Europe; this in turn helps to deter potential shareholders. The national grudge against tax, the national fondness for secrecy, operate powerfully throughout the investment field, making the stock exchanges sensitive to the tiniest puff of fiscal wind. Interest on bonds is paid in full, and hardly anyone ever declares it in his tax-returns; the authorities close their eyes to this, but try to catch those who don't pay tax on their dividends from shares. Successive Italian governments, trying in vain to pin down rich shareholders and make them pay, have given the stock market some bad moments. A special withholding tax on dividends was introduced in 1962, and the law forced shareholders to disclose their holdings, or tried to. This caused an uproar, and huge quantities of shares were sold, not to avoid the fifteen per cent tax, which was only an advance payment on the final bill, but to avoid giving details of shareholdings. Cash was smuggled out to Switzerland, taking the route it always does in time of trouble, and the flight of capital was so serious that some Italians have even blamed it for the slump that affected their economy soon after. Most of it probably crossed the border by road, hidden in false-bottomed suitcases or under clothing, or simply piled high inside a van—or so a Swiss banker in Zurich told me; when I asked how it got past the Customs, he looked at me as if I were a child, and rubbed his thumb and forefinger together.

Literally hundreds of billions of lire went north and straight into Swiss bank accounts, speeded on their way by a general feeling that Left-wing politicians were going to make life difficult. As an Italian economist wrote later in a British publication, using economist's circumspect language, 'the misgivings that some of the internal political trends had inspired prompted a capital outflow which reduced the volume of finance available for industry on the home market.' Most of the money was then reinvested in Italian securities by the Swiss banks, on behalf on their anonymous clients in Milan and Turin.[2]

The net result was to drain away funds and make the Government look foolish, and so in 1964 the dividend tax was changed again. The rate came down from fifteen to five per cent, but at the same time, shareholders were offered the alternative of paying a thirty per cent withholding tax and no questions asked. This seemed a concession to the really rich, since only those with incomes above roughly $170,000

[2] Extract from the Segré Report: 'From 1962 to 1964 Italian residents made large transfers in banknotes to Switzerland. These transfers have been estimated to be $762 million in 1962, $1,456 million in 1963 and $557 million in 1964. The bulk of the funds transferred . . . was repatriated by the owners under the cover of Swiss names, to finance portfolio and direct investment in Italy.' It's not often that large-scale smuggling and tax evasion are so well documented.

or £70,000 a year would normally pay more than thirty per cent of it in income tax and surtax; anyone earning less than £70,000 would have to hand over less than thirty per cent of it (an almost unbelievably low proportion by British standards), and so would apparently lose money by opting for the thirty per cent tax.

In fact, thousands of shareholders chose to pay it, since it enabled them to conceal their overall shareholding, and go on fiddling their tax; it was the 'no questions asked' part that appealed to them. The rules made in 1964 ran for three years, and when they expired in 1967, and the Government made it clear that shareholders would lose the option of paying more and keeping their secrets, prices on the stock exchanges fell by ten per cent. The Government was called a lot of impolite names, and no doubt the traffic in lire across the Swiss border speeded up.

'We have very little sense of State,' a stockbroker said to me a few months later. 'We are always afraid that what they do next will be worse.' He wasn't apologising, only explaining. The tax system wasn't fair, he said, that was the trouble. He sat in a small room with period furniture while the telephone bells rang softly in other rooms, and said it wasn't paying taxes they minded, it was having their names put in files. Once they had you, they squeezed you. 'You make a good income one year of ten million lire [£7,000, $17,000] but the next year you only earn six million. They will just laugh at you and tax you on eleven million, and the year after that it will be twelve million. Yes, they will say, we know you had a bad year, we read it in the newspapers, but we are going to tax you on twelve million.'

Why, he asked, was private aviation in Italy so limited? It was because outward signs of wealth like private aircraft were best avoided. 'I am an Italian pilot,' he said, 'but I fly a Swiss plane which I keep in Switzerland. If you have a plane in this country, they think you must be a Paul Getty.'

He was called to the telephone. I remembered having seen a narrow airfield between the mountains, not far inside the Swiss border, with little blue planes on the grass. I also remembered the banker in Basle who said that half the Italians of his acquaintance pretended to have a residence in Switzerland for tax purposes. He knew an Italian with a flat in Lugano that he hardly ever visited; a friend went there regularly to empty the letter box, otherwise it would explode.

The stockbroker came back and said that funnily enough it had been a call from a woman who was worried about the need to disclose her shareholdings. There were many worried people in Italy; there were people who would rip up their dividends and throw them through the window, rather than cash them and find themselves filed by the authorities. It was inevitable that money should be smuggled out to Switzerland. The man who wished to sell his shares and export the cash was unstoppable; if asked where the money had gone, he could say, 'I spent it on a pretty woman.' Such men with such desires were part of human nature and not to be stopped by anything, said the stockbroker. He grinned; he liked the idea; an English stockbroker might have liked it, too, but unless drunk would not have been so explicit. 'You can't', said the stockbroker, 'keep money in a country if it wants to get out. If the authorities announce that anyone caught crossing the English Channel with more than five pounds will be hanged, it will merely cost a little extra to smuggle it out. That's all.'

This straightforward attitude isn't quite the official one, as expressed by the Italian Treasury, some of whose income-tax advisers I met, to ask delicately if all I had heard was true. Their department was in a tower block at E.U.R., the grandiose estate by the Tiber outside Rome, with lake and sports ground, that was started by Mussolini, who wanted to hold a world fair there, but never did. (A man on the train going out said, 'Instead he started the war. Which he lost'.) The departmental windows looked out on avenues, trees and white facades swept by rain, like palaces from a film-set. Everyone talked at once. I asked about the thirty per cent option and the no-disclosure concession, now withdrawn; was it true that this had been really a device to encourage tax evasion, as being a lesser evil than damaging the stock markets and letting lots of money escape? 'No', said an official. 'It was not a fraud. It was not an evasion. It was a matter of political economy.'

They drew sketches and graphs to explain what was happening. I mentioned multiple balance sheets; they all shook their heads, and said that an occasional deception by an occasional company should not be mistaken for a principle.

I asked about bonds, as opposed to shares. In Italy, virtually all bonds (whether the borrowing is being done by industry or the

Government) escape tax on the interest; nothing is deducted at source, the securities are in bearer form, and there is no undue pressure from the authorities. This makes it harder for companies to raise equity capital in the form of Ordinary shares. The officials nodded and looked grave. Income from bonds should be declared, of course; it was the law. 'But I can make this admission,' said one of them. 'As a rule it isn't.'

They weren't keen on questions about tax evasion, seeing them as reminders of the past, and there's little doubt that the scene is going to change fairly rapidly within the next few years, as Italy grows more deeply into Europe. This is true of taxation and of the country's financial attitudes in general. Italy's part in the Eurobond market—which provides a legitimate and quite profitable means of exporting money—points to this process of integration.

So the tax men were disturbed to think I had been hearing slanders, even if I had been hearing them from Italians themselves. The senior official said that Italy was not the only country in the world where people evaded tax. Admittedly the system had its faults, but for many years the authorities had been working towards a new fiscal system. When it was approved by Parliament, it would put Italy in the forefront of modern nations.

When would that be? Soon, they said, it would be soon.

The Vatican

If income-tax reform is only a matter of time, the Vatican is beyond time altogether. When the last trumpet sounds and everyone's accounts are balanced, perhaps the Vatican's will be revealed; not before. Glimmers of information suggest worldwide investment in shares and estates, industries and buildings, but the Vatican, being accountable to no one on earth, can work in silence and publish nothing. The idea of anyone's secret riches is intriguing, and doubly so if they belong to the Church. It must cost a lot of money to run the Roman Catholic Church, and in the absence of a general movement towards saintly poverty it's hard to see what the money-men of Vatican City can do, except to follow their present policy of getting a good, safe return on their assets.

The Italian Finance Minister estimated in 1968 that the Vatican held $160 million in Italian securities. This was the first figure to be produced that seemed more than a guess. In 1965 the London *Economist* thought the figure might be $560 million, and quoted an opinion 'close to Vatican sources' that the Italian holdings were one-tenth of the world total. Assuming the $160 million figure to be correct, and that it really is one tenth of the total, the overall investment might be expected to produce an annual income of, say, $100 million a year, some of it subject to withholding tax by the countries involved. But even if the gross sum were divided among the world's 600 million Catholics, it wouldn't provide them with more than about 15 cents a year per head (which is the kind of statistic the Church's P.R.O.s would produce, if it had any). The Church is rich but it's possible to argue that it's also poor.

One assumes that the Vatican would be unable to put a figure on its total assets, since these include the indefinable wealth of palaces, paintings, sculptures and books. Property assets must be more measureable, though the holdings of the Amministrazione dei Beni della Santa Sede, the Administration of Holy See Property, include estates in Italy (among them Chianti vineyards), other European countries and the American continent. This centrally-owned property is distinct from the possessions of Catholic churches, convents, colleges and other ecclesiastical bodies—a substructure of immense complexity, since Church ownership is often prudently concealed. In Italy, religious orders remember how their property was seized by the State in the past, and put their material possessions in the hands of societies run by trustworthy Catholic laymen. But these are local, autonomous assets, and nothing to do with the central Church.

The Vatican itself is the smallest State in the world, area about 109 acres. It has dozens of churches, and palaces, radio, printing presses, hotel, bank and railway station. There are 1,000 citizens, most of whom have had their citizenship conferred by the Pope because they need it for their work, chiefly as Vatican officials. When the need for citizenship ceases, the Pope takes it away again; while they have it, Italians lose their Italian citizenship, and can't vote at elections.

The original source of the cash that has since multiplied so profitably, though just how profitably no one knows, was a lump-sum settlement of 1929, when the Italian Government paid over the equivalent of about £20 million at existing exchange rates, to compensate the Vatican for finally abandoning its rights to the Papal

States. This solved the 'Roman Question' and left Pope Pius XI, a Milanese who was good with money, sitting on a fortune in banknotes and Italian Government bonds. To administer it he set up the Amministrazione Speciale, the Special Administration, which he put in charge of a clever financier called Bernardino Nogara. Nogara (who died in 1958) spread his investments, pleasing Catholic businessmen in many countries, which was probably incidental, and safeguarding the fund by not having too many eggs in one basket. Now part of a reorganised financial set-up with a cardinal at its head, the Special Administration is run by the safest of all kinds of banker, a Swiss—the Marchese Henri de Maillardoz, formerly of the Swiss Credit Bank. His staff numbers about forty. The portfolios of shares are actively supervised—the management isn't left to banks and brokers—but the general approach is as one would expect. 'When they make an investment they like to stay in it for a long time,' said a banker who once worked there, unsealing his lips for a second.

Alongside the Special Administration is the Vatican bank, the Istituto per le Opere di Religione, which handles selected accounts for individuals but is important chiefly because all money being moved into and out of the Vatican goes through it. This includes the annual offering of 'St Peter's Pence', collected in Catholic churches on St Peter's Day, June 29, and estimated (another guess) to be worth half a million pounds a time.

Foreign banks named in conversations and articles as having close working associations with the Vatican include Morgan Guaranty and Chase Manhattan in the U.S.; Hambros in London, and the Swiss Credit Bank. In Italy, the Vatican has its tiny shareholding and perhaps its larger, shadowier interest in the Banco di Santo Spirito; together with another small shareholding but more open degree of influence in the No. 3 'bank of national interest' the Banco di Roma, whose chairman is a former leader of Catholic Action in Italy. The Banco di Roma has a Swiss subsidiary, just over the Italian border in Lugano, the Banco di Roma per la Svizzera; this is owned jointly with the Vatican's Institute for Religious Works, and its chairman is Prince Giulio Pacelli, nephew of a former Pope.

Other smaller banks are variously reported to be linked with the Vatican. A sober book called 'Banks of the World' (1967) mentions the Banca Ambrosiano as owing 'direct obedience' to the Vatican, a suggestion that was promptly dismissed by the bank when I went there, though they didn't seem surprised by the reference. 'We hear it often,' they said, 'no doubt because we were created as a bank for Catholics in 1896. Only Catholics could be shareholders then, but the articles of association have been altered. We don't owe obedience to the Vatican or to anyone else.'

Italy's widespread anti-clericalism makes it natural for the Church to be suspected of hidden powers and mysterious energies, operating for its own benefit under the nose of the State. The Vatican's known investments in Italy are enough to make nervous Socialists suspect that the true total is alarmingly high. There are the Finsider and Bastogi interests. The Vatican has a large stake in the leading cement firm, Italcementi, which is also a holding company; Dr. Spada is on the board. It has a share of a building and holding group, Societa Generale Immobiliare, which has interests in Rome, including blocks of flats and the Hilton Hotel, as well as in transport and tourism; various noble and other friends of the Vatican are directors. The Vatican is in *pasta*, gas, trams and insurance; it would be surprising if it *weren't* a sore point with Italy's political Left.

Predictably, taxation is involved. When the 1962 withholding tax on dividends was introduced, some foreign investors were exempted. The Vatican claimed exemption on the grounds that it was a foreign State and that it had charitable responsibilities in Italy, but it made the claim in private, and the Italian Government agreed to it equally privately. Italian companies received a confidential circular telling them to pay dividends to the Vatican free of tax, and the matter came to light only when a Socialist became Minister of Finance. The ensuing row used up the usual amounts of energy, and seemed likely to last for years.

Since then, fears that the Vatican, if forced to start paying, might retaliate by selling all its Italian shares have been blamed for slumps in the markets. It sounds improbable, but one never knows. Italian finance has a flavour of its own.

(ii) **Germany:** The Giants

An American banker based in Europe, addressing colleagues at an Atlantic City meeting, gave a tongue-in-cheek definition of the well-rounded world banker as someone who would combine 'the punctuality of a Spaniard, the tax morality of an Italian, the charm of a Prussian, the happy-go-lucky humour of the Swiss, the modesty of a Frenchman, the long working hours of the British, plus the quiet banking habits of us little New York bankers.' All the ironical attributions have grains of truth in them; perhaps the unkindest is the suggestion that the German are charmless, though it's a natural enough response to their tough sobriety and the roaring commercial success it has brought them since the war.

When the war ended in 1945, the German economy was ruined, and the country suffered all the pains of defeat. But it had to be quickly revived so that it could become a contributing member of non-Communist Europe, and by 1946 it was absorbing a substantial part of the aid that the U.S. was sending to Europe. About $1,300 million arrived as post-war relief between 1946 and 1948, followed by nearly twice that amount under the more formal Marshall Aid programme up to 1952. After 1952 American aid dwindled sharply and within a few years had virtually stopped; Germany, restored to life, rebuilt factories and cities, and in the 12 years after 1954 succeeded in doubling its gross national product. Twenty years after the days when rats and refugees roamed the land, and cigarettes were used as currency, Germany's industrial output and foreign trade were the largest of any Western country after the U.S. Its reserves of gold and other countries' currencies gave it the strongest foreign-exchange position of any industrialised nation. Germany was powerful again, a model of diligence for others to admire, and perhaps fear a little.

A British banker in Hamburg, where the British have held a financial beach-head since the nineteenth century, said that when his seniors came over from London they were sadly out of their depth. The Germans were so meticulous and industrious that they made their visitors uneasy. An official from the British banker's head office in the City had seen him at his desk early one morning and advised him not to work so hard. The man in Hamburg was enraged, remarking that he was merely following the local custom of starting at 8.30. 'When people turn up for work in London, the first thing they say is, "What's in the mail, Miss Smith?" In Germany it's the other way round. The top men turn up first and pounce on the letters to open the important ones themselves.

'I go into the office in London, and they're standing around, working at two miles an hour. Here they're working at fifty miles an hour. They may live longer in London, but they don't have financial surpluses.'

The financial system that has helped the economy to perform so admirably has had to develop from a chaotic state of affairs, in which the Western allies were at first determined to keep power from accumulating in any one quarter. No proper currency existed until June 1948, when the old Reichsmark, the 'Imperial' mark, was abolished by the allies and replaced by a new unit, the less grandiloquent 'German' or Deutsche mark. The central bank, the Reichsbank, had already disappeared in 1946, after seventy years of existence. It seems to have been ignored rather than corrupted by Hitler during most of his regime—its boss in the 1930s, Dr. Hjalmar Schacht, was acquitted by the Nuremburg war crimes tribunal of having helped to prepare Germany for aggression. But the Reichsbank had to go, and under the new system, each of West Germany's 11 provinces was given an autonomous central bank of its own, with a single federal bank above them all.

Money and its management were decentralised. What remained of the commercial banks after the war was broken down. The Deutsche Bank found itself in ten pieces. But before long the theories of the victors were being modified by reality. The West needed a strong Germany, and Germany itself, afloat once more on the tide of American aid, began to grope for the financial instruments it needed to make the economy work. National banks began to take shape again, and eventually all pretence of decentralisation was dropped. The various central banks were also merged—brought under one roof in one place and renamed the Bundesbank.

One legacy from the post-war system is the number of business centres. Munich, Cologne, Hamburg, Dusseldorf and Frankfurt are all important, with Frankfurt established as the commercial capital, now that Berlin is no longer part of West Germany. Though Frankfurt is only the seventh city, with a population of 700,000, its central position, and a long tradition of being good with money, gave it the strongest claim after 1945. But enforced decentralisation has left its mark, and the three leading banks—Deutsche, Dresdner and Commerz, in that order— have what looks like a preposterously awkward division of management between Hamburg, which is Germany's largest port and manufacturing city; Dusseldorf, in the industrial Ruhr, and Frankfurt.

Even in an age of rapid movement, German bankers seem to move on perpetual roller-skates; they must commute between cities in order to meet one another, while important industrialists expect to be visited on their own territory. The Dresdner Bank has two managing directors in Hamburg, five in Dusseldorf and seven in Frankfurt, where each Friday a list of their movements for the coming week is drawn up, so that if they all look like being away on the same day, someone can try to change his schedule. 'Unfortunately we have a very spoiled clientele,' said a Dresdner man; it was far from being the most convenient system, and they were gradually favouring Frankfurt at the expense of the others, but for the moment, a company chairman in Hamburg or the Ruhr expected there to be a bank director nearby at all times.

The managing directors must come together for important decisions, which makes travelling schedules still more tiresome. Decision-taking at a German bank is thorough. The managing directors, who exert collective authority as the Vorstand, or board, need to agree unanimously. Since a dozen busy men travelling fast around Europe may be involved, this looks like a system for achieving little. In practice it isn't like that, as an official at the Dresdner Bank explained: 'If a managing director disagrees with his colleagues, they try to get him to change his mind, so that he still disagrees but now he says Yes'. What appears to be another complication, the hundreds of industrialists named in annual reports as members of 'advisory boards' (the Deutsche Bank's fill eighteen large pages), is immaterial, since the boards exist largely as a gesture to clients who like to see their names in print. The Vorstand does the work, but everyone is comforted to see page after page of old pals. It looks thorough and business-like.

There is something solid and harsh and overpowering about the big German banks, which are always having to defend themselves against charges of omnipotence. Mention, to a German banker, the suggestion that banks dominate industry and manipulate the stock exchanges, and his face either twitches with annoyance or, more probably, creases with boredom at hearing what he will call 'those stale old stories.' But the stories continue to be told, partly because they have elements of truth, partly because they satisfy every country's regrettable weakness for caricaturing every other country.

A Swiss financier who accused the Germans of being greedy and bloody-minded over international bond issues, grabbing the best business for themselves, said they were all right as long as you betrayed no weakness. One must be strong, as with dogs and horses, he said rudely, which seems to be taking caricature to extremes—not to mention the fact that the Swiss themselves are frequently accused of being greedy. But a feeling that the Germans are not easy to deal with persists.

Their banks offer a comprehensive range of services that impresses bankers in countries where there is more specialisation. They do the work of stockbrokers and investment bankers, managing new issues of shares, holding large share portfolios, both for themselves and on behalf of customers, and handling all the stock-exchange trading. They run investment trusts. They lend to industrial firms that in Britain and America would be more likely to raise money by issuing shares or loan-stock. They do all the obvious things like financing trade, they have a variety of lending schemes for small borrowers and many deposit rates for different kinds of lending; and, since banking precepts are in the melting pot everywhere, the Germans' 'department store' approach is watched with interest from outside.

The Big Three banks have only a seventh of the country's deposits, the rest being distributed among hundreds of municipally-owned savings banks and thousands of local co-operative institutions, with everyone competing furiously. Altogether Germany has nearly 12,000 separate credit institutions, with more than 36,000 banking offices. About two-fifths of these offices belong to the savings banks, which offer a wider range of services than in Britain, and are very much a part of local life. Working in regional groups, they regard themselves as the backbone of the local community, middle-class establishments that are closer to small business men, shopkeepers and housewives than the commercial banks, with their big-business associations.

The large banks are no less devoted to wealthy industrial clients than they were. What they are now attempting is to befriend the smaller customer as well. But in this as in other ways they tread warily —they would probably buy up more smaller regional banks than they have done, but for Germany's continuing prejudice against too much centralised financial power.

The big banks carefully avoid suggestions of size and power, and especially the Deutsche Bank. This has 24,000 employees, and finances a third of Germany's foreign trade. But it is the variety of pies in which it has a finger that count. Asked if it's true that the Deutsche Bank comprises what in other countries would be split up among a range of deposit banks, investment banks, stockbrokers and finance houses, officials can only express polite astonishment. City men, who know the scope of the Deutsche Bank, are astonished at their astonishment. A merchant banker of German origin said that one shouldn't be fooled by their modesty, and compared their importance in the German economy to a combination, in the U.S., of Chase Manhattan, Morgan Guaranty, Dillon, Reed (the investment bankers), Merrill Lynch and a few investment trusts for good measure.

The title is an advantage—just as Lloyds Bank in London is confused by some people with the insurance syndicates that make up Lloyd's (the insurers have an apostrophe, and there's no connection), so 'German Bank' sounds official and gilt-edged. At its head until recently was one of the West's best-known bankers, Dr. Hermann Abs, who retired as 'Speaker' of the Vorstand in 1967, became chairman of the Supervisory Board, and continued to be much sought after as a financial adviser and ideas-man. But while bankers in Britain are learning to boast in the American style, the Germans move cautiously. An American banker in Frankfurt called the Deutsche Bank 'the holier-than-the-Pope bank', and said it reminded him of the Frankfurter Hof, the best hotel in town, where, if a stranger asked for a reservation, they would reply, 'We will consider your application, sir.' In an odd way, the Deutsche Bank (founded 1870) is more formal than the older City banks, which have abandoned much of their reserve in the last ten years.

A dilemma for bankers throughout Europe is that it is both fashionable and necessary to merge and form powerful units, yet at the same time it can be dangerous if the concentration of power leads governments to think of nationalisation. There is the constant reminder of France and Italy, where Government banks are dominant. The big German banks prefer not to attract attention to their importance. It is politically tactful for an institution like the Deutsche Bank to say how ordinary it is.

Private Parlours

All non-Government banks are 'private' in the sense that they are independently owned, but to say that a man is a 'private banker' implies in Europe that his bank is small and select and closely held, often by a family and its friends. Sometimes they are called 'houses', the word, like the banker's 'parlour', hopefully suggesting something safe and cosy. The Swiss still have plenty of them. A few struggle on in Paris and Amsterdam, looking down their noses at the vulgar new bankers, or selling out to them and retiring to a chateau or a chalet. In London, a core of family names and memories survives at the centre of some of the merchant banks, but few, if any, belong to the private banker's world; they wouldn't last long in the City if they did.

The breed is dying out, but they are still to be found on the Continent—most successful where (as in Switzerland) they have made a virtue of their privateness. Their past is sprinkled with resounding names: the Kings they loaned money to, the canals and railways they financed in the industrial revolution, the despots they survived. Often the furniture in their offices—inlaid tables, delicate bureaux, painted cupboards—seems interchangeable. Sometimes a monstrous antiquity will dominate the room—the stove in the parlour at the house of La Roche in Basle, sitting there like an enormous blue-tiled boiler, under the moulded ceiling that depicts Swiss scenes, circa 1763. Frequently English prints or pictures decorate the walls. La Roche has nineteenth century engravings with titles like 'Bolton Abbey in the Olden Time'. Georg Hauck & Sohn in Frankfurt has an oil-painting of a nineteenth-century Hauck by a painter of the time whose signature was recognised by a present-day partner when he was at Kleinwort Benson, the London merchant bank, under one of their old paintings.

Germany has more private bankers than anywhere else in Europe. There's a long tradition of family banking, and places like Frankfurt and Hamburg, powerful for centuries, have produced some of the most famous names in finance. But in general, all that the little old banks have become is little new banks. The going has been hard for half a century, and the 2,000 or more that existed in 1928 had shrunk by a third in the 1930s, to fewer than a thousand by 1939, to 300 after the war, and now to about 200. Only a handful are of importance, led by C. G. Trinkaus of Cologne.

In Frankfurt, the big banks look like concrete battleships from the outside; the private bankers cling to quainter premises. They note with pleasure that Frankfurt has regained the financial primacy it lost to Berlin in the 1870s, but know it doesn't belong to them any more. The men in the battleships have taken over, squeezing their smaller colleagues harder than (for instance) private bankers were ever squeezed in London, where, turned into limited and sometimes public companies, they have gone on making their reputations and their fortunes as merchant bankers. The Germans weren't able to do this. What they specialised in was investment and the floating of stock exchange loans, both domestic and by foreigners in Germany; the first war and the subsequent economic upheaval ended stock-market borrowing by foreigners and upset the pattern of domestic borrowing. Germany was afflicted with the worst inflation in history, and this was followed by Nazi rule, which deliberately isolated the country from the rest of Europe. The private bankers withered away, and those who survived were never able to expand and become international names.

One of the shrewd survivors is Gebrüder Bethmann, a family business with two active partners, Baron von Bethmann and a friend, and three inactive ones, Baron von Bethmann's wife and two sisters. Bethmanns began on New Year's Day, 1748, raised money for clients who included the Emperor of Russia and various Scandinavian kings, became banker to the court of Vienna, helped to finance Germany's railways and the first line to Baghdad, and has now cut a modest niche for itself in industrial lending. It runs small savings accounts for anyone who wants to save with it, and promises a more personal service than the commercial banks. 'Some people like to go to a private bank with its own coat of arms on their savings book,' said the Baron. 'There is a snob appeal, isn't there?'

Sitting in his office, through a courtyard off Bethmannstrasse, under a painting of an eighteenth-century Bethmann cavalry officer on his horse, he put in a nutshell what it feels like to be a survivor. 'Our problem is that we are condemned to grow. We must have the staff, and this is more expensive year by year. We must increase our capital. But by growing too much, we risk losing what we are proud of, the individual character of private banking—the service for customers, the overseeing of accounts. Another problem is that although we give special services, the larger banker gives them as well. I hate to be the fifth wheel on a car, serving the big industrial companies. They treat the private bankers as nice people, but you always feel that they think the large banks are the most important—which they are, of course . . .'

Something else has helped to weaken the old bankers of Germany—the Nazi persecution of the Jews, who have traditionally played a bigger part in finance in Germany than in most countries. For obvious reasons I found no banker in Germany who was anxious to talk about it. Even in the City (where Jews are plentiful) it has become much harder to make neutral references to the place of Jews in business; one either seems to be defending or criticising. I once wrote that in the City there appeared to me to be fewer Jews at Lloyd's than at the Stock Exchange, and a man telephoned me at midnight and demanded to know if I was anti-Semitic or what?[3]

The most famous bankers of all time were German Jews, the Rothschilds of Frankfurt, who began as nothing when Bethmanns were already a great institution, and sent their five sons over Europe to establish the dynasties that still flourish in London and Paris—but not Frankfurt, where few traces remain, and even the original house has gone, destroyed in the war. The Rothschilds left because expansion was in their blood. In the 1930s many bankers were among the Jews who left because they had to. A number of Jewish houses disappeared. Some had to change their names—Salomon Oppenheim in Cologne became Pferdmenges & Co (Robert Pfermendges, an anti-Nazi Protestant, was a close friend of the late Chancellor Adenauer), but is now Sal. Oppenheim again.

[3] It was easier once. The *Bankers' Magazine* could write in 1888 that 'the Jews excel on every Bourse in Europe; they have a pre-eminence there wholly out of proportion to their numbers, or even their wealth. Some part of that pre-eminence is, no doubt, owing to their peculiar position as a race; for nearly two thousand years they have been a small nation diffused over a wide area; that diffusion has made them the money-lenders for most of the nations with whom they lived; and the exchange of money between country and country is a business of fine calculation which prepared them for other calculations.'

The most striking banking emigration of the 1930s was probably that of Siegmund Warburg, who left Hamburg for London in 1934, later emerged as the most original merchant banker in the City, and was knighted in 1966. Other Warburgs settled in New York. Originally the family came from the Westphalian town of Warburg, where they were pawnbrokers and money-dealers. They began business in Hamburg in 1798, and had a successful career until Hitler came to power. The bank ceased to exist in its old form, though the name of M. M. Warburg & Co lasted until 1942, when it became Brinckmann, Wirtz, the present name of the house. A Warburg is now back in partnership there, and Sir Siegmund Warburg in London has a personal shareholding. The London bank, S. G. Warburg & Co, is also back in Germany as S. G. Warburg of Frankfurt, after taking over a small bank there and renaming it. But it's through London that the name of Warburg has its international flavour: and but for Hitler it's unlikely that it would ever have happened.

Banks and Industry

Continental Europe knows all about inflation, invasion, loss of property and the crumbling of institutions that were supposed to be permanent. Germany knows more than most, and the much-written-about, much-denied but undeniably close and curious connection between German banks and German industry is one result. Industry has used the banks because for a variety of reasons, most of them connected with wars and disasters, it has been more difficult than it is in the U.S. and Britain for a private firm to raise money through the stock exchange. All the Common Market countries have a similar problem; State agencies to lend funds are one answer, Italy's I.R.I. complex is another; but in Germany it has fallen particularly to the ordinary banking system to produce large amounts of money, and thus to find itself involved with industry in a way that upsets bankers in other countries. There have even been tax advantages in keeping a company private, and not raising money from the public.

The case of Krupp, the industrial group that finally ran out of credit in 1966, and was saved only by a Government guarantee of $75 million, is like an episode from some lost world of high finance. Herr Alfried Krupp left gaol in 1951, having been sentenced on charges of looting and employing slave labour, and carried on cheerfully, the fifth generation of his family to avoid issuing shares and becoming a public company. Krupp was being carried by loans from 150 banks when the leading lenders, headed by the Deutsche and Dresdner banks, decided it was time to drag Herr Krupp and his one-man empire into the twentieth century. He died soon after, just as the bankers' consortium was beginning to set slow wheels in motion, and make the group into a limited company, Fried. Krupp, owned by a broadly-based foundation.

Germany's capital market looks large but is less useful to industry than its size suggests. It includes large amounts of borrowing that in Britain would not take the form of stock-exchange issues at all. Germany has about 50 mortgage banks that issue bonds to raise money for housing loans, and housing finance has come to represent a large slice of stock-exchange issues. In Britain, people lend to and borrow from building societies direct, or rent their houses from local authorities who have raised only part of the money by issuing stock exchange securities. Local authorities in Germany pour their bonds on to the market; in Britain, cities and counties frequently solicit money in the form of straight loans.

'Official' borrowing dominates the German market, and the exchanges, like all those on the Continent, have nothing like the range of active industrial securities found in London. Figures are frequently quoted on the Continent to try to prove that criticisms of their capital markets are nonsense, and that they are really comparable to those of Britain and America. The impartial view seems to be that the public certainly provides the money, but that the markets can't make the most efficient use of it. The subject is abstruse, and everyone tends to fall back on generalisations. This is one from an enlightened source, the 1966 Segré Report: 'The shortcomings of the capital markets in the various member countries are, in reality, due not to any lack of overall savings, but rather to an imbalance between supply and demand for capital, the markets being too narrow and the investors' liquidity preference too strong.'

A manager at the Deutsche Bank admitted that 'traditionally our market has always been hectic and not too good—overshadowed by the borrowings of the State and the railways and the post office.' It isn't that no one buys bonds, but that so many of the bonds channel money into housing, public utilities and so on. It isn't that people don't save, but that a strong feeling persists that money in the bank is safer than money in securities—even semi-official bonds, let alone industrial shares.

The banks have the money; and even when a company goes to the stock market to raise cash, it is the banks that dominate the market. All buying and selling by the public must be done through banks; they are the stockbrokers, trading both on behalf of their clients and for their own account, using the stock exchange when it suits them but often bypassing it and dealing direct with another bank outside.

It's sometimes said that a German private company is reluctant to offer shares to the public because it fears that a large slice of them will never travel farther than a bank, which then puts directors on the board and has a perpetual interest. An American banker in Frankfurt said that what happened in Germany was horribly obvious: 'Banks lend and lend and lend to a company, then they turn off the faucet. You can justify this as a banker by telling them they haven't got a sound capital structure, and you can't lend them any more. The chairman of the company says, "Gee whiz, you must lend me some more or I'll collapse." So the bank says, "In that case, you must convert part of the ten million marks you owe us into stock, and since we've lent you the money, we'll keep the stock. Now we've got twenty-five per cent of you." This is what people have been speculating on in the case of Krupp—that a portion of the loans will be converted into equity and that the banks will get it. So instead of the banks being creditors they'll be the owners.'

This is the sort of view that infuriates German bankers, who say that it obviously suits incoming Americans in search of business to make the local scene appear as inbred and unfair as possible. They deplore the widespread view that German industry is in the palm of the banker's hand. They say that banks have to fight so hard for business that it's really the other way round: Krupp, according to this argument, was able to play off its 150 banks against one another (there is an old saying that if a man owes a bank a few thousand pounds, he is in its power; but if he owes it a million, it is effectively in his).

Shareholdings by banks are substantial, but not as great as some critics suggest. The big commercial banks own about five per cent of the total capital of German joint-stock companies. Major holdings must now be disclosed by law. The Deutsche Bank owns more than a quarter of the shares in Daimler-Benz of Stuttgart, the oldest automobile firm in the world, which makes Mercedes cars; and more than half the shares in the Hamburg-Amerika liner firm. Karstadt, a department-store chain, is mainly in the hands of the Deutsche Bank and the Commerzbank. Kaufhof, the largest chain of department stores, has Commerzbank and the Dresdner as major shareholders. Gelsenkirchener Bergwerks, a big oil, coal, chemical and power group, is one-third owned by the Dresdner Bank, which also has a large stake in Metallgesellschaft, a sizeable chemical and metals firm; the Norddeutscher Lloyd shipping line; two breweries (Elbschloss-Brauerei and Dortmunder Ritterbrauerei) and two construction companies (Grün & Bilfinger and Julius Berger). The list is impressive (the one above is far from exhaustive), but after comparatively few important names it tails away into a scattering of smaller firms.

Bankers appear frequently on the boards of industrial companies, and until recently a single banker might be a director of twenty or thirty undertakings; a law limiting each man to ten directorships was joked about as the 'Lex Abs,' after Dr. Abs of the Deutsche Bank, who was a director of more than thirty companies. A managing director of the Dresdner Bank said that even where they held substantial shareholdings, their influence on the company wasn't necessarily great. He agreed reluctantly that a bank could 'supervise policies'—but 'I ask myself how far the chaps I know are striving for this responsibility.' He produced the 'exceptional case' of a company that was told by the Dresdner Bank to dismiss workers or it would have its credit cut off, but insisted that the bank was only advising: if the company could have raised the money somewhere else, it was free to do so.

As well as owning shares in companies, banks (in their role as stockbrokers) hold them on behalf of clients. Where the clients give no instructions, banks may use voting shares to make their views felt at company meetings.

The position of companies that are heavily indebted to banks, as opposed to being partly owned by them, is even harder to assess. Industry, and especially smaller firms, borrows large amounts of medium-term money, and loans that are theoretically for a short period are often 'rolled over' regularly and made to last practically for ever; British and American bankers aren't keen on this sort of thing. Savings banks in particular lend to the smaller family firms that struggle on, short of capital and trained management, a dying breed but still to be found in large numbers ('They've got that old Teutonic way of thinking,' said a foreign financier in Frankfurt. 'There's only one boss-man, and he has to decide everything, down to whether they're going to build a new john'.)

Industry of all shapes and sizes, when it wants to finance new plant and machinery, is likely to turn to the banks and not the capital market. Events at Krupp show what happens when the banks are dissatisfied with the way things are going: they intervene and make the company change direction. It was their refusal to go on granting credit that precipitated the crisis. Estimates of Krupp's total debts to the banks went as high as $600 or $700 million, though at the time, publicity was conveniently circumscribed by the banker's professionally sealed lips. An official at the Bundesbank, who had been telling me how important it was to have full public discussion of financial matters, changed direction sharply when I mentioned Krupp: the banker-and-client relationship was private, he said, and one couldn't go discussing *that* in public. So the stronger the hold of the banks, the less one knows of what's really going on inside a company.

The concensus of non-German expert opinion is that their banks are unhealthily involved with industry. German banks naturally resent the idea, and they resent still more the suggestion that they manipulate the stock exchanges. 'There are many misconceptions in other countries,' said a man from the Dresdner Bank. 'When I was in Scotland a few years ago, I went to see some investment trusts and insurance companies, and the first thing they said was, "What about the banks and their links with industry? It means you know things about companies before anyone else does, and we're the last on the list to hear." While I was struggling to answer this, they said, "What about the way the stock markets work? We're afraid that if we invest in German stocks we're at the mercy of the banks."' It was a laughable misconception, he said.

But money-men with bizarre systems are always talking about 'misconceptions'; the tax havens of Liechtenstein and Luxembourg are full of authoritative spokesmen who say they are baffled at the way the rest of the world misunderstands them. The German banks are so omnipotent in the stock markets that even if they invariably put their clients' interests before their own, people would still have their suspicions. An official of the Frankfurt Stock Exchange said he denied there was any abuse: he wouldn't deny that abuse was possible. There was plenty of scope for banks to match their orders outside the market, and to deal direct with one another, by-passing the exchange. They denied that they abused their position, but unfortunately, he said, the public didn't believe them.

The German banks do it all. Besides the shares they own as long-term investments they hold large 'trading inventories'. They manage the original issue of securities, and take what they want for themselves. Even if they have no shareholding in a company, they may be close to it as a result of massive loans. So they have a good deal of information about companies, they have an interest in trading profitably in their shares, they are rich enough to buy and sell in quantity; and at the same time they are acting as stockbrokers for clients who have no option but to put their orders through a bank.

Under U.S. law, a bank may not both take deposits, and underwrite or deal in securities: it must opt for one or the other. Britain has no law about it, but in practice the investment and deposit business is kept fairly well apart; in any case, London has a strong stockbroker community to look after the clients, besides a range of powerful 'institutional' clients, such as insurance companies and pension funds, who are well able to look after themselves. German investors don't have the same institutional backbone: there are no private pension funds on the same scale, no insurance companies with enormous income from life-insurance premiums that they are free to invest. Heavyweight investors like these set the tone of a stock market; when they are pouring millions of pounds into securities every week, the market's air of deference isn't surprising. Stockbrokers and company directors take investment managers of insurance companies out to lunch, listen to their ideas, and in the end behave better than they would if there were none of these grey, upright, canny institutions to be reckoned with.

The Continent hasn't yet cultivated this kind of investor. The markets are old-fashioned; too many companies keep too much information to themselves; people aren't shareholder-oriented. A Dresdner man described how he went to see the chairman of a company where three-quarters of the shares were in the hands of the family. The chairman remarked with pleasure that their annual meetings gave no trouble. The last one had taken three minutes. A non-family shareholder had turned up by train but arrived ten minutes late. 'What do you want?' they asked him. 'The meeting,' he said. 'Sorry', they told him, 'that was seven minutes ago.'

American stockbrokers with offices in Germany have a good supply of anti-bank stories. They are in a position to see what happens; they are also (as the banks point out) in the position of newcomers who would profit if the banks' monopoly were broken, and so have a vested interest in being critical. But the stories often coincide; and the brokers sound genuinely indignant about the German system. 'We feel that commercial banking and investment banking under the same roof is an obvious conflict of interest,' said one broker. 'When credit is tight, a bank is looking for money. You, as a client of the bank, may be interested in buying securities. When you visit your bank, the man you see may be under instructions to talk you out of investing your money in securities and into having a savings account.'

German banks are now beginning to admit that in the past their investment advice has been third-rate. An official of the Dresdner Bank, where (in common with their rivals) they have been polishing up the investment service, said that discreet investigation, at their own branches and those of competitors, had shown that there was 'no systematic method for dealing with inquiries at the counters, in the way that we think appropriate.' This is just what the Americans have discovered.

Visiting brokers dwell gloomily on the way the market is rigged. A third or more of the business, they say, doesn't go through the stock exchanges at all. Many of the shares that in theory are available for trading are really locked away in bank portfolios. A financial newspaper can report that 'business came to a complete standstill on the Frankfurt market yesterday afternoon on an acute lack of orders', which is an odd state of affairs for a financial centre. Under such conditions, small amounts of trading can move the price of a share in whatever direction suits the bank. A bank that wants to sell may go into the market and buy a small block of shares, which moves the price up, then start recommending the shares to his clients, and sell from its own portfolio. 'I'd be in gaol for twenty years if I did in New York the things they do around here,' said a broker. 'There's no real control—no national stock exchange authority. Now, if there's an American financial scandal, and sometimes there is, the German Press is quick to pick it up. But the American scandal is caused by some guy violating a system that's basically honest. You can always violate systems. Here, their system is lousy.'

Plans to improve it have been framed and widely discussed in Germany, though the bankers, who have an effective political lobby, keep denying that anything is wrong. They want to keep the system; the American brokers, who are busy setting up shop in Germany as they are all over the Continent, want to change it. Both have interests of their own, so the attitude of the Segré Report is worth noting, since it's presumably as impartial a view as one is likely to hear. The group that prepared it consisted of twelve members and six associates from banks, universities and E.E.C. official institutions. One of the group told me privately: 'The banks in Germany are plain dishonest. We have said this in the report in polite and veiled terms, but it's true. It is a manipulated stock market. The German stock market is a scandal.' The report itself, very polite and very veiled, confined itself to remarking that for banks to combine the three functions of (a) acting on the stock exchange as an intermediary; (b) holding securities on one's own account, and (c) making transactions outside the exchange by 'matching customers' purchase and sale orders with stock held for their own account' was 'obviously apt to be detrimental to the good functioning of the market, because of the conflicts of interest that may result, and is therefore best avoided.'

The Segré Report wasn't interested in the German market for its own sake, but because it was looking towards the day when capital markets throughout Europe are integrated with one another. Local idiosyncracies are already less local than they were. It's impossible for money-men to be as parochial as they might find it convenient to be. In Germany, the arrival in 1967 of an American stockbroking firm, Bache & Co, caused alarm. Bache are the second largest stockbrokers in the world (another New York firm, Merrill Lynch, are the largest), with about two dozen branches outside the U.S., half of them in Europe. Bache began in Germany as most incoming stockbrokers do, co-operating with the banks and not trying to deal directly with Germans who might want to buy U.S. securities. Later the firm became more aggressive, and later still, to the annoyance of German bankers, Bache bought its way into the Frankfurt Stock Exchange by taking over a local bank, Bankhaus Kessler. Renamed Bankhaus Bache and installed in elegant offices full of Telex machines and direct lines, the American broker-bankers have an effective beach-head into the German system. Others are expected to follow.

The World Outside

What is happening in the German stock market is simply that outsiders are intervening to suit themselves. This kind of thing is going on all over the Continent, as financial markets of every type gradually penetrate one another; but it has a special interest in Germany because it is a country whose recent history has set it a little apart, at least in people's minds. The Germans themselves felt this after the war. Their country was ruined and so was their image. They felt unwelcome in the world at large. The attitude of bankers, according to one of them now, was that 'they didn't want to go in for foreign branches, and they would prefer banks from other countries not to go to Germany. But the Government was for freedom of trade, and so the Bundesbank let the foreign banks in.' While the French, the Belgians, the Japanese, the Americans and the British have all been expanding outside their own countries, few German banks have opened branches overseas. 'There is a psychological objection among the older generation,' said a man from the Dresdner. When the Dresdner opened a London branch in 1967, it was the first German bank to go there since before the first world war.

As Germany became an industrial power again, its commercial ties with other countries developed quickly. American firms alone have more than three billion dollars invested in Germany. While the big German banks have been inclined to look inwards, despite their involvement in trade-financing, two individual bankers have emerged as international figures—Abs of the Deutsche Bank and the wily Dr. Otmar Emminger, vice-president of the Bundesbank.

Emminger is the foreign specialist, and among the cleverest and most influential of the European central bankers whose lives have been one long round of monetary crises (over other people's money, not theirs) in recent years. Abs is a more stately character, a Rhineland lawyer's son who was a banker under the Nazis but never joined the Party, and was brought in to help organise the distribution of Marshall Aid after the war. Earlier in his career, as a private banker, he worked in several European capitals and in the United States. Germany was short of cosmopolitan money-men after 1945: too many had fled or been killed; and after twelve years of Nazi isolationism, too many of those who survived weren't cosmopolitan enough. Abs spoke English, French, Dutch and Spanish, and he knew what the world was like outside—a German banker, who kept referring to him sarcastically and perhaps enviously as 'Hermann Joseph the Great Abs,' said it was this cosmopolitanism that pushed him to the top so quickly. 'Maybe', he said, 'he was the only man in the Deutsche Bank who knew that Louisiana was in the south of the U.S.A. Under the Nazis, going abroad was decadent. Abs can talk in many tongues without losing touch with what he really wants.'

With his multiple directorships and influential contacts—he was a close friend of the former Chancellor, Konrad Adenauer—Abs emerged as the most formidable businessman in the land. Among the companies where he is still chairman of the Supervisory Board are Daimler-Benz, Lufthansa and the reconstituted Krupp. Abs became better known outside his own country when, after 1958, Germany re-entered the international-lending business. Germany was prosperous enough to let borrowers outside the country use her capital market to raise loans, and the Deutsche Bank under Abs was involved from the beginning as chief organiser.

Later, when the Eurobond market developed, German banks carved themselves profitable slices of business. After half a century of war, inflation, dictatorship and more war, Germany was once more a respectable figure in the world's money circles, and rather more respectable than poor old debt-laden Britain. 'More than at any time since 1914,' says Dr. Karl Blessing, president of the Bundesbank, 'Germany is both economically and financially involved with foreign countries.'

One striking instance of Germany's new posture was the support that came from Frankfurt in 1967 for a Eurobond loan to Israel. The Industrial Development Bank of Israel was borrowing $15 million. One of the seven banks in the syndicate that organised the loan was the Deutsche Bank; other German institutions came in to help sell the bonds. So here were the Germans publicly raising money for the Jews, and incidentally running the risk of offending Arab clients and losing their business. 'I consider it only normal that Deutsche Bank did not withhold its normal co-operation,' says Abs, adding that 'we heard, of course, a few critical comments from some Arab sources.' The syndicate was led by S. G. Warburg of London, the bank that moved on from Hamburg because of Hitler. Some kind of wheel had come full circle.

(iii) **Holland:** Honest Men

The great vein of the River Rhine runs through Europe from Switzerland to the North Sea, carrying millions of tons of Common Market trade each year. Where it reaches the sea at Rotterdam the Dutch have built the world's largest port outside the United States. Along the river-sides around Rotterdam the black and silver skyline of oil refineries and petrochemical plants is like New Jersey's seen from the Hudson River. It is one of Europe's major industrial complexes, and the sea-winds that blow sharply in between the pale new skyscrapers smell of fire and metal.

But the financial centre is somewhere else—forty miles away in Amsterdam, which is quite a distance in a country as small as the Netherlands. Holland is just twice the size of Wales and supports more than twelve million people; nowhere else in the world is so densely populated, and Holland, like Britain, depends on extensive foreign trade. It became a commercial power in the seventeenth century, and Amsterdam emerged as the leading financial city in Europe; by 1611 there was already a stock exchange of sorts, perhaps the first in the world (ten years later it was sufficiently well organised to ban swearing.)

Amsterdam developed as a centre in the way that London did—a port that handled trade, which attracted bankers and brokers, whose presence in turn brought more business. Like London, it was the cornerstone of a colonial empire, and many buildings in Amsterdam date from the golden age of two or three centuries ago. If they were to begin again, Rotterdam would be the natural centre; but Amsterdam, afloat on its canals, has the history. Many of the business offices are in old buildings along the once-superior canals of Keizersgracht and Herengracht, where the houses were more spacious. The bigger banks are in streets full of trams and dust, but there are plenty of money-men tucked away around corners, beside bridges, behind churches and museums.

There's a certain nostalgia for the past, a recognition that it won't be the same again. Long after Holland had ceased to be a world power, Amsterdam continued to be a centre of international importance. In the last century, when Europe was the exporter of capital and America was on the receiving end, Amsterdam raised large sums that (among other things) helped to build America's railways, and by 1900, Amsterdam was the most important centre for dealing in American shares outside the U.S. It was one of Europe's largest security markets between the wars; besides dealing in many foreign shares, it raised large sums for investment in the Dutch East Indies, Holland's colonial empire for centuries, which produced rubber, oil, coffee, tea, tobacco and much else, to the benefit of the mother country, until the war swept it away. The Japanese occupied parts of the long chain of islands—the land area is fifty times that of Holland—and in 1949, the former colony broke away and became the independent State of Indonesia. Dutch firms and property were seized: the commonplace humiliation for Europe's old colonialists. Meanwhile Amsterdam's business in foreign securities had dwindled, so that now when non-Dutchmen talk about it, they make kind remarks, as though sympathising. Most of Holland's overseas holdings had to be sold after the war to pay off debts, and Marshall Aid had to be pumped in to get the economy going. It was the end of the old order.

In the nineteenth century, the money went from east to west across the Atlantic, from Europe to the United States. Now it comes the other way. Amsterdam, like London, has lost its status as an international centre for raising capital. 'It still looks impressive on paper,' said a Stock Exchange man, 'but most of it is what's been left over from history. There are more than two hundred American stocks, but most of them date back to the turn of the century. Only a few have been added since the war, and their importance keeps declining. In the twenties and thirties, American stocks mattered more than domestic ones. Now the emphasis has shifted. People talk of "internationalising" Amsterdam and some of the other exchanges. But domestic needs come first, and they'll absorb all the Continent's capacity to save, and more.'

The Dutch have had to come to terms with their times, and considering the smallness of the country, they haven't done badly. Of the numerous countries that give Britain a fellow-feeling because they, too, have lost their empires, perhaps Holland is the nearest in temperament. It's an accommodating place. Most bankers and merchants speak English; offices rarely fail to produce coffee, cakes and assorted cigars for visitors. The Dutch have a solid God-fearing air that makes for commercial confidence—'for traditional standards of conduct,' wrote a London merchant banker, 'Amsterdam stands head and shoulders above all the capital markets of the Common Market countries.' It's a difficult point to press with money-men, since the conventional attitude is that nowadays there is nothing to choose between one centre's morals and another's. But foreign-exchange dealers, in particular, will sometimes wink when asked if it's true that one is more likely to be double-crossed in Paris or Milan than in Stockholm or London; and Amsterdam always gets an approving nod in this kind of conversation. 'We have an astonishing regard for legality,' said a stockbroker. 'We pay a great deal of money to income-tax consultants, but we do not fiddle. In this we resemble the Germans. During the Occupation, many Jews came forward and registered with the Nazis—not because they were Jews but because they were Dutchmen.'

Moral uprightness by itself wouldn't make Holland so prominent in the financial league. Natural-gas deposits, first proved in 1959 and now being piped for export as well as used at home, are one source of prosperity. So is Europort at Rotterdam, where 30,000 ships arrive in a year—three times as many as at Amsterdam—and oil imports of 100 million tons a year are envisaged in the near future. Traffic through Rotterdam is especially important for Germany, a hundred miles down the Rhine. ('Rotterdam is virtually a German port,' said an Amsterdam banker, 'but don't write that down or you won't sell a single copy in Holland').

Another element in Holland's affluence is that it has three of the biggest industrial companies in the world. The *Fortune* list of the 200 largest industrials outside the U.S. is headed by the Royal Dutch-Shell group, the joint Anglo-Dutch oil and chemicals corporation that is a giant by any standards. It is carefully (and at times awkwardly) run both from London and The Hague, Holland's political capital, and is slightly more Dutch than British. *Fortune's* second largest company is another hybrid, the Unilever food and detergents group, which is slightly more British than Dutch. In seventh place is Philips Lamps—the electrical and electronics firm, which took over the British firm of Pye in 1967—coming after British Petroleum, Germany's Volkswagen, Britain's Imperial Chemical Industries and Britain's National Coal Board. These Anglo-Dutch corporations, and especially Royal Dutch and Unilever, have come to dominate the stock market, and help make it outward-looking. When Philips made a $210 million share issue in 1962, the largest ever floated in Holland, foreign investors bought half the shares.

There is a sharp division between companies like these and the traditional family-run firms that are still thick on the ground. Holland has been busy industrialising itself since the second world war, and now fewer than a tenth of the working population is in agriculture, compared with a fifth before 1939. (France still has a sixth of its workers on the land; Germany has around 12 per cent, Britain 3 per cent.) But as a banker put it, 'the old customs of Dutch companies, emerging from the days of the family-owned business, have been slow to disappear. The old ways are reflected in a shortage of information and the secretiveness of managers.' Daf, the car manufacturer, is privately owned, with no stock exchange quotation. So is the still bigger department-store firm of C & A, owned by the Brenninkmeyer family (C and A were the initials of Clement and Augustus, the first of the family), who opened their first shop around 1840. The Brenninkmeyers are a rich family who have managed to keep some of their secrets; they may be going against the tide, but there must be a lot of industrialists who envy them. They were quick to take advantage of a provision of Britain's 1967 Companies Act, which allows an ordinary limited company to become 'unlimited', and withhold information about profits and management changes. Their British subsidiary, C & A Modes, which runs more than forty stores, was made into three unlimited-liability companies, with at least one director personally liable for the company's debts, if it had any.

Holland's capital market is usually described as being the nearest to London's, just as London's is the nearest to New York's. The institutional investors are strong and varied; private pensions and life assurance are more popular in Holland than in most parts of Europe, providing large sums that can be invested in bonds, shares and, most of all, in privately placed loans—highly popular in Holland as in Britain, with firms going direct to the institutions in order to raise long-term capital.

At the same time, Holland has its private firms without a stock market quotation, and a number of firms that have quotations but do their best to discourage shareholders from interfering in the company by doing such irritating things as voting. 'Companies that go public often keep control with non-voting shares,' said a securities manager at the Amsterdam-Rotterdam Bank. 'We have many devices, some of which are unique in the world.' He described a method of dealing indirectly in shares, via 'certificates' that are issued by a trustee or holding company. The company issues the shares; the trustee takes them up and issues certificates; these are what the customer buys, worth just as much but minus their votes. 'As a matter of fact,' said the banker, 'the average investor is little interested in voting, because there isn't much he can do even if he does.' This isn't the view that stock-market men in London like to take.

Another substantial difference between Amsterdam's market and London's is that in Amsterdam the banks have most of the power. In Germany the banks do all the trading and are accused of selfishness and worse. In Holland they are members and traders, but there are also several hundred independent stockbrokers, anxious not to be elbowed out. The Stock Exchange is among old streets beyond the Royal Palace, and the stockbrokers sit tight behind their traditions and regard the banks with dismay. 'You don't have to dig far to find hatred of the big banks,' said a stockbroker. 'They have a network of branches and so they can reach the clients. The poor downtrodden Amsterdam stockbrokers can't—at least, that's what the poor downtrodden Amsterdam stockbrokers say, though to my mind it's nonsense. If we aren't efficient we don't deserve to survive.'

The banks, as usual, are accused of bypassing the exchange and dealing with one another direct, and although they naturally deny any malpractice, they regard the brokers (in private) in a way that confirms the brokers' fears. 'Oh, they're a very minor element,' said a banker. Angry mutterings were heard in Amsterdam when Lloyds

Bank Europe, the Continental subsidiary of the London deposit bank, bought up a small private bank called Theodoor Gilissen, thereby gaining entry to the Stock Exchange. A broker said the feeling was that banks were bad enough, let alone a foreign bank. Once upon a time, he said, banks were excluded from the exchange; then one of them bought up a stockbroker, and the rot set in. Now it was foreign banks. What would happen if the Deutsche Bank wanted to get a foot in the door? It would point to the precedent of Lloyds Bank Europe, and that would be that.

Dutch banks have been busy amalgamating in recent years to form large units in the approved manner, and well over half the deposits are held by two of them, the Algemene Bank Nederland and the Amsterdam-Rotterdam Bank, or Amro for short. Everyday banking has a good deal in common with Britain's, except that in Holland, cheques are used less. It is not a criminal offence to pass a dud cheque, and a shop is correspondingly reluctant to take one from a customer. A type of guaranteed cheque, to be used with a special identity card, has now been introduced. There is much popular advertising aimed at small customers, who are all too often wedded to the post office's giro. As often happens on the Continent, the banks are in the odd position of trying to attract the public away from somebody else's giro, while most of their own employees, including many of the senior ones, use it themselves. The trouble, said a banker, was that the post office giro was becoming more human. In the old days it automatically rejected a transfer if the money wasn't available to meet it, no matter how small the deficit; there was no such thing as an overdraft. But now the giro would let it through if it was only for 20 or 30 guilders, and tell the customer to hurry up and pay something in. That was progress, said the banker grudgingly.

As well as its large commercial banks, where idiosyncracies and character are, as usual, hard to find under the layers of rectitude, carpets and posh panelling, Holland has many small banks, relics of better days, where the bankers sound more relaxed and claim to be more flexible. The 1966 edition of Auburn's *Comparative Banking* lists seventeen 'private banks', but a year later the number was down to fourteen at most: Gilissen had been bought by Lloyds, a bank called Mees and another called Hope had amalgamated to make Mees & Hope, and an impressive-sounding house called Teixeira de

Mattos—founded 1852, and described in another book published at about the same time as belonging to 'a class of bankers who compel respect by their adherence to the traditions of their long-established firms'—had collapsed, and a man was in gaol. Others on the list, like an increasing number of European banks, were not quite what they seemed on paper. The Americans had a stake in at least three of them.

The two private banks that are best-known outside the country are Piersons, which doesn't advertise at all, and Mees & Hope, which will go so far as to advertise its name, without giving details. Both have found allies, ready for the fighting years ahead—considering the size of Holland, it's doubtful whether any other European country has had so many banking mergers and alliances. The Amro and Algemene banks are both the result of extensive amalgamations. Piersons, which isn't a particularly old firm, has taken a joint share in a larger Dutch bank with Chase Manhattan. Mees & Hope has sold a modest slice of its holding company, Bankierscompagnie, to Morgan Guaranty of New York, and another to the Hongkong & Shanghai Bank.

Mees & Hope (the Mees part founded in Rotterdam in 1720; the Hope part in Amsterdam in 1762) overlooks one of the grander Amsterdam canals, the Keizersgracht, and has a long-standing friendship with Barings, of London. When I was there, one of the partners apologised for having to leave on official business; after he had gone, they told me that he held a position at court, and was off to change into uniform and help receive the King and Queen of Nepal, who were visiting Amsterdam. It sounded like the City: a piece of ritual, a flash of something reflected from the past. A Mees & Hope man mentioned another historical oddity, the prejudice among Protestant bankers—the majority, by tradition—against Roman Catholics. It was fading now, he said, but ten years before when he worked in the personnel department, he needed special permission from the partners before he could engage a Catholic (Holland has about equal numbers of Catholics and Protestants, but in the past the Catholics were generally less well educated, and are still poorly represented at the top in business. Only one of Amro Bank's fourteen directors is a Catholic).

The rivalry between Amsterdam and Rotterdam, which goes back a long way, is echoed in every letter that goes out from Mees & Hope. The bank's title after the amalgamation put Mees, the Rotterdam partner, first; the letter heading and all the bank's literature carefully redress this slight to Amsterdam by putting the Amsterdam address first, followed by the Rotterdam one. 'That was an important decision,' said a former Hope man in Rotterdam, adding that overseas clients were sometimes so confused that they wrote 'Amsterdam and Rotterdam' on the envelope, just to be on the safe side.

They laughed when I asked which really was the head office and said they were equal. This is the answer, complete with laugh, that one gets from most Dutch banks, including the largest; Amro Bank, created by amalgamating the Amsterdam and Rotterdam banks, is particularly careful to say that it has two head offices. Everyone knows that the real head office is the one in Amsterdam, though it's difficult to find anyone who will admit it to an outsider. Holland's prosperous present is reflected in the reddened sky above Rotterdam, but Amsterdam is where the memories are.

(iv) **Belgium:** Centrally Situated

Business capitals like to claim they are central or otherwise geographically convenient. Frankfurt stands where the old trading routes crossed and where rail and air lines still intersect. Switzerland is nicely juxtaposed with the rest of Western Europe. The Dutch, according to publicity put out by the Robeco investment trust of Rotterdam, are 'ideally placed', when it comes to assessing international stock markets, 'by virtue of their central geographical position'. The claim is vitiated by Telex, direct dialling between countries, communications satellites and the aeroplane, but it shows how hard people try to sound close to the heart of things in a crowded peninsula like Europe where there is so much manoeuvring for place.

The Belgians are particularly keen to be thought of as well situated, and can point to the number of times their country has been a battlefield as evidence that they are at some kind of Continental junction. Other people's armies have fought there for centuries. (Ypres today has smooth fields and little brown and white houses. Waterloo is a village on a main road south of Brussels, where business men commute by car). The area was important for trade and communications from medieval times, when there was no

Belgium as such, but a group of Catholic-oriented provinces, linked with a group of Protestant provinces to the north that later become Holland.

Not far south of Holland's Rotterdam and the mouth of the Rhine is Belgium's Antwerp and the mouth of the Scheldt. Bruges, to the west of Antwerp, was a trading centre from the thirteenth century, and the Van der Buerse family there is said to be the origin of the word 'bourse' for a money or trading exchange. In the middle of the sixteenth century the Catholic Low Countries (now Belgium) came under the thumb of the Calvinist United Provinces (now Holland); it was not until 1830 that an independent Belgium finally emerged, just in time to join Europe's industrial leap forward. By the end of the century it was one of the world's most tightly packed manufacturing countries, with an African empire in the Congo that had another sixty years to go before it turned sour on its owners.

Belgium's present claim to be at the centre of things rests in particular on the solid fact that the Common Market has had its headquarters in Brussels since 1958. A cluster of skyscrapers has gone up on the edge of the city, replacing scattered premises, to house 5,000 officials, librarians, statisticians, translators and secretaries. The Commission, the executive body, is divided into more than twenty 'directorates', from 'budgets' and 'competition policy' to 'financial policy' and 'social affairs'. The total Common Market budget, contributed by the six member countries, is now more than $2 billion a year; the E.E.C. and its agencies spend money on, among other things, farm subsidies, nuclear reactors, coal and steel projects.

Newspapers christen the supra-national Civil Servants 'Eurocrats' and Brussels 'Euro-city', a label that conjures up some gleaming urban landscape unlike the real Brussels, which is a plain, harsh place, not notably cosmopolitan. Because the E.E.C. executive is there, it's possible for the Belgians to feel that nothing could be more natural than for Brussels to become the economic and financial capital of a united Europe. But it is one thing to be the capital of the planners and theorists, another to be part of the daily business machine.

Brussels has other assets. Belgium's geographical position still counts. Antwerp and Rotterdam are near, both Paris and the industrial Ruhr are a few hours by train, and London is a short air journey away. A circle drawn around Brussels with a radius of 200 miles takes in London, Paris, Luxembourg, Amsterdam, Rotterdam, Bonn, Frankfurt, Cologne and Dusseldorf. This makes Brussels a useful base for the banker who wants to visit clients. It appeals to other organisations besides the E.E.C. The Council of the North Atlantic Treaty Organisation has its headquarters in Brussels, with a staff of 2,000.

Foreign firms have flocked there, especially when Switzerland, an early favourite with American industry, grew too crowded for comfort, and labour became scarce (the same thing is now happening in Belgium). A succession of governments have fallen over themselves to attract firms and capital from outside, even offering deferred-payment facilities, so that foreigners can buy up bits of Belgium now and pay for it later. Hundreds of firms from Germany, Britain, the Netherlands and of course the United States have set up subsidiaries or bought their way into Belgian companies, encouraged by tempting investment subsidies and tax concessions. Antwerp and a wide area around the port are thick with new plants.

Among British firms operating in Belgium are Imperial Chemical Industries, Fisons (chemicals), Watney Mann and Allied Breweries (both beer), Schweppes (soft drinks and food), Tate & Lyle (sugar) and British Petroleum. U.S. capital directly invested in the country is not less than $750 million. Half this amount is in manufacturing industry, giving Belgium, for its size, the biggest concentration of American factories on the Continent.[4] As well as plant, many American firms have set up their European headquarters in Brussels, including some of the biggest, such as Pfizer, Texaco, General Foods, Coco-Cola and International Telephone and Telegraph; the latter has M. Paul-Henri Spaak, former Belgian Prime Minister and long standing advocate of U.S. investment, on the board of its principal company in Belgium. The city has an American business community of several thousand.

Small countries must be free-traders, and the Belgians have taken kindly to economic invasion. Perhaps the heterogeneous nature of

[4] Holland has rather more capital invested, but much of this is in the oil refineries around Rotterdam. Switzerland has not less than $1,200 million, by far the highest American investment in relation to population, but little of this is in either manufacturing or oil: most of the money has gone into finance, holding and service companies.

the place helps to curb any budding sense of economic nationalism; an official Government booklet talks of Belgium as 'an astonishing digest of Western Europe.' (With Luxembourg and the Netherlands it forms a single Customs union, 'Benelux', within the Common Market. An agreement with Luxembourg dates from 1921; in matters of trade and foreign exchange the two countries act as one. The Customs union between the three began in 1948.)

As a financial centre, Brussels has grown more important as foreign capital has come into Belgium; so has Antwerp, thirty miles away. Few Continental centres have more American banks than Brussels, and many Wall Street stockbrokers have offices there. It's a common picture in Europe—the Americans busy building their business empires, alongside local institutions that helped to build empires now defunct—but the contrast is sharper than usual in Brussels. The local banks in Belgium trail some splendid vestiges of imperial glory, especially the august Société Générale de Banque, where attendants in black ties glide across marble floors, and the electric lights are set in gilded brackets. The Royal Palace is down the road; the basement garage is full of black Mercedes. Talking to two officials, I asked if the bank had a motto, and was told it hadn't, but that there was once a little joke among the directors—they both smiled and looked away, but finally one of them leaned across and said, 'It was, *We fear nothing but God and the expense*.' Years ago the expense would have mattered less; but that was before Belgium lost the Congo.

When Belgium had an empire, the bank helped to administer it, and its atmosphere today combines a dignified awareness of its past with a strenuous desire to face the future, which it has been doing by (among other things) reorganising management and rebuilding its offices. The bank, like all banks of importance in Belgium, is closely tied to a holding company, in this case the shy but gargantuan Société Générale de Belgique, one of the two or three largest investment concerns in Europe. The Société is so big and has been there so long that it is credited with even more power than the substantial amount it possesses—'We are a picture of horror for the Socialists,' said an official.

All the holding companies are well entrenched, a part of the scene since Belgium was industrialised. The Société outdoes them all, colouring the country's economy, said to control a fifth of it. Less important than it was—the Congo nationalised its main interests there, and at home it is only now beginning to move into new industries such as electronics and petrochemicals—its name still has a persuasive ring. Shareholders are thought to include members of both the Belgian and Dutch royal families. An officer of the Belgian court, the Grand Maréchal de la Cour, is always on the Société's Board of Auditors, which at present has two former Grand Marshals as well, one of them a prince and the other a count.

The Société was founded early in the nineteenth century, before Belgium and Holland had separate identities, as a development company whose only substantial asset was the Fôret de Soignes to the south of Brussels. This was sold to the Government—it's still there, stretching nearly to Waterloo—and the proceeds used to start empire-building. The Société was bank and finance company combined, investing (together with similar, smaller concerns) in Belgian industry at home and public utilities in under-developed parts of the world like America. For years it issued Belgium's currency and to all intents was the national bank. It made its fortune in the Congo, and continued as combined bank and investment company until 1934, when, as in other countries hit by the crisis, banking and investing had to be separated. In Italy the banks' industrial shareholdings were gathered up into a State corporation, I.R.I. In Belgium they were left with holding companies, which then set up banks as subsidiaries. The three main Belgian banks began like this, though the holding companies have reduced their direct influence over the years.

The worst thing that ever happened to the Société was independence for the Congo, which led to massive interference with its interests there, and in particular the nationalisation in 1966 of the Union Minière du Haut-Katanga, the copper-and-cobalt-producing company in which the Société was a major shareholder. Union Minière called it 'the greatest grab in history' and the Société now says it lost assets worth $800 million; but a surge in the price of copper, of which it held large stocks, enabled it to carry on, and start investing in Canada, among other places.

In the Congo, another member of the Société's family, the Société Générale des Minerais, appeared on the scene to handle the producing, processing and selling of copper on behalf of Gécomin, the

Congolese company that had taken over. The Belgians had lost enormously but they hadn't lost everything; big business is usually too ubiquitous to be disposed of by decree, too practical to let sentiment stand in the way of making money. It suits both the Belgians and the Congolese to go on working together; the Société's annual report refers angrily on one page to the way Union Minière was 'unjustly dispossessed,' and on another, concludes that Société Générale des Minerais looks like having a good year. As an economist back at headquarters in Brussels remarked, 'You cannot fool realities. Psychologically, Gécomin was necessary because the Congolese didn't want to hear any more about the Union Minère. It was a nasty word for them and it had to go. In fact, it was the same people who signed the agreement on behalf of Société Générale des Minerais. But everybody's face was saved.'

Inside Belgium, the Société's holdings extend throughout heavy industry—steel, engineering, chemicals, glass, textiles, cement, zinc and shipping. It is in public utilities and nuclear power. It has an important holding in Petrofina, the Belgian petroleum company, through its stake in another holding group, Compagnie d'Anvers. Many companies are interlocked, or thought to be, and Socialists have spent much effort trying to unravel the truth. Solvay, the biggest company in Belgium, is described as being 'close' to the Société. Solvay controlled a bank which was merged with the Société Générale de Banque a few years ago, and Solvay men now appear on its board.

Belgium's bank-and-finance groups can have seemingly endless ramifications. After the Société comes 'Brufina,' the Société de Bruxelles pour la Finance et l'Industrie, which holds about a sixth of the capital in Belgium's second bank, the Banque de Bruxelles. Banque Lambert, the fourth largest bank in Belgium, developed about the middle of the nineteenth century from the Antwerp agency of the Paris arm of the Rothschilds. The Lamberts ran the agency, and the boss's son married a Rothschild daughter. The bank is now part of a holding company, the Compagnie Lambert pour I'Industrie et la Finance. It's an elegant house of the old school with partners who include a diplomat or two and a couple of barons. It was one of the first European banks to sponsor Eurobonds. It looks after private portfolios for the rich, has a subsidiary in Luxembourg, and is also a deposit bank with about fifty-five branches.

The holding company's interests include property, petrol, food and mining. In Africa, the ingenious Lambert men have joined forces with bankers from France, another country that has lost its possessions there, to run a chain of banks through their countries' old territories—from the former Belgian Congo to the former French Cameroons. Altogether there are banks in ten African States, controlled by a company called Société Financière pour les Pays d'Outre-Mer, which has its headquarters in Geneva (not to be confused with a big French-dominated holding company in Africa, the Compagnie Financière pour l'Outre-Mer). The French are represented in Société Financière by the Banque Nationale de Paris. Germany and the U.S. are also represented—another bit of ingenuity. Partly to have more money and partly for political reasons, the Bank of America and Germany's Commerzbank were invited to join the African group. As a partner said at Banque Lambert, high up in its glittering new office-block near the palace, it would never have done for the Belgians and French to appear in Africa as 'the sole representatives of former political powers.'

The holding companies were criticised by a Government commission that reported in 1967 on ways of modernising the financial system; some of its members thought they were too aloof and old-fashioned, and pointed to their fondness for traditional industries. They enervate the Belgian stock market, where only a tiny proportion of companies have a quotation—among those without one are the largest in brewing, sugar and chocolate. There are many family firms, not all of them small. The Solvay chemical group has existed since 1863, when Ernest Solvay invented the soda-making process which took his name, but it didn't make a public issue until 1967. Solvay has dozens of subsidiaries in many countries. It trundled out figures that showed it to have annual sales of $560 million, and 46th place among Continental companies in the *Fortune* list. Even then the Solvay family and associates remained in control, selling off only a small part of the equity.

The Stock Exchange has a pillared exterior where pigeons strut; inside, men shout and bells ring as if this really was the financial nexus; an old man in a battered black hat sits on a public bench staring through a pair of green binoculars at the lists of prices across the floor. It's a restricted market because industry finds so much of its money elsewhere—either from the holding companies or from official institutions like the Société Nationale de Crédit a l'Industrie, which issues torrents of bonds to raise money from the public, and has about $1 billion invested in Belgian industry. These and other official issues of bonds mop up much of the country's available savings. Arriving late to see a manager at the Société Générale de Banque, I apologised and said I had been delayed at the Stock Exchange. He smiled thinly and said 'Was it worth it?' It's the old story in Europe, where people feel safer with a more rigid and State-controlled system. The national savings bank, the Caisse Générale d'Epargne et de Retraite, is well to the fore, presided over by His Royal Highness Prince Albert, with more than $2 billion in deposits, which it lends out to build houses and finance industry and farmers. The Post Office also runs a large giro, and public authorities have to keep their accounts with it. Continental post offices are always on the look-out for new business. A Brussels banker explained that when a child's birth was registered in Belgium, the parents received a note to say that an account had been opened for him at the national savings bank and credited with 50 or 100 francs (something under £1). The baby would not withdraw the money for the next 21 years; it cost the State nothing till then, and it helped to ensure that the new citizen took the straight and narrow path of national savers.

For all its banks and Eurocrats, Brussels doesn't *feel* like the prospective centre of financial Europe (in fairness to the Belgians, they don't often lay claim to the title). If there were nothing else, the country's bitter race-and-language quarrel between Flemings and Walloons gives Belgium a parochial look. Just over half the population, mainly in the north, speak Flemish, which is exactly the same as Dutch; the rest, mainly in the south speak French. The French-speaking Walloons, traditionally the ruling class, have been faced with mounting Flemish nationalism. The decline of heavy industry in the south, and the new developments around Antwerp, which is the heart of the Flemish area, have helped to upset the balance. Antwerp already handles more general cargo than any other port in Europe (Rotterdam's total is swollen by oil), and the city is still offering inducements to new industry, despite a cluster of factories, from General Motors and Ford to Union Carbide and the German Bayer, that would be the envy of an undeveloped area. Part of the original intention in developing Antwerp was probably to help the Flemings; instead, the boom in their area is giving them a taste for power. The Flemings still act the role of the oppressed—'They feel they're servants,' said a banker—but now they are armed with more influence then they ever had before.

Officially the two languages go hand in hand, and the effects range from duplicated staffing in some public departments, to street names posted in French and Flemish, one above the other. Flemish extremists, of whom there is no shortage, attack signposts in Flemish parts of the country, covering the French version of the words with tar; sometimes loyal Walloons retaliate by tarring the Flemish word as well. The leading banks are Walloon-oriented, except for the Kredietbank, the country's third largest, where Flemish is normally spoken, especially by the management. The language question provides an oddly parochial background to Belgium's position in economic Europe.

(v) **Luxembourg:** Tax Haven

A stockbroker called X with an office in a block of flats, half a mile from the centre of the city of Luxembourg, was explaining why he worked there. 'It's an oasis,' he said, relighting a small black cigar that kept going out. Children were playing in a courtyard, their voices muted; doves were audible; greenstuff was in view, framing a bland blue sky.

X isn't a Luxembourg stockbroker—the last one closed in 1960, leaving only the representatives of the country's thirteen banks. X runs, and more or less is, the branch of a London firm of brokers, one of the few to have invaded Europe. He punched a button on his telephone and it began to dial a Rotterdam number by itself; such phones, which can be preset to connect with up to fifty chosen number-groups, are useful for money-men who dial direct around Europe at twelve or thirteen digits per call. 'When the directors decided they wanted an office on the Continent,' he said, 'I put my foot down and told them it must be here. I like it here. But where you are sitting is an extension of London.'

The machine finished dialling and we waited for the connection to click and start ringing. Nothing happened, only the characteristic near-silence of the European telephone, with tiny sounds like insects on a summer day. In the bookcase alongside his desk I saw the title *Mr Executive: Keep Well—Live Longer*. X fiddled patiently with the telephone and began again, explaining, before the connection was finally made, that Luxembourg was both central and salubrious, and had other merits besides. It was necessary to stay on the right side of banks by channelling business through them; one mustn't steal clients and keep them to oneself by placing the business direct through London. If, let's say, he had set up shop in Paris, the local stockbrokers might have suspected that he was after their clients. But in Luxembourg there were scarcely any local clients anyway, and so there wasn't much to be suspicious of.

Luxembourg may sound a financial backwater, but it isn't. The Stock Exchange is not very busy, yet a large proportion of the international bonds that have been issued in Europe in the last ten years have a Luxembourg Stock Exchange quotation. There is more in Luxembourg than meets the eye. There are 999 square miles of it, a pear-shaped country about the size of Derbyshire or Rhode Island, bordering Belgium, Germany and France. Officially the Grand Duchy of Luxembourg, it has a population of a third of a million, nearly a quarter of whom live in the city itself. It has its own Germanic-French language, Letzeburgesche, a steel industry producing above three million tons a year, and a large number of company headquarters to which no one, or hardly anyone, ever goes. As a holiday resort it is slightly unfashionable; as a financial centre it is eccentric, successful and brushed, just brushed, with a suspicion of something not quite nice. It is a tax haven, 'the Switzerland of the Common Market' according to one of its operators, though the Swiss would rather not have such comparisons bandied about.

The train from Brussels takes two and a half hours and a cheap return costs under £5. As Belgium and Luxembourg form an economic union, there is no Customs barrier between the two; the British Board of Trade's *Hints to Business Men Visiting Belgium and Luxembourg* warns of 'frontier posts where passports and baggage may be examined,' but in practice the traveller from Belgium, like his money, is likely to pass without hindrance. Luxembourg has its own coins and low-denomination banknotes. Belgian money, which is worth exactly the same, circulates alongside the local currency, though travellers going in the other direction find that Luxembourg money isn't welcome in Belgian shops.

The city of Luxembourg's railway station is a modest place where telephone boxes are hard to find. The cobbled squares are attractive, the cafes are pretty, the cars don't hoot very much, and new buildings are not allowed to rise more than a few storeys above the street. It used to be the headquarters of the Coal and Steel Community before this moved to Brussels and was merged into the main body of the E.E.C., but the steel and glass tower building was put up outside the city. The beauty of Luxembourg and its importance to money-men is that as a sovereign State it can make its own laws, and its laws are framed to deal liberally with the finance companies that go there. The company needn't go there in anything but name. There may be an actual staff in an actual office; usually there's a plate on the door or a post office box number, with a lawyer or, more likely, a bank to look after the company's interests. The State of Luxembourg profits by taking a little tax from the company; it isn't very much, but Luxembourg isn't very big. The banks that have set up in Luxembourg, to deal with the companies that have gone there because it's such a permissive place to be, add to the country's prosperity. It makes everyone happy, except for governments who feel they are being deprived of money that they might be entitled to if the companies had stayed away from Luxembourg; but even the critics of Luxembourg usually give the impression that they are making a gesture more than anything else—as if they know in their hearts that when it comes to looking after their own interests, business men are unstoppable.

The crux of the matter is that when a company is established in Luxembourg for the purpose of receiving income, it can take in the money from abroad, and pay it out again to whoever it likes, without seeing it shrunk by tax. The holding company may retain some of the money, but if it does, and eventually dissolves itself, it can walk off with the money, tax-free as far as Luxembourg is concerned. The income may have been taxed already in the country where it originated; and when it has passed through Luxembourg and is paid over to a citizen of any country, he should pay tax on it in the normal way. But in practice it can be highly advantageous to use a Luxembourg company to collect and distribute money. First, its costs are going to be low because the local taxes are so small. Second, the recipient of income paid out by the company knows that he is going to get it gross, without any taxes withheld. Even if he must later pay tax, he will think it better to receive the full amount to begin with; and if his conscience and the tax inspectors don't intervene, he may well be able to conceal the income, and so never pay tax at all.

A large country would find it difficult to act like Luxembourg: it would be a matter of pride, of not wanting to be caught acting like a fly financier instead of a dignified statesman. Luxembourg is too small to have delusions of grandeur, and over the years has exploited the fact that it's little but sovereign. Some little countries sell their Crown Jewels; Luxembourg sells its services to the international business community, among them Radio Luxembourg, which broadcasts sponsored programmes all over Europe.

The original Luxembourg law on holding companies goes back to 1929, and thousands of companies have been set up since then. Increasing co-operation between money-men in different countries makes it natural to look for some neutral, low-tax area where the operation can be managed. The Alexander Hamilton Fund (Chapter 3) is one example. Here are some more:

Eurunion is a Luxembourg investment trust, set up by banks in six countries (including the State-owned Mediobanca in Italy, and Banque Lambert in Brussels) that specialises in Continental shares. Another called Finance-Union, set up by another group of banks (including Hill, Samuel in London and Piersons in Amsterdam) invests in North America as well.

ADELA, formed 1964, is a 'multinational private investment company,' which invests in Latin America on behalf of institutional shareholders who range from Italy's Monte dei Paschi di Siena, the world's oldest bank, Rothschilds and Barings in the City and the three leading banks in Switzerland, to Coca-Cola, General Motors and Britain's Dunlop Rubber. The operations office is in Peru, the registered office in Luxembourg.

European Enterprises Development Co. was formed in 1963 to supply capital and management assistance to new companies. The shareholders are more than forty banks and financial institutions, including the Amsterdam-Rotterdam Bank, Banca Commerciale Italiana, Banque Nationale de Paris, Dresdner Bank, Mees & Hope and the Midland Bank in London. The company is run from Paris but is registered in Luxembourg. 'Why?' I asked a member-banker. 'For tax reasons,' he said. (A more direct answer than usual. Spokesmen tend to hedge and say things like, 'Oh the tax angle is very much overdone').

Since the roll-call includes half the best names in Europe, it must be perfectly respectable to have or be a Luxembourg company; yet it's an aspect of things that one is asked not to keep emphasising. The Société Financière Européenne is backed by some of the biggest banks in Europe plus the Bank of America. It is organised as two companies, one based in France and the other in Luxembourg. An official at the French participant, the Banque Nationale de Paris, said they used Luxembourg as a convenient centre where a holding company would 'allow everyone to get the same amount of profit,' but added that 'I wouldn't like you to say too much about it.' He pointed out that the French authorities had attacked Luxembourg as a Common Market tax-haven, adding that in this case, though, the arrangement had been made 'in perfect agreement' with the French Government (since the Banque Nationale de Paris is owned by the State, it could hardly be otherwise).

What has enhanced and extended the Luxembourg-type operation has been the use of holding companies to float loans in the Eurodollar market. Banks and consortiums lend dollars for anything from a day to a couple of years, but from about 1963 a market developed in long-term borrowing against the issue of bonds. Previously, European borrowers (who were mainly governments and local authorities) had been queuing up to make bond issues through the New York markets —the source of all riches after 1945. Then, in 1964, the Americans grew worried at rising expenditure overseas, and acted to inhibit dollar borrowers, who had to organise a market of their own. The result was the Eurobond market,[5] a home-grown European market to tap the pool of Eurodollars. It quickly became so effective that U.S. companies, pressed by their Government to limit overseas spending, decided to use it themselves.

In order to do so, they had to find a way of paying interest on the bonds without deducting withholding tax. This sounds a technicality, but a lot of energy has been used up, trying to get it right. Withhold-

[5] For a fuller account of Eurobonds, see Chapter 10.

ing taxes are imposed in most countries as a means of ensuring that investors' income is tapped at source. For honest citizens who declare their income, the amount withheld by the paying agent (and passed on to the authorities) becomes a first instalment against the final bill for the year. U.S. withholding tax is about 30 per cent. Securities issued by foreign borrowers are usually exempt, and when the international market was centred on New York—before 1963—European borrowers didn't have to withhold tax on their interest payments.

When the borrowing moved to Europe, payments had to go on being made in full if international investors, many of them seasoned tax-dodgers, were to be kept happy. National and quasi-national borrowers were able to oblige simply by deciding for themselves that they would pay the gross amount—a government can tell itself what to do. Every prospectus for every issue was careful to explain that interest would be paid in full. Whether it was the Republic of Austria, the Government of New Zealand, the City of Copenhagen or the European Coal and Steel Community, they all promised much the same thing: 'All payments of principal and interest will be made without deduction of or an account of any taxes, imposts or duties, present or future.' Large sums are involved. One year's interest on a billion dollars worth of bonds (the Eurobond total is now far greater) wouldn't amount to less than $60 or $70 million, and withholding taxes might easily take $20 million of this.

The Continental attitude towards income tax is complicated. Compared with Britain and the U.S., most Continental countries raise a smaller proportion of their revenue by direct taxation.[6] This means that the income tax dodger, though active, has less to dodge. 'Of course,' said a London stockbroker, 'plenty of people on the Continent don't declare their tax. But there are plenty of others who do pay their tax, but who don't want to feel they've *got* to'.

When U.S. firms came to use the Eurobond market, they found they couldn't do it successfully unless they, too, could pay their interest free of tax. The answer proved to be Luxembourg and its all-embracing holding companies. Luxembourg was already a centre for international bonds. Some countries forbid their institutions to invest

[6] Proportion of taxes on income as percentage of gross national product; 1965 figures: U.S., 15·1. Netherlands, 14·1. Britain, 13·0. Germany, 12·0. Belgium, 10·1. France, 7·9. Italy, 7·5.

in securities unless they are quoted on a stock exchange, and Luxembourg, which will provide a quotation quickly, cheaply and without red tape, is the natural answer. Another reason for using Luxembourg is so that securities can change hands there without the aggravating stamp duties that bigger financial centres have a habit of levying. There has to be a trading centre where securities can be legally transferred from one owner to another as they are re-sold and re-bought through their life; Luxembourg is the most convenient. Scores of issues are listed on the Stock Exchange (the introduction fee is a modest $500 or so) and bonds can be transferred without stamp duty or other taxes. One local bank remarks in a booklet that the existence of such taxes in other countries 'gave rise to problems', quickly adding the good news that the local situation is 'completely unrestricted and free.'

The U.S. corporations moved in because they discovered that by setting up financial subsidiaries in Luxembourg, and guaranteeing each one with its parent's good name, they could raise sums of 20 or 30 million dollars, spend the money on worldwide operations, and pay the lenders their interest in full. The first to move was Mobil Oil Holdings, constituted on May 17 1965, which borrowed $28 million. Luxembourg had to change the rules slightly to make this particular kind of finance company possible, and the Minister of Finance's circular on the subject is dated 9 September 1965. I asked a man at the Ministry of Finance what had been happening between May and September. He said coldly: 'The facts in Luxembourg always come before the interpretation.' After Mobil came U.S. Rubber, Standard Oil of Indiana, Du Pont, Honeywell, International Telephone and Telegraph, Bankers Trust and many more. Other Luxembourg borrowers include Philips Lamps (Holland), Beechams (Britain) and Siemens (Germany). Their Luxembourg holding companies are usually looked after by a bank, which redirects mail and organises the annual meeting; directors fly in to the small airport or catch the train from Brussels, meet briefly, have lunch and depart for another year.

Later came other refinements. It appeared that Holland was equally convenient from the tax point of view. Some British companies floated loans direct, without creating a Luxembourg subsidiary, though they had to go to great lengths in order to avoid British withholding tax. U.S. tax experts found they could use a law which allows a company to escape withholding tax if it elects to be a foreign company, and eventually this became standard practice. As long as most of its business is outside the U.S., the subsidiary has as much freedom as it would have had in Luxembourg—this is the 'Delaware company', named after the State of Delaware, which happens to be the place where it's cheapest to form a company.

But Luxembourg found plenty to do, tempting the Eurodollar investor in a variety of ways. This investor is a shadowy figure; bankers, anxious to keep their clients for themselves, talk guardedly of oil-sheikhs and Greek ship-owners, South American financiers and rich family trusts. Increasingly, the investors may be international pension funds and insurance companies. It's a market for the rich, run by banks, trading in large quantities on behalf of clients who, whatever they are, aren't small men. A list of the 200 leading investors in the Eurobond market would be as interesting as *Fortune's* list of the 200 leading industrial companies. Eurobonds soon became so fashionable that advertisements designed to attract comparatively small investors appeared in Continental papers. I answered one for an investment trust, registered in Luxembourg but managed in Switzerland, which had climbed on the band-wagon by offering its own Eurobonds at $1,000 a time to the public, the money to be invested in various dollar enterprises. The literature that came by return of post spoke passionately of the need for a better return on one's capital in this era of rockets to the moon and planets, and continued with almost lyrical references to the tax-free joys of the Eurobond.

Many Eurodollar investment trusts have been started in Luxembourg, paying tax-free interest to holders of bearer shares whose tax authorities would be none the wiser. The Luxembourg banks also organised private Eurodollar loans on behalf of small firms (or even large ones that didn't want everyone to know they were borrowing).

Luxembourg, busy out of all proportion to its size, sits blinking in the sun, purposeful but discreet, Most of its banks are owned by or associated with interests outside Luxembourg. Banque Lambert is there with the Banque Européenne du Luxembourg. The Banque de Bruxelles has a substantial shareholding in the Banque Internationale à Luxembourg. Busiest of all is Luxembourg's Kredietbank, a subsidiary of the Belgian bank, which has looked after the Luxembourg end of things for many of the Eurobond companies, beginning with the first one, Mobil.

Between them the Luxembourg banks hold a fortune in bonds for their clients. A Kredietbank manager pointed to a car park across the road, on the edge of the gorge that runs beside the old part of the city. The Kredietbank vaults were under the cars, he said, excavated in the rock; they contained bonds worth about 20 billion Luxembourg francs, say $400 million.

Humbler clients turn up in person at Luxembourg banks to cash the interest coupon on their bonds, often travelling down from Brussels for a day out. A man at the Kredietbank, which employs fifty people in its coupon department at Luxembourg, said that bondholders didn't need to go there. 'They can leave the securities with a bank, which sends the interest twice a year. But they may not want to pay the bank's fees for keeping them, and anyway, they like to take them out every so often and look at them. They come here especially on July the twenty-first, which is a national fete in Belgium but not in Luxembourg—they drive down by coach and bring their friends' bonds as well in suitcases.' He made it sound like a jolly day out, all money and cafes and girls. It didn't mean that the bank had anything to do with improper practices. As another banker explained, 'We act on the principle that tax evasion takes place at the moment someone fills in his tax return. The dishonesty isn't in cashing the coupons in Luxembourg but in not declaring the income. We leave it to the individual's fiscal conscience. The only criticism one could make is that by providing the facilities, banks encourage tax evasion. This is not true because they do not publicise it. They don't need to—people know damned well what they can do.'

Most business men naturally get away with what they can, but would prefer not to be shown too often in close-up, sailing near the wind. The Luxembourg authorities are charmingly prepared to answer questions on this delicate matter, but what they say, predictably, is that they want to be left in peace to do what others would do if the Luxembourg authorities weren't doing it themselves. 'Our aim', said an official of the Bank Control Commission, 'is to use the law but not to abuse it. We would like to keep quiet about it and go ahead doing things legally and quietly.' He agreed that criticism had come from certain quarters, particularly France, whose Finance Ministry had complained that Luxembourg holding companies were disturbing the Continent's capital markets, and asked that the system be abolished. But such attacks, he said, were unjustified, since they were not technical but political. The French were determined to make Paris the financial capital of Europe, and they couldn't bear to meet opposition from within the Common Market itself. They wouldn't succeed, of course. 'I have been told by companies that they don't have full confidence in the French authorities, or in the German authorities for that matter,' he said stiffly. 'There has been retrospective legislation to impose taxes. But these things don't happen here. It is a question of confidence—that is why people come to Luxembourg.'

As the official pointed out, Luxembourg isn't the only tax haven. Liechtenstein flourishes between Switzerland and Austria. The Caribbean is well supplied with comforting little countries where a man can form a company that pays few taxes on its income; Panama and the Bahamas[7] are both well-known havens. So are the semi-British Channel Isles. Gibraltar, of all places, has gone into the business because of trouble with its economy, encouraging investment firms to set up brass-plate companies. Nobody likes to pay taxes. If it weren't Luxembourg, it would only be somewhere else.

(vi) **France:** State Enterprise

The French have the most volatile, complex, Government-dominated financial system on the Continent; they are proud of it but touchy, and in the last few years they haven't been able to stop meddling with it in order to make it better. They have also been busy improving

[7] A curious sidelight on the Bahamas was the case of the subpoena served in 1967 on the New York representative of Barclays DCO, the British overseas bank. A Congressional committee was inquiring into the affairs of the Rev. Adam Clayton Powell, the Negro member of Congress whose right to take his seat had been challenged. Barclays was ordered to produce records relating to accounts alleged to be held by Representative Powell at the bank's branch in the Bahamas, but declined on the grounds that the Bahamas, being part of the Commonwealth, were beyond the committee's jurisdiction—no bank likes to be forced to publicise the affairs of its customers. The gesture was obviously appreciated. As soon as the story was published, said a Barclays official in London, 'there was a rush of deposits to our New York office for transfer to the Bahamas.'

their economy. Anglo-Saxons have watched with interest, polite applause and then growing irritation as the French, penniless after the war, and bruised by seven currency devaluations between 1945 and 1958, took themselves in hand, made money, kept most of it in gold, lectured the West on finance, insisted that in matters of monetary reform it was they who were right and the rest of the world that was out of step, and declared privately in a whisper just loud enough to be heard across the English Channel that Paris was going to be the financial key to Europe. Although France's credibility as the wise man of international money[8] has a bearing on her claims to make Paris the belle of the E.E.C., these claims will be vigorously pressed, whatever happens on the world-money-crisis front.

French pride and ambition took some hard knocks in the summer of 1968, when student uprisings led to a national strike and a state of near-revolution that paralysed the economy for weeks. The usual round of financial gloom and panic followed, with fears that the franc might be devalued, and temporary exchange controls imposed to stop money pouring out of France. Bankers braced themselves over the border in Geneva and were duly inundated with funds in search of calm waters. The promise of higher pay for the country's grossly underpaid workers was part of de Gaulle's package that ended the strikes, and this in turn helped undermine other countries' confidence in the French economy. The Government found itself spending some of its hoarded gold, and borrowing heavily from the International Monetary Fund. It was all very embarrassing for the French, after their decade of prosperity, though the British were in no fit state to enjoy a feeling of revenge. The pound is so shaky that it simply becomes shakier still at the prospect of sickness among other currencies. And the French themselves, though plagued by money worries, showed little inclination to play a more unassuming part in world finance. They pressed on with their plans to make Paris shine.

What Paris has to offer includes a centre for foreign-exchange and gold, and (strikes and riots permitting) a large degree of the freedom to move one's currency around the world that countries aspire to. London, which is the rival that Paris watches, has survived as the financial centre of Europe in spite of lacking this freedom. The irony of Britain's situation is that about a quarter of the world's trade

[8] See Chapter 11.

is still arranged in sterling, yet Britain is perpetually anxious lest the owners of sterling around the world should want to realise their claims on London and collect other currencies instead. The foreign holders of sterling can't be stopped (short of draconian controls that would ruin London overnight) from converting their sterling into something else, but British holders can be, and are. Britain nowadays is a bank with insufficient reserves of its own, relying heavily, in its role as international banker, on sterling left in London by foreigners who can take it away at any time.

The French don't act as an international bank; but because their financial position is stronger they have ample reserves to meet their needs. Francs can be used by Frenchmen outside their country more freely than pounds can be used by Britons outside theirs, and especially since there was a general easing of controls in 1967. After that time, a Frenchman travelling anywhere in the world could write a cheque, in his own or any other currency, and present it for payment. Whether it would be accepted by a London shop or a Bombay hotel was another matter, but he was free to do so as far as his own exchange-control regulations were concerned. This sort of thing continues to be illegal for the travelling Briton. The freedom covers movements of private capital into and out of France—say, to buy shares or houses in another country. Private citizens can import and export gold as freely as bars of chocolate, which puts the French alongside the Swiss, Germans, Belgians and Dutch; when the law permitting this was introduced in 1967, it ended extensive gold smuggling between France and Switzerland. By allowing private demand to make itself felt through Paris, the French authorities made their gold market that much busier.

The French authorities still control the movement of large capital sums for industrial investment (if a French firm wants to transfer francs to build a factory in another country), but in general it has become easier for French banks and companies to spend and borrow abroad. The intention is that an increasing number of foreign loans should be raised on the French Stock Exchange, as well as French loans in other countries—the kind of two-way traffic that would enhance Paris's claims to be an international centre.

Its present assets include a range of powerful banks that has been reorganised by order of the Government, which owns most of the big ones. The biggest of all, the Banque Nationale de Paris, was created in 1966 by the Finance Minister, M. Michel Debré, who squeezed two existing banks together to make the largest on the Continent. With $6 billion in deposits, it's among the world's ten largest, outranked in Europe only by Britain's Barclays and Westminster groups. Paris is also the headquarters of the extraordinary Banque de Paris et des Pays-Bas, a *banque d'affaires* with extensive financial and industrial interests; like the other *banques d'affaires*, it isn't State-controlled.

American bankers, looking with mistrust at the way governments intervene in credit systems in Western Europe, have an especially cold eye for the way they do it in France. They see a planned economy in which banks and a range of dour-looking credit institutions dole out the money as the Government directs. In reply, the French can point to the merits of national guidance and co-operation, as they do officially, and at the same time can offer a high-powered Civil Service, probably of the highest intellectual calibre in Europe, that both runs this official money-system and is often (when it comes to individual views) sharply critical of it. Essentially it consists of a handful of men, 150 or so, of the few who are appointed by competitive examination to be *inspecteur des finances*, the grade peculiar to France, with its own mystique and snobberies, that provides an academic equivalent to the old school tie. Deceptively young, eyes glittering, the *inspecteur des finances* puts an edge on France's arguing and negotiating ability inside the Common Market, and adds materially to Paris's weight as a centre.

The French confidence in themselves is a useful weapon. The trouble with the French, as a banker said in Belgium, is that they are agonisingly pro-French. Money-men in other parts of the Continent shrug their shoulders and put it down to a streak of inferiority for which the French must compensate, a feeling that their country has been outclassed in the world, making them touchy about their language and their currency. Britain has lost her empire and is still groping for economic security, but the pound sterling remains one of the two world currencies. Who finances trade in French francs? It may be troublesome to be an international banker, but it carries much prestige—a point that British spokesmen like to overlook when they talk about the burdens of sterling. The French don't overlook it, and are incensed at what they see, not unfairly, as the well-known

British hypocrisy in action. It makes them cross to see the pound still on its pedestal. A year before the 1967 devaluation of sterling, and the slump in Anglo-French relations that accompanied it, one heard London bankers talk about the 'emotional resentment' of Paris at the fact that the pound had so far survived the troubles of the preceding years. Despite devaluation, it still has its international role, and still upsets the French.

As for language, English is spoken in business, even more than it was. The Eurobond market is largely conducted in English; it involves bankers, lawyers and accountants from so many countries that a common language is necessary. Even when an Italian banker is talking to another Italian about a Eurobond issue, the conversation will be thick with English words like *management group*, *underwriters* and *withholding tax*. 'English is the language of the whole Eurodollar market,' said a German, 'except that the French try to do it in French.' I found that when I wrote to bankers in different parts of Europe, nearly all the replies were in English; except from Paris, where they either didn't reply at all, or replied in French. When it came to meeting, the Paris bankers, brokers and Civil Servants were friendly, talkative and usually bi-lingual; but first they made the gesture.

The British have always looked outward in business. The French are more private and acquisitive. Fred Hirsch, who devotes a chapter to French financial attitudes in his book *Money International*, suggests that while the English instinct is to lend gold, the French instinct is to bury it (the French not only hold large amounts in their national reserves. *Individuals* who keep it in bank vaults, up the chimney or under the bed have been estimated to have at least $5 billion worth). Religion comes into it. It has been argued that Protestants (who made individual effort and material profit respectable) make better business men than Catholics (who have always been more uneasy about money); this conveniently explains why the Dutch, the British and the Scandinavians are more advanced in banking today, and have achieved more in the past, than the French and Italians.

The English were risk-takers, a maritime nation whose economic system was based on an exchange of produce and merchandise. England looked outward through London; the French looked inward through Paris. 'Your banks went overseas and risked everything,' said a manager at the Banque de Paris et des Pays-Bas, which has reversed the tradition in the last twenty years. 'Paris is far from the sea, built from an inland point of view.' And a young *inspecteur des finances* said that although France was changing, the transition was painful. It was hard to say but it was true. 'Unless they are positively obliged to look outwards, they are still a nation of peasants.'

Great Grey Institutions

The French have a formal banking code, which amuses the English, just as the English have no formal banking code at all, which amuses the French. In this respect it is Britain which is the odd man out, not only in Europe but throughout the world; most countries regulate their credit systems more formally than the British. But in France it is not just a matter of rules for banking and credit, but of direct participation by the State. Italy is the only other country in Western Europe where the authorities are in such a powerful position, and there, the central control is exercised less thoroughly than in France. The big Italian banks are all State-owned, but they and the I.R.I. complex of State holding companies always seem to have one foot in the private-enterprise camp. Business men sit on the I.R.I. boards; the State is less pervasive, perhaps because it is less able to cope with the technicalities of business.

The French have no shortage of technicians to work their central machinery, which handles most of the country's current money. Deposits at banks, credit institutes and post offices go in at one end and may emerge as loans for industry, agriculture and house-building, on lines dictated by the State, working through the Treasury and the Banque de France. Always in the background is the current French economic strategy—'Le Plan,' in full 'Le Plan de Modernisation et d'Equipement.' Plan No. 5 began in 1966 and was designed to run till 1970. Plans are not compulsory as far as French industry is concerned, but General de Gaulle calls it a moral obligation, and in any case official control over so much investment puts the Government in a strong position.

Local authorities and nationalised industries such as gas and electricity swallow money, raised by issues of bonds that have tax advantages over other kinds of Stock Exchange investment; many of these bonds are issued over-the-counter by banks, leaving the Stock

Exchange itself to make a thin, secondary market in them. 'The Treasury's main job is to collect money for the nationalised industries and so on,' said an *inspecteur des finances*. 'The head of the Treasury would be furious if he heard me, but there is a real fear of seeing money go too far away from the public sector. Regulations are made to favour the public sector—for instance, the poor old insurance companies have been obliged by law to keep 50 per cent of their funds in Government securities. The Treasury is reluctant to see real competition for people's money.'

The Stock Exchange is kept on a tight rein. Anyone who wants to use it to make a new issue must obtain permission from the Treasury, which is one of many things not in its favour as a capital market; the Paris Bourse is a famous place, and even noisier than expected when one visits it for the first time, but it plays a comparatively humble part in the system.

The Treasury, the Banque de France and half a dozen official and semi-official institutions form the hard core of this system. Of all the big European central banks, the Banque de France has the least autonomy; staffed near the top by officials who may have been at the Treasury last year and who will duly move on to a neighbouring institution, it lacks the sombre exclusiveness of the Bank of England, and to a lesser extent of the central banks in Germany and Italy.

The bank (which has the usual enormous central bank building with barred windows, where an occasional soldier with a sub-machine gun mooches disconcertingly in a deserted corridor) also houses the secretariat of an imposing-sounding body called the Conseil National du Crédit. Nearly fifty members, headed by the Finance Minister and the Governor of the Banque de France, represent all branches of the economy, and supposedly advise the Government how to manage its affairs. It doesn't seem a very workable proposition, and turns out to be a polite fiction, set up after the war when the Government was strongly Left-wing, and bankers and financiers were particularly unpopular. Power was supposed to be taken away from the old gang and redistributed on more egalitarian lines. It happened to some extent; the Banque de France was nationalised and so were the four largest commercial banks; but there are still private fortunes and private bankers in France, and still an absence of steam behind the Conseil National du Crédit. 'In 1945—remember how it was?—we had a sort of revolutionary atmosphere,' said M. Q., an *inspecteur des finances*. 'It originated with mistrust of the Banque de France and the banking community, but after a few years the Treasury and the Banque reached some kind of agreement, and now the Conseil acts as a screen. It doesn't do much. It meets two or three times a year for two hours. But suppose the Minister goes to the Banque and says, "Such-and-such has been decided," and the Governor replies "*I* didn't decide that". In those cases, to have the Conseil is psychologically very useful.'

Long before the banks were nationalised in 1945, the State already had the largest slice of the banking system through the other official institutions. Such places have a glum sound, whether they are in Paris or Brussels or Milan; Agricultural Credit Institutes and National Savings Banks are even less glamorous than straightforward commercial banks. But they rake in so much money, from people who have always trusted them more and liked their tax privileges, that they can dominate the whole system. In France, people's savings are drawn into the State through four channels, and the deposits are far greater than in all the commercial banks put together. First there are the savings banks, with thirty million depositors, three in five of the population. Some are private, some run by the Post Office, and their deposits, about $14 billion in all, are managed by the venerable Caisse des Dépôts et Consignations; this was founded as a sort of public trustee in the year after the Battle of Waterloo, and General de Gaulle attended its 150th anniversary in 1966. The Caisse disposes of another $4 billion or so in money from pension funds, insurance funds and sundry sources; the $18 billion at its disposal, growing at the rate of 6 or 7 per cent a year, is about the same as the total of deposits at Chase Manhattan, the second largest bank in the world. A staff of 1,500, headed by *inspecteurs des finances*, works in a grey palace on the Left Bank, and puts the money into public works, cheap State-owned flats and houses, Government bonds, Treasury bills and other places where the State needs funds. It's the biggest single operator on the Paris Stock Exchange, and as a manager of Government securities, buying and selling as necessary to keep the market stable, its role is similar to that of the Government Broker in London.

The State's second source of money from the public is the giro, the

Service des Chèques Postaux that it runs through about 20,000 post offices. Begun in 1918, it is now the most highly developed in the world. Like all the Continental giros, its service of postal cheques, with the accounts kept centrally, competes effectively with the banks (most bank officials use it themselves) and constitutes a permanent loan to the Government. People use it because it's cheap and convenient, though it pays no interest. The best way to use a giro (or a current account in a bank, unless it carries interest) is to keep the balance as low as possible. But the French Treasury can count on a float of more than $5 billion of giro money at any one time (which shows how the inability of individuals to manage their money expertly can be turned to the profit of money-managers who wouldn't dream of letting funds lie idle).

Thirdly, the State has a network of nearly 100 agricultural banks, begun in the nineteenth century as farmers' co-operatives, which take deposits from some farmers and lend the money to others ('It's more extensive than it looks,' said a man at the Banque de France. 'If you have a garden and three trees, I don't know that you aren't a farmer'). The agricultural banks are organised around a head office in Paris, the Crédit Agricole, which takes their surplus funds. Finally there is a network of 'popular banks', intended for smaller traders and business men, with a central Crédit Populaire in Paris.

It is unexciting but effective, a system for concentrating money where the Government can oversee it or actually lay hands on it. Three other solid Paris institutions, raising their money by different means, complete the picture. The Crédit National is the principal lender to industry in France, raising about $300 million for the purpose each year by issuing long-term bonds, and also approving medium-term loans that banks wish to make to industry. When the Crédit National's signature is added to the commercial bills against which the banks are making these loans, they can be rediscounted at the Banque de France (that is, the money can be borrowed there until the bills fall due for payment) at a low rate of interest. The Crédit National has private shareholders and in theory is only semi-official; a manager bridled at the suggestion that they were Civil Servants and said the situation was that they could do anything, anything at all, as long as the Government approved. This is the point; industrial ending can be arranged in accordance with the best interests of Le Plan. The chairman and senior managers of the Crédit National are appointed by the Government, as they are at the Crédit Foncier, founded as a private company, which borrows from the public and lends much of its money as mortgages on houses and other property. Third and last is a newer institution, the Banque Française du Commerce Extérieur, formed after the second war to help finance French trade.

The Inspectors of Finance

In all these heavy-sounding establishments, as well as in the Treasury, the Banque de France and the three nationalised deposit banks that sit close to them, *les inspecteurs des finances* can be found in key positions. They are the flesh-and-blood expression of Government surveillance; and the fact that the most successful of them often leave Government service and move into industry or private banking helps to define the particular French answer to the perennial question of what relationship the State should bear to private enterprise. In Britain the movement of senior Civil Servants and central bankers into private firms has increased in recent years but is still the exception. In France the *inspecteurs des finances* are highly mobile and create their own framework of contacts on both sides of the private/public fence. Jacques Rueff, the French economist who has been blamed or credited for helping to mould de Gaulle's acquisitive ideas about gold, is an *inspecteur des finances*. So are most Finance Ministers. Those who want to move on find equal scope. A former Finance Minister and Governor of the Banque de France, Wilfrid Baumgartner, is now boss of the biggest industrial group in France, the Rhône-Poulenc textile and chemical complex: the Governor of the Bank of England may go back to being head of the bank (Lord Cromer, who returned to Barings in 1966), but has yet to move on to be chairman of I.C.I. or even the National Coal Board.

The biggest non-Government bank, the Banque de Paris et des Pays-Bas, has two *inspecteurs des finances* in its management; the man who built up the bank after the war, Jean Reyre, isn't one of them, though the man named to succeed him, a financial impresario called Jacques de Fouchier, is. Fouchier left Government service after the second war, but instead of joining someone else's bank he began his own, and later developed it, with the aid of other banks, into a housing-mortgage and hire-purchase finance company, a new idea in France at the time, called Compagnie Bancaire. 'In an economy such as ours', says Fouchier, 'it is necessary to have people in the private sector who have experience of the public service', adding sardonically that 'those who are your friends are frequently in a position to be less libellous about you than if they didn't know you.' 'It means that we all speak the same language,' said another banker, recalling the City of London's affection for its public-school, old-boy solidarity. 'If our chairman has someone he can visit at the Ministry of Finance and say "tu" to, that's obviously a good idea.'

The way in to the *Inspection générale des Finances* is through a two-year course at the illustrious academy for producing career Civil Servants and diplomats, l'Ecole Nationale d'Administration, where postgraduate students go at the age of twenty-three or twenty-four. About a thousand candidates present themselves yearly and a hundred are admitted. 'The first year, I did no classwork,' said M.Y., another *inspecteur des finances*. 'I spent it in Morocco, in the field. Then back to Paris, reading diplomatic history, law and economics. It was work, work, work.' When students take their final examination they are graded competitively, and can choose their jobs according to rank. There are usually vacancies in the *Inspection générale des Finances* for the top seven or eight candidates, if they want to go there, which they usually do.

This creaming-off process should guarantee some quality in those who survive it. *Inspecteurs des finances* resent the idea that they are merely clever; personality is considered as well as intellect. Politically, they are of all alignments. 'What they have in common, by right of being hatched there, is to be the highest Civil Servants in France, and so influence the economic life of the country,' said a banker who failed the examination. A successful candidate, with no fear that anyone might think it sour grapes, remarked that it was a hell of a difficult examination, but somehow it didn't stop stupid people getting in.

At first the work is dull. For several years they literally inspect finances, usually in the provinces, plodding through such things as local taxation and Post Office accounts. 'Some remain all their lives, inspecting,' said one of them who hasn't. 'Most, when they have done this rather bleak job for four or five years, move into the Treasury.'

Thus launched, in their late twenties or early thirties, they can rise at surprising speed. Because the French (like most Continentals) give more weight to academic qualities than the British, to be an *inspecteur des finances* is to carry a recognisable badge that has no real equivalent in the City. The cleverest may hold important posts at the Treasury or the Banque de France by the time they reach their mid-thirties—ten years or more before they might expect to have equivalent office in London. Wilfrid Baumgartner was director of the Treasury at the Finance Ministry when he was thirty-three.

Those who move on to private firms begin to do so in their thirties, when they are still young enough to accept a comparatively junior post; if they wait till they are older and greyer in Government service, they will want something nearer the chairmanship. Of the 250 or so *inspecteurs des finances* who are active, about 150 work for the Government, either directly or at the central establishments like the Crédit National and the Caisse des Dépôts; and perhaps sixty or more are in private business, often banking.

Banking Empires

In rearranging the financial scene, the French Government hopes to get the best of both worlds, leaving the official establishments in a privileged position, but within a freer, simpler and more competitive system. The changes are part of a pattern that was imposed on France by the times. Competition was growing inside the Common Market. The end of Customs duties on industrial goods (in 1968) was in sight. French planners, looking at the country's industry, saw that large sums would have to be invested in coming years, and that the financial system wasn't adequate for the task. The need to overhaul the mechanics of banking and investment coincided with the desire to make France the leader of Europe; it was a practical move with political overtones, elegantly framed and pushed through with single-mindedness. Among other things the changes affected interest rates, the mechanics of borrowing, industrial finance and the Stock Exchange, as well as France's financial relations with the rest of the world. Everyone connected with money was concerned with the changes, but bankers most of all.

Numerically most French bankers are Civil Servants, and the

senior ones are inclined to be touchy if one hints at any idiosyncracy about their kind of banking—suggesting that, for instance, it isn't as good at making profits as the private kind. The nationalised banks still have their old names, remember their nineteenth-century origins, and compete strenuously. The law that nationalised them, along with the Banque de France, was passed soon after the war ended, on 2 December 1945. There were four of them at the time: the Crédit Lyonnais, the Société Générale, the Comptoir National d'Escompte de Paris and the Banque Nationale pour le Commerce et l'Industrie. Reform was in the air; Communists were at the door. 'I think that if one could have a new world,' said an official at the Banque de France, 'they would not be nationalised now. The atmosphere is different today.' As it was, their shares were transferred to the State, and they became part of the machine. In their daily operations they are largely left alone, but they play a game whose rules are made, and remade, by the State.

The Government's reforms are meant to light a little fire in their bellies. Whether they would have been more efficient and profitable had they stayed in private hands is arguable. They are overstaffed in relation to the business they do, but this may be the fault of the system as a whole. Lending money makes extravagant use of manpower in France. The method of borrowing from a bank by a straight overdraft—allowing the customer's account to run into debt up to an agreed amount—isn't popular in France. In Britain it is the standard method; elsewhere in Europe, banks often prefer to lend against the security of bills of exchange and promissory notes, which mature on a fixed date in the future, and so guarantee the point at which the bank (or whoever the bank may have passed the bill to, in the meantime) will get its money back. France is particularly keen on this method, and every conceivable kind of business transaction generates clouds of paper. Much of it can be rediscounted at a low rate of interest at the Banque de France, which means that the banks are, in effect, getting from the Government the money which they have failed to attract in deposits from the public, who prefer the savings banks, the giro and so on.

Attempts to simplify the system and reduce the paperwork are being made as part of the march of progress. The French have been attached to their bills of exchange; they say it makes lending safer and borrowing easier (for honest men), and like the reassurance of a piece of paper inscribed with a date and a sum of money. Individual bills may be drawn to finance each consignment or each invoice involved. The head office of the Banque Nationale de Paris gets 200,000 bills a day, and, when it analysed them not long ago, discovered to its alarm that half were for less than £85. No one had realised things were as bad as this.

The staff at that time (1967) was 34,000, which must have made it the biggest bank in the world in terms of employees. The bank was formed the year before by a rather brutal merger between the antiquated Comptoir National d'Escompte de Paris and the livelier Banque National pour le Commerce et l'Industrie. It was rushed through by the Ministry of Finance, which seems to have wanted an event that would crystallise the new look in French banking. The enormous staff was expected to shrink rapidly over the next few years. Of the 34,000 employed before the shrinking began, a manager said that he supposed a third were doing one of two things. Either they were handling bills and promissory notes, or they were selling Government and private bonds to the public. Government bond-business is another never-ending task for the nationalised banks, which have to take quantities of them each year, and sell them over the counter as best they can.

The profits of the nationalised banks are tiny—'Much less than that of privately-owned banks,' said an *inspecteur des finances* in Government service, 'but it is not discussed much in gentlemanly circles.' They are providing cheap finance for industry, they have to compete with the savings banks, they employ large staffs, and, perhaps, they lack the incentive that the existence of shareholders is supposed to provide.

It wasn't clear whether the reforms would make the nationalised banks more profitable, but there was no doubt that they would make the system work better. The tax advantages that savings banks possessed over commercial banks were narrowed or removed. Commercial banks were allowed to open branches wherever they liked without seeking official permission, They were encouraged by various technical devices to lend, direct to industry for long and medium terms, more of the deposits that they were now supposed to be attracting from the public. They were encouraged to put money into house-mortgages. And a general bringing-together of banks into fewer, bigger units got under way.

The French authorities encouraged mergers by ending a rigid distinction that had existed between deposits and investment banks—the *banques de dépôts* and *banques d'affaires*. The first category includes the three nationalised banks, and a number of smaller privately-owned ones; the second is made up entirely of non-Government banks. The distinction is the usual one between a bank that takes deposits and lends them out again, and a bank that doesn't take deposits but uses its own resources to invest in industrial companies. Some European countries maintain the distinction by law, having nasty memories of the financial crises between the wars, when large amounts of the public's money, deposited with banks, were tied up with industry, and disappeared for good when the crash came. Britain maintains a distinction in practice, between the clearing banks that take deposits, and the merchant banks that do more specialist financing; there is no law on the subject, but in any case, the British merchant banks don't have large shareholdings of their own in industry.

In France the two kinds of bank were largely separate, though they weren't compelled to be until after 1945, when they had to opt for one or the other. Twenty years later, the Government began to blur the distinction by deciding that deposit banks could put more of their money into industry, and that investment banks could have more freedom to accept deposits from the public. This drew more money towards industry; it threw everyone into competition with everyone else, and precipitated mergers with rivals in some cases; it energised banks in general, but especially the *banques d'affaires*.

The largest of these (and the one that needed energising least) is the Banque de Paris et des Pays-Bas. Founded in 1872, this is the biggest of its kind in Europe, with assets of nearly a billion dollars, and money invested in every French industry, but especially in chemicals, electronics, steel, gas, paper, publishing and building. The list of nearly 200 domestic holdings runs from the leading French companies in petroleum (Compagnie Française des Pétroles) and computers (Compagnie des Machines Bull, which is controlled by America's General Electric) to a stake in garage facilities at Paris's airport (Garage Auto Service Orly) and champagne (Maison Moët et

Chandon). The bank has helped to develop many areas of industry, including television, oil refining, insurance and cars, especially Citröen. It has participations in other banks and financial institutions, among them the old Crédit National and the new Compagnie Bancaire, with which it is closely associated. Outside France the bank has branches or offices in North Africa, Belgium, the Netherlands and Switzerland. In the United States, where it's close to the Bank of America, it turns up as an investment bank called Paribas Corporation. In London it is Banque de Paris et des Pays-Bas Ltd, two-thirds owned by the head office, with the other third shared among nineteen local participants who include the merchant bankers Warburgs and Barings, and the Prudential and Pearl insurance companies.

The ramifications of the bank extend to every part of the world, difficult for the outsider to trace. It's linked with banks and finance companies in Latin America, Turkey, Africa, Spain, Holland, Switzerland and Italy, among—no doubt—others. It has an important interest in Libby, the American food canners, and a large piece of Columbia Pictures, which it cheekily tried to take over in 1966, and might have succeeded in doing if the Federal Communications Commission hadn't intervened. In Africa it owns parts of companies that mine copper and manganese, build railways and make aluminium. In Belgium it controls a holding company with interests in steel, electricity, gas and department stores. Harry Oppenheimer, the South African diamonds, gold and minerals king, is on the board of the bank, which has joined with Oppenheimer's rich Anglo-American Corporation to form a Luxembourg investment trust.

Politics make no difference. Looking East, the Banque de Paris has financed industrial plant and oil refineries in Soviet-bloc countries. Looking West, it has, like all the best banks, joined one of the groups formed hopefully in the 1960s to finance the projected Channel Tunnel between England and France (with Warburgs and White, Weld, the New York investment bankers). It has a share in S. G. Warburg of Frankfurt, which is a subsidiary of the London bank. It's in chemicals in Norway and mortgages in Canada.

So many interests in so many places are guaranteed to arouse the suspicions of the Left, and the French *banques d'affaires* have often been targets of political criticism. The big ones were nearly nationalised in 1945, along with the deposit banks. It's said that one of the things that saved the Banque de Paris then were its overseas interests, especially those in the U.S., where action by the French Government would have led to all sorts of embarrassments. If so, nationalisation would be even more unthinkable today. Its chairman, Jean Reyre, isn't regarded as a particular crony of the Government, but the bank is too powerful and widely dispersed to be interfered with.

Since 1948, when Reyre, an economist who had made his career with the bank, became chairman, its assets have multiplied tenfold. Reyre would be a phenomenon anywhere, but even more so in Paris, since he has succeeded in becoming one of the country's most influential financiers without being an *inspecteur des finances*, even without showing much deference to them as a clique. Aware of the opposition that could be aroused by making enemies among such a powerful establishment, he has gone through some complicated manoeuvres when appointing executives, so as to protect himself from criticism. 'It's like a game of chess,' said a colleague.

Reyre's office is suitably elaborate. The bank itself occupies an eighteenth-century building that used to be a civic hall, and the chairman uses a richly furnished saloon where Napoleon Bonoparte married his mistress, Josephine, in 1796. (It's an historic monument, and must be opened to the public once a year). Now an elderly man, Reyre is reputedly cold and self-sufficient. One of his colleagues told me that the strategy behind the Columbia Pictures episode was still not clear—he had never been sure whether Reyre had seriously meant to try to take over the corporation and make it a permanent part of the bank's empire.

The middle-to-senior staff at the Banque de Paris includes a high proportion of technologists and scientists, on Reyre's principle that specialist knowledge is essential in banking, and that it's easier to make a trained scientist into a banker than vice-versa (there is a similar tendency in American banking). Industrial reorganisations and mergers form an important part of the bank's business. The organisation is comparatively small in terms of people—the staff in Paris totals 1,400—and it can move more swiftly than the deposit banks. In style and *élan*, it belongs to the same school as the sprightlier merchant banks in London. Entering the Eurobond market along with dozens of other hungry banks, it had become the leading

European manager of loan-raising syndicates by 1967. Its managers like to feel they are casual as well as clever. 'We do not take ourselves seriously,' said one. 'We take our business seriously.' This is characteristic of merchant and investment bankers—they relish a taste for informality that a duller business man will try vainly to acquire by hanging a card on the wall that says *You don't have to be crazy to work here but it helps*.

When banking mergers and alliances were becoming an almost weekly occurence in 1966 and 1967, the Banque de Paris had its share of them. The webs grow so complicated at times that it looks as though everyone will end by owning everyone else, by accident if not design. The bank edged into deposit-banking by joining with the largest privately-owned deposit group the 700-branch Crédit Industriel et Commercial. It drew closer to a smaller but important *banque d'affaires*, Banque Worms, which also sold part of itself to Bolsa, Britain's Bank of London and South America, and the Bank of Scotland.

Perhaps the surprising thing about the new alignments was not that they were occurring but that they had been delayed for so long. The history of the Worms group is the history of a rich family holding that clung to its old-fashioned status until it was forced to change, a commoner story on the Continent than in Britain and the U.S. Even now, Worms is still largely in private hands. It began in 1848, undercutting imports of Belgian coal by buying it from Britain instead, and later built coaling stations in the Mediterranean and along the Suez Canal. The family put in four million francs at the beginning, and for more than a century the company was self-sufficient, feeding on its own profits. The offices have old leather sofas with big buttons, and models of cargo ships in long glass cases. A grandson of the founder headed the firm till he died a few years ago, but by this time the group had proliferated and moved on.

A banking department was formed in 1929, but for a long time after that, the family would have described themselves as 'financiers' rather than 'bankers'. 'We were very rich,' says M. Meynial, the present head of the group. Its interests include ship-building and ship-owning, and it runs a third of France's privately-owned tankers. It has holdings in chemicals and insurance, in Air France—which it helped to form in the 1930s—and controls Paris stores and hotels, including the Crillon. With the Rothschilds it runs a Saharan oil company. But most of its interests are in France, and when it decided to join the fashion and expand overseas, money and partners were needed. In 1965 a separate Banque Worms was hived off as a subsidiary of the holding company, whose main shareholder was now the widow of the founder's grandson, Mme. Worms (her maiden name was Morgan, which has led observant bankers to suppose that Worms is intermarried with the American bankers of that name. But she was a Welsh woman from Cardiff, where her husband used to go in connection with the coal trade). Before long Banque Worms was linked with the two British banks and the Banque de Paris, as well as a German bank and a large regional group in France, the Crédit du Nord.

M. Meynial, spelling out their overseas role as he sees it, sounds remarkably like a London merchant banker, with his emphasis on personal favours and *quid pro quos*: 'Let us say that Imperial Chemical Industries are a client of the Bank of Scotland in London. If I.C.I. want to do something in France or in Germany, we will help them. You see, Paris isn't very big, and we know everyone. If all they want is an architect, we'll know where he is. The banker is often what we call a *confesseur*. Perhaps a client will ask us for help in South America. If so, we can go and ask Bolsa. There is an enormous amount of help we can give, and especially if England joins the Common Market.'

Other moves in the French financial game included a grouping of forces around the two largest *banques d'affaires* after the Banque de Paris—the Banque de l'Indochine, with worldwide interests, and the Banque de Suez et de l'Union des Mines, formed from the remnants of France's Suez Canal interests and a sequence of mergers (one result of which was to give the British Government an indirect shareholding through its former Suez connections).

Two private banks with international names, both remaining as partnerships of the old kind, joined the merry-go-round. Lazards, who have three independent but closely co-operating houses, in London, New York and Paris, formed a joint subsidiary in Paris for international business. And the Paris Rothschilds, who not long before had issued a thousand golden credit cards to selected clients for use at selected shops, formed themselves into a bank and asked the public to deposit money with them. This Rothschild venture provided the family with marvellous publicity; the world, fascinated by them when they remained aloof, was apparently just as ready to be impressed when they unveiled a few of their secrets.

The question of 'what the Rothschilds are really like' has engaged many writers, who usually assume that there is some essence to be distilled. The chairman of Lazards in London, Lord Poole reviewing a book about them, once wrote, 'What is it like to be a Rothschild?... I also asked myself that question about forty years ago, when, as a schoolboy, I galloped about the Forest of Compiegne behind Baron James and Baron Philippe with their hounds. I did not learn the answer then and I have not learnt now . . .'

To be a Rothschild is presumably not to be bothered about what people think. After a few generations of behaving as rather withdrawn financiers, the French branch of the family, found themselves in a more competitive situation, and promptly adjusted to it; they chose the year that celebrated their 150th annivarsary, and almost contrived to make it sound like a victory. They had made the usual fortune in the nineteenth century but then had grown fat and comparatively idle. Between the wars the Paris house did little more than manage the family fortunes, but after 1945, when a new generation took over, it branched out into proper banking, financing trade and accepting long-term deposits from large customers, and behaving in general more like the London house, which had gone into banking earlier and stayed there.

The three French financier-Rothschilds are Guy, Alain and Elie, all now middle-aged; there's also Edmond, in his early forties, who is nothing to do with the bank, but runs a private organisation of his own called Compagnie Financière, which finances such modern-living projects as holiday resorts, supermarkets and pipelines. Frederic Morton in his book 'The Rothschilds' says he's the richest of them all and 'probably the largest multiple millionaire in Europe.'

In 1967, Guy, Alain and Elie reorganised their industrial interests, mainly within a holding company called Compagnie du Nord—originally a Rothschild railway, Compagnie des Chemins de Fer du Nord, before it was nationalised in the 1930s. A limited number of shares was offered to the public in 1968. The family remained in control, as well as retaining all manner of private holdings outside the Compagnie du Nord. But investors were now able to have at least a cursory interest in the company's $85 million assets, which include new areas such as refrigerated transport, computers (with John Diebold, the American consultant) and the Club Mediterranée, as well as petrol, mining, shipbuilding and the rest. Deposits from the public were being politely asked for by the newly created Banque Rothschild; according to Guy, the chief baron, this was to become a 'mini-mini-mini Crédit Lyonnais' with branches all over the country.

They also strengthened their position outside France. The name of the family is still good for business because everyone recognises it and thinks instantly of money-bags, but in resources and management skills the Rothschilds today are small stuff beside First National City Bank or even the Banque de Paris et des Pays-Bas; friends and allies are needed. After having been financially separated from their British cousins since before the first world war, new business associations were struck up with the London branch of the family, which is in banking as N. M. Rothschild & Co., the only true partnership left in British banking; the four London partners are Edmond, Leopold, Evelyn and Jacob. Both the London and Paris branches joined to form a New York investment bank, New Court Securities (New Court is the bank's address in the City). With them in the New York firm was Banque Privée of Geneva, controlled by the French cousin, Edmond; Banque Lambert of Brussels, the one that was founded in the 19th century by a former Rothschild agent who married into the family; and Piersons, the Dutch private bank. The times were changing and so were the Rothschilds.

The Case for Paris

No European city outside London has such an impressive range of banks and bankers as Paris. Zurich is more cosmopolitan than Paris because so many foreigners put their money there for safety, but its banks are comparatively small. Paris is ambitious to provide a range of international services, though it has some obvious disadvantages. The Government's hold on the system means that the place is not as 'profit oriented' as it might be. 'We're not making value judgments,' said an American banker in Paris, 'but if it's theoretically possible to produce twice the profits with half the staff, it doesn't take the banker long to decide where to go. That's one of the reasons you see such a proliferation of banks in London. It's acceptable for a variety of reasons, one of which is that it's market oriented. If the market here in Paris is designed to be at best marginally profitable, the foreign banker, too, must be prepared to be marginally profitable.'

Against this, anyone who was measuring the claims of each city in Europe would have to set the pruning and liberalising of Paris in recent years, the comparative freedom for money to come and go at will, and its desire to be at the head of affairs. In the end, though, it looks as though Paris is still unsatisfactory in some essential respects. The State may have loosened its hold, by, for instance, encouraging banks to lend direct to industry without going first to the Crédit National, but it still has many hands on many levers. Money-raising by industry is closely controlled. The central weakness of Paris as a money-centre is that it is an unsatisfactory capital market beside those of London and New York. About 900 shares are quoted, against 9,000 in London, and many of them are inactive. Family concerns abound, company information is inadequate. Not one of the world's largest fifty firms is French. There is no institutional backbone of insurance companies and pension funds with a continual flow of money coming in from the public.

Official bonds overshadow the market—gas and electricity, roads and railways, city of Paris and the Crédit Foncier. There are tax inducements to make them more attractive, and the nationalised banks devote much effort to hard-selling this Government paper to the public. People buy it because they are not yet very sophisticated investors. 'After fifty years of inflation,' said a manager at the Banque Nationale de Paris, 'the French people have become frightened. We really sell the bonds one by one to our small clients.'

A Paris stockbroker, one of the eighty-odd *agents de change* who are appointed by the authorities (another black mark in the eyes of London and New York), said disgustedly that bank salesmen received commission on what was sold, so that 'naturally they flog them as hard as they can, which I think is immoral.' Why was it immoral? He said it was because the purchasers knew no better. Next day I heard an *inspecteur des finances* in a senior Government post say much the same thing. 'Retail selling by the banks is a costly business,' he said, 'and we don't like it very much. Unfortunately we don't know what would happen if we floated the loans straight on the market. We don't like it because it's a bit immoral. An issue of bonds is sold at par to small people through the network of banks and salesmen. A few weeks later the issue is quoted on the Bourse at two or three per cent under par, and at that point the more sophisticated investors will buy. You see, it's a bit of a swindle for small people. They buy bonds at a hundred francs, and perhaps six months later the salesman calls and says, "That's not very good. You'd do better to buy this one." So they sell at a small loss and buy the new one. I simplify a bit, but it is rather like this.'

He agreed it seemed incredible that people could be induced to co-operate in cheating themselves, but pointed out that they got their 6 or 7 per cent interest, which was what really concerned them. He smiled a bureaucrat's smile, as though apologising for the fact that in France it was still possible to get away with such things. 'The truth is,' he said, 'that people have little choice. Prices go up, prices go down. Small people do not know very well.'

The words suggest a frame of mind. It's not that men are un-swindleable in London, but that the official establishment doesn't acquiesce in the swindling. Paris doesn't shine as a capital market. In all ways, the government casts too many shadows. The place doesn't inspire quite the right degree of confidence—not to mention that uprising of passionate students and dissident workers whose memory will continue to cast a shadow of its own. As a European centre, Paris still lags far behind London.

5 *City Character*

The City is always being redefined and reassessed. In the eyes of some it stands for full-blooded materialism, with a cast of cunning bankers and gross-minded stockbrokers. When the *Guardian* printed an article on the vulgar art of petomania, it remarked the next day that copies of the newspaper, price fivepence, had been changing hands on the Stock Exchange at two shillings and sixpence—reporting the fact as though this provided a reliable gauge of rudeness. The City can stand for drudgery and boredom, with its strange sea-noise of feet shuffling over London Bridge in the morning, and shuffling away again at night. It was T. S. Eliot's 'Unreal City, under the brown fog of a winter dawn,' where

> . . . each man fixed his eyes before his feet.
> Flowed up the hill and down King William Street,
> To where Saint Mary Woolnoth kept the hours
> With a dead sound on the final stroke of nine.

The city is as old as the hills. Lost rivers and Roman walls run below streets whose electoral wards still correspond to the estates of City families who lived there, centuries ago, before it became fashionable to start moving west, shifting the centre of gravity away from the original City that was once the whole of London. It can be made to represent Britain's vanished glories or her hopes for the future. The City has slipped back in the world, losing first place to New York. It has a lingering obsession with old customs and ceremonial. But it continues to be good at making money, and its invisible earnings of foreign exchange from banking, broking, insurance and merchanting are more than £250 million a year. The City probably works harder and more skilfully than it did: it must do, in order to compensate for Britain's changed circumstances. There are not only foreigners in other countries to compete with, but foreigners on the spot, their numbers swelling all the time. Most of the new arrivals are American bankers, but they come from all quarters. 'About five o'clock in the afternoon the doors open,' said a managing director, 'and a lot of little brown men come out and go down the Underground.'

The remarks betrays the arrogance that goes naturally with the City, like its pubs and window-boxes and traffic jams. They are sure of themselves. Their confidence is their strongest point, the thing you notice first when you meet a merchant banker, a bill broker, a stockbroker, an insurance underwriter. It's not that they are always right. August merchant bankers have been swindled by wide boys who left school at fourteen, share issues have been recommended at times that turn out to be hopelessly wrong, new trends have been misinterpreted; Hambros Bank called the Eurodollar market a 'temporary phenomenon' in 1962. But they have the look of men who expect to be right, and their sense of expectation is catching. Under the courteous exterior of chaps who went to public school is the good old commercial bounce.

Much of the City's atmosphere derives from the fact that its senior managers and directors often went to the same schools, share the same circle of acquaintances, and spend their working lives within a few hundred yards of one another. I once heard an old-fashioned tailor near the Stock Exchange say that his clients were mainly stockbrokers, and add that he never saw an insurance underwriter from Lloyd's because that would be too far away. It takes about three minutes to walk between Lloyd's and the tailor. The City is a little place, its strictly financial area much smaller even than the 'Square Mile' of the guide books. Within this tiny enclave used to flourish fine gradations of respectability, depending on one's address, incomprehensible to anyone but a sociologist or an Englishman. It was based on distance from the Bank of England and the Stock Exchange across the road, and still survives, up to a point. The heart of the City might be defined as the area that a middle-aged messenger who has had a couple of pints of beer and a ham sandwich for his lunch can cover on foot in the last ten minutes before 3 o'clock, visiting the head offices of the big clearing banks to collect and deliver the final multi-thousand-pound cheques of the money market so that it can balance its books for the day. Annual office rents in Cornhill, opposite the great walls and skylights of the Bank of England, could be £6 per square foot. A hundred yards to the east they could be little more than half as much. The gaunt new tower blocks along London Wall, to the north of the City, rent at around £3 a square foot, but those on the south of the road are slightly more expensive than those on the north.

Space is one of the City's preoccupations, as it has been for a long time. In the year of the Great Fire, 1666, about a quarter of a million people lived there. Now scarcely anyone does. A population map showing the ten million who live in Greater London would be almost blank where the City is. At night it has four or five thousand if one includes caretakers, policemen, the residents of a Salvation Army hostel and other special cases; but by day nearly half a million arrive by bus, train and car, or walk across London Bridge from the railway stations on the other side of the Thames. The City Corporation is hoping to tempt residents with blocks of flats, as part of its plans to make it a more balanced community. To help make the place less nerve-racking to work in, property developers have had their arms discreetly twisted by officials who agree to their projects on condition that extra money is spent on good causes, such as overhead walkways for pedestrians. The City preserves gardens and plants trees, sometimes spending several hundred pounds per tree when the cost of diverting underground pipes and cables is taken into account.

It can afford to do this sort of thing because as an administrative unit the City is self-sufficient, with its own Lord Mayor, aldermen, common councilmen and officials, and an additional private income from estates and properties that makes it the richest local authority, for its size, in Britain. It was the original London, with a royal charter granted by William the Conqueror, and it has managed to go on living a life of its own. There are City police and City courts; the Central Criminal Court, which serves the whole country, is largely run and paid for by the City; at one time it nearly had its own airport. The Lord Mayor lives in the Mansion House during his year of office, surrounded by henchmen bearing titles like Sheriff and Swordbearer, with a footman to answer the door, and a glittering round of banquets and receptions that would exhaust anyone but a hardened public-speaker and handshaker, who had spent years looking forward to it. The daily password to the Tower of London is kept at the Mansion House, and no troops are supposed to cross the City boundary without mayoral permission. The Lord Mayor, and anyone with social ambitions in the City, will be a member of one of the guilds, or 'livery companies', the trade associations of the past. They still flourish, for ceremonial and sentimental reasons, and also because they are a useful means of bringing City men into the open, where they can be scrutinised by their fellows. There are Drapers, Grocers, Goldsmiths, Ironmongers, Waxchandlers and many more, encouraging clubmanship and the atmosphere of the closed shop that so many City men cherish.

In one sense all this ritual, traditional side of the City is irrelevant. It has nothing to do with financial London—except that it provides a suitable setting for the bankers and brokers, one that colours their view of themselves, and makes them more able to impress the rest of the world. I used to think the City's sense of ritual was absurd, and I still think it sometimes wallows in it, to the point of caricature. But it seems to be necessary to the City's confidence in itself, and this in turn is useful in helping to persuade others to have similar confidence in the place. The City has fared better than it might have done, considering that it's so hedged in with exchange-control restrictions, and is based on an international currency that has been almost continuously in trouble for twenty years. One reason is the local skill but another is the local air of confidence. The Eurobond market was first organised from London because the banks were technically clever, but bound up with their cleverness was the fact that their style somehow bedazzled the opposition. By the time the others realised what was happening, London's place in the market was established. Yet few of the dollar bonds have ever been sold in Britain because of the cost of buying investment dollars to use for their purchase. It was, as City bankers will say gleefully in private, a confidence trick of the very best kind.

It would be an exaggeration but one with a grain of truth to say that the City lives on its wits; this is why it is so fond of the phrase, 'my word is my bond,' since at times it has nothing else to offer. The very use of the phrase, 'the City', is part of the game; the meaning can expand or contract to suit the purpose. *The City thinks* implies one meaning (the most senior money-men, blurring into central bankers and even Treasury officials); *the City has built a car-park* implies another (its administrative, local-government function); *he's something in the City* implies almost anything, and could mean that a man is in insurance, ship-broking or commodity-dealing as well as in banking or stockbroking. When people refer to 'the City' they include banks of all kinds, the money market and the stock market; the foreign-exchange and gold markets; and to greater or lesser degree the markets in ship- and aircraft-chartering, insurance, metals, rubber, tin, cocoa, sugar and other products. Most of the dealing in raw materials and commodities is on paper, but considerable quantities of merchandise still pass through the City, providing a link with the past to remind people that river, port and trade were the foundation of London as a financial centre. There are offices along Mincing Lane, which was a thoroughfare leading to the river before the Great Fire, where bags and parcels of nuts, feathers, spices and waxes fill the air with improbable smells. Even furs and diamonds are part of the City's business.

As commonly used, 'the City' is convenient shorthand for 'the financial system of London,' and saves having to define it further. Most of the definitions are colourful rather than explanatory; they are about the City's morals or its profitability, its role in the British economy or tomorrow's world. They aren't about the way it works because it works in very complicated ways, reflecting in part the mysterious official attitude to the place, which, under Labour governments as well as Conservatives, implies a benevolent watch from on high, with freedom to act within a code of behaviour that is implied rather than stated.

This is what the City means by 'flexibility', a quality that money-men everywhere like to have or claim, but nowhere so loudly as in London. Banking is free—perhaps too free, as occasional disasters at small finance companies suggest, though these are all far removed from true banks. There is no British equivalent of the U.S. banking examiners who audit the books on behalf of the authorities, nor is there any legal distinction between investment and commercial banks.

Every Continental banker knows the joke about the definition of a bank in Britain, which is that it's a place that carries on the business of banking; except that it isn't a joke but a fact. The Bank of England Act of 1946, which virtually nationalised the central bank, laid down that it could issue legally binding directives to bankers, but didn't define who these bankers were—not that this appears to matter, since no directives have ever been issued. Just as Britain has no formal, unified banking code, so the relationship between the Bank of England and the rest of the system, which establishes a working code of conduct, rests on precedent and orderly behaviour. The banks keep their own accounts with the Bank of England, which (like most central banks) can call for 'special deposits' to reduce the amount of money that the banks have available for lending. Otherwise the Governor of the Bank works by 'requests'. As the Bank describes it, 'direct control of credit has been achieved through the Governor's requests to the banks . . . and to other financial institutions—imposing a quantitative ceiling on credit, or recommending or discouraging certain categories of lending.'

'It's almost as if we were a public utility,' said an economist at one of the clearing banks. 'The authorities talk about a thing, such as credit restrictions, and we do it.' The banks understand their role in life: they are private-enterprise firms with shareholders, but they know when to defer to officialdom; they are independent institutions with headquarter buildings that ooze dignity and prestige, but they are all within a few minutes' walk of the Bank of England. 'We have to confer with the Governor of the Bank,' said the chief general manager at one of the largest, 'but in theory we could defy him. There is no legislation governing the conduct of banking in this country—the only such country in the world. Of course, the authorities have now got the Bank of England Act behind the scenes which gives them the power to say "Thou Shalt Not," but it's never been invoked.'

A City phrase refers to 'the Governor's eyebrows' and means that merely by raising them he can show sufficient displeasure to stop a bank doing whatever it shouldn't have been doing. There are all kinds of nasty courses the Bank of England can take without invoking the 1946 Act, such as withdrawing foreign-exchange business, or, in the case of a foreign bank in London, refusing to renew its licence to stay there. In the last resort the system behaves itself because it would find life unbearable if it didn't. But the moral pressures are important, and City men enjoy the feeling that it is these and not the sanctions in the background that keep everyone in line. (A foreigner might call this another example of English hypocrisy.)

The methods of the money market show the process at work in its purest form, since this is where the Bank of England has its most regular dealings with the rest of the City. The term 'money market' is increasingly used to include a number of parallel markets (described later), but in its classical sense it means the same as 'discount market'. This is an arrangement for handling surplus money in the City, and is operated by a dozen banks of a special kind called discount houses, which borrow and lend up to £800 or £900 million each day. They pass the money from one part of the banking system to another, as and when individual sectors have too much or too little, and they alone have recourse to the Bank of England when the system as a whole is short of money—the clearing banks haven't been going there direct for a hundred years. The discount office at the Bank is its window on the City. The Bank can use the market to exercise a daily check on the amount of money in circulation, and it can influence interest rates by its willingness or reluctance to make extra money available without charging an uncomfortably high rate of interest for the privilege.

The money market is at the centre of the system, and its efficiency in finding borrowers for money that may be available for only a day or two helps to attract foreign funds to London. But it's run in a way that is almost a caricature of the gentlemen's-agreement, play-the-game aspect of London. The discount brokers, usually called bill brokers, follow a ritual of morning visits to all the banks in person, formally dressed. They have polite conversations before getting down to business, which they conclude without actually putting anything on paper in a banker's office. If a discount house needs to borrow from the Bank of England, to balance its books before the banks close at 3 p.m., a managing director must go to the Bank's discount office, form a queue with his fellows, and do the borrowing in person. The Bank is never explicit where a hint will do. Representatives of the market visit the Governor before the weekly tender for Treasury bills—I.O.U.s issued by the Government, against which it does its short-term borrowing, and which are bought by the discount market in large numbers—but are never given more than a general idea of the price they ought to be paying. 'It's a very informal market,' said a banker. 'The Bank of England expects everyone to do their best. If they're slightly wrong, well, the Bank will accept it.'

It's easy to laugh at some aspects of the discount market, and see it as composed of good chaps with nice manners; gentlemen-financiers, top-hatted and deferential, strolling about the City with public school smiles stamped on their faces. They have the Englishman's fondness for being thought amateurs, though not amateurish. 'Securities are kept in a tin box and are lodged each night in the vault of a clearing bank,' says a booklet issued by one of the twelve houses, as though *tin* box adds a tiny joke, suggesting a battered old container to keep the valuables in. But the discount market has bestirred itself and begun to change, adapting its functions to new streams of money, including the dollars that now circulate in the City. One could argue that the small number of people involved in the market (not more than a hundred executives), their close but informal relations with one another and with the Bank of England, and the Bank's benevolent oversight of the system, have all combined to make the changes smooth and unobtrusive. If 'flexibility' means anything, this is how it looks in action.

The word for the Bank of England's attitude is paternal, or rather maternal, since its sobriquet is 'the Old Lady of Threadneedle Street', a phrase one often sees in print but never hears an Englishman use. It is supposed to have originated in 1797, by which time the Bank was more than a century old, when Gilray, the cartoonist, published a drawing which showed Pitt, the Prime Minister, trying to rob an old woman—a reference to the Government's demands on the Bank for gold to fight Napoleon. The caption read, 'Political Ravishment, or the Old Lady of Threadneedle Street in Danger.' The nickname stuck because it suited. The building has occupied the same site since 1734—the first Governor had his private house there—and now stands, overpoweringly solid and stony, where six main roads meet. The Underground station and bus-stops here are known simply as 'Bank'. Surrounding it on its island site is a curtain of high windowless walls, put there as a defence after the Gordon Riots of 1780. The place is lofty and remote. After the great metal doors have closed at the end of the afternoon, a caller feels like a man in a rowing boat going alongside an aircraft carrier. Beside the main entrance is a small contraption, with notice: *To deliver letters etc. ring bell and await instructions through speaking tube.* Each day an armed guard arrives from barracks on the other side of London soon after 5 p.m.—until a few years ago it used to march through the City in the middle of the rush-hour, but now travels by lorry—and adds its deterrent to those of the locks, bolts, armoured steel and electronic devices that protect the gold and banknotes in the vaults.

It would be impossible for an institution like the Bank, in a place like the City, in a country like England, in a tradition laid down over centuries, not to have a highly developed sense of its own importance. Its remoteness is part of its personality, though politicians have tried to make it more accountable—Parliament's Select Committee on Nationalised Industries began to make angry noises in 1968. Unlike every other nationalised industry, the Bank conceals the salaries it pays. When suede shoes were approved for its executives a few years ago, the fact was sufficiently remarkable to be reported. But the Bank is less stuffy than it was. Its activities are better publicised, its officials can be interviewed. Changes at the Bank reflect changes in the City in general. Its Economic Intelligence Department, which used to be a mere 'statistics office', has grown. Intellectual distinction now commands better prospects than it did; dons and bright young men have been brought in, including one, Jeremy Morse, who became an executive director in 1965, at the age of 36. This would have been thought impossibly young a few years ago.

The Bank is unlikely, or less likely than it was, to find itself run by a Governor who was appointed for the kind of personal reasons that gave it Montagu Norman, who ruled there and influenced British economic policy from 1920 to 1944. Norman was a member of a well-known City family who quarrelled with his girl-friend, had a nervous breakdown, left his firm of merchant bankers, and was given a job at the Bank out of compassion. The story, both hilarious and alarming, is told in Andrew Boyle's biography of Norman; as the *Economist* said when it reviewed the book, 'The key to the commanding control over the British economy in the interwar years was thus given to a well connected scion of a respected City family chiefly as a therapeutic kindness because he had recently gone out of his mind . . .

[it is] a sort of horror story: reflecting not on Norman, but on the system of inheritance and feudal virtues and personal loyalty and family friendships in the City that elevated him to a high office for which he was impossibly unsuited.'

This system hasn't entirely vanished, as the *Economist* remarked. But nepotism has waned in the City. It used to flourish at merchant banks; nowadays a member of the family is unlikely to be appointed on his name alone, and bank after bank has reorganised, enlarging its inner group of managing directors by promoting its own managers, or bringing in people from industry, accountancy and the law. The trend is illustrated by Schroder Wagg, who appointed four new directors of whom the eldest was thirty-nine, and Kleinwort Benson, who appointed seven new directors at the same time, three of them in their mid-thirties.

The typical clearing banker and the typical merchant banker are still divided by their backgrounds. The former is more likely to have gone to a grammar school; most top positions are still held by safe, solid men who joined at the age of sixteen and rose slowly through the ranks. 'What are we doing about university entrants?' said a clearing-bank official as late as 1965. 'The answer is, as little as possible. Most of the general managers have worked their way up more by guess and by God than anything else. In the United States there's a much clearer division: they recruit for clerical work on the one hand and bankers on the other. In Britain we recruit for clerical work, and those who are best at it become the top bankers. This is entirely wrong. We ought to be attracting the second-class honours men to work in the ordinary branches, and first-class honours men for the big branches. A pass would do for head office.' (This was a joke, he added hastily).

There are now signs of improvement, including such straws in the wind as a Barclays advertisement for graduates promising that 'Top bankers earn as much as Cabinet Ministers.' (Really top bankers earn considerably more, even at a clearing bank. At a merchant bank, £20,000 and upwards for a senior executive is not uncommon. A 1968 advertisement for the head of the domestic banking department at an unnamed merchant bank offered a salary of not less than £17,500 for a man of 45).

If the average clearing banker is still the bright-but-not-brilliant ex-grammar schoolboy, the average merchant banker is the well-spoken ex-public schoolboy. But the merchant banks have had to adopt new standards, now that straitened circumstances and painful competition have forced them to abandon nepotism. Able to change direction more swiftly because they are smaller, they have begun to find room for intellectuals and clever outsiders. It would be difficult or impossible to find a banker who also teaches at university, which sometimes happens in France and Italy, but easier than it used to be to find senior men who have crossed over from the Civil Service. 'To put it crudely,' said a former Treasury man who went east to a banking directorship, 'before the war no one would have dreamt of leaving the higher echelons of the Civil Service and going into commerce or the City. Commerce was a dirty word. Then power shifted and one felt that commerce was more important. In addition, one must admit, there has been a certain amount of financial incentive.'

Sir Richard Powell went from the Board of Trade, where he was Permanent Secretary, to be a director of Hill, Samuel; earlier recruits to the same bank were J. R. Colville, who had been private secretary to prime ministers and Princess Elizabeth, and Sir Philip de Zulueta, who also served under a number of prime ministers. Sir Eric Roll, head of the Department of Economic Affairs, joined the boards of the Bank of London and South America and of S. G. Warburg—the City's most enterprising merchant bank since the war, with a bold policy of recruitment. Senior posts there may be filled by barristers, journalists and classical scholars. Sir Siegmund Warburg, the former Hamburg banker, and scholar in his own right, who has made the bank very much in his own image, remarked once that he liked to have graduates who had read classics, since it was a suitable preparation for the banking business. 'The fellow who is a good classical scholar has a sense of style. One of the things he should be able to do is to write a letter, to be able to express himself. I hate boring letters, without sex-appeal and punch.' Other bankers have different theories about the qualities that will produce a good recruit to the cause, like Jean Reyre at the Banque de Paris et des Pays-Bas with his swarms of young technologists; what matters about Warburg's policy isn't that he has a weakness for men who read classics but that he has an open door for talent. He says that he looks for 'a sound attitude towards life from people who are at the same time noncomformists,' which is not the kind of remark that would have been associated with the City twenty years ago.

Warburg was harshly criticised as an outsider by the old guard when the City began to feel his impact in the early 1950s. He took over a merchant bank, Seligman Brothers, one of the inner ring that brought with it membership of the coveted Accepting Houses Committee, and from this position at the heart of the City built up a diversified bank that could offer, among other things, a wide range of expert services to industry. Warburgs made much of its reputation with the ingenuity and will-power it exercised in mergers and takeovers. Eventually Siegmund Warburg got a knighthood and everyone said that a bank like his was an example to us all, but to begin with, he had to steer through minefields of disapproval. He was a necessary element in the resurgence of the City, which had become hidebound and went through a particularly unflexible phase immediately after the second world war. Another City figure whose electric and unconventional approach suits the times is Kenneth Keith, chairman of the Philip Hill Investment Trust, who helped develop the Philip Hill merchant bank (now Hill, Samuel, where he is chief executive). Keith is one of the best-known City figures, on the boards of Eagle Star Insurance, National Provincial Bank and *The Times*: a big-shouldered, physically restless man, very different from Warburg, who sits hunched and reflective, but has the same contempt for inertia. It's still possible to be a languid City banker, but it's no longer desirable.

There are fewer City snobberies today because they are an increasingly expensive luxury. I was told of a £25,000 fee that had been declined not long before by one of the hoarier merchant banks, since to accept would have meant joining the same consortium as a brasher bank of which it didn't approve. The point of the story was that such gestures were becoming so rare as to be collector's pieces. Two bankers said at different times that in the old days, if X's (they both named the same bank) declined a piece of business, there was no point in trying to find anyone who would accept it. Nowadays if X's were fool enough to say No because they didn't like the colour of the client's socks, there would be plenty willing to say Yes.

The rise of a managerial class in the City is seen clearly in the business of investment. Statisticians and economists have moved into stockbroking, and machines clatter away in back rooms. For the moment, the Stock Exchange is a strange mixture of new methods and old idiosyncracies. It has a powerful sense of what it is, a private club as well as a public industry, with many rules and traditions that no doubt will survive the move to the new tower block which is being built on the same site as the old Exchange. Advertising by individual stockbrokers is forbidden, though the Stock Exchange itself goes in for prestige advertising. Second only to New York in the value of transactions, and largest in the world in the number and range of securities traded, it is self-organised and managed; there are no laws and no Government officials; the State makes itself felt only indirectly, by, for instance, imposing a short-term capital gains tax, and a Government stamp duty on the purchase of securities.

It's a masculine place, often hearty and facetious; telegraphic addresses of stockbrokers include Fiddle, Oddness, Overmodest and Contrive. Women may not be members—a poll in 1967 turned down a proposal that would have admitted them to membership as long as they didn't set foot on the trading floor during business hours. The floor of the Stock Exchange is still sacred ground, a place where a man can swear a little or play the fool with his friends. (A Milan stockbroker said he had been told by an English colleague that if a broker carried a newspaper under his arm for long enough in the London Stock Exchange, some joker would be sure to set fire to the end of it. 'That couldn't happen in Milan,' he said severely, 'and if it did, the person would be suspended for a fortnight'). Sons and nephews still slide into family firms; some brokers still exist on a shoestring, managing a few portfolios and mouldering away with a certain elegance. But mergers between Stock Exchange firms are creating fewer and larger units, especially among stockjobbers—the English brand of specialists, who trade as wholesalers in securities, for their own account, and so need greater resources.

Stockbrokers have to spend more of their time dealing with institutional investors, and less with the affairs of old Lord Moneybags, who comes to have lunch with the partners once a year. The ownership of industrial shares is slowly passing from individuals to financial institutions. In 1957, it's estimated, two-thirds of Ordinary shares in Britain were owned by individuals, roughly one-sixth by financial institutions, and the other sixth by non-financial institutions, such as colleges and charities, and overseas holdings. Ten years later, 'personal' shareholdings had fallen to half, while the financial institutions now had nearly 30 per cent. These institutions are insurance companies, pension funds, and investment and unit trusts, all of which draw in immense sums of money from the public. To invest their income through the stock market they use professional managers who have no option but to employ strict, well-informed criteria. Insurance premiums bring in more than £2,500 million a year, of which at least two-thirds goes into the stock-market—making £7 million of new money to be invested each working day. About one-eighth of everything invested in the British stock market (£100,000 million at end-of-1967 values) is insurance money. Unit trusts now own more than £1,000 million worth.

The scale of institutional investment imposes its own values. Traditions are less important than results. The investment managers of the institutions, each one of them with more funds at his disposal than the wealthiest of individuals, are powerful men, whose displeasure with a company that conceals information or issues shares on poor terms can make itself felt. 'They are dictators,' said a stockbroker. 'They're constantly exerting pressure on the Stock Exchange and on companies. It's the morality of the accountants and the investment managers that forces company boards into telling the public a great deal more than they *would* tell them if they were left to themselves.'

When an industrial take-over is in the offing, the attitude of the institutions is studied minutely. When the General Electric Company was bidding for Associated Electrical Industries in 1967, the City didn't take its eyes off Prudential Assurance, Pearl Assurance, Legal & General Assurance, the Church Commissioners for England and the rest. After G.E.C. had won, making it Britain's biggest industrial take-over, the *Economist* remarked that, in contrast with the goings-on of ten years before, 'the City has grown up. The investment analysts and professional managers are now in charge. The consequence of their new pre-eminence is that this time both sides have had to show that their arguments made sense in terms of long-term industrial economics as well as short-term cash.'

The investment analysts still have a long way to go before they are as numerous and important as they are in Wall Street. But if the City's new competence is a fact, and if sterling is ever strong enough to let foreign borrowers float loans on the London Stock Exchange again, then the City might be an incomparable home for a European capital market. It's unlikely to be so straightforward. Already the dollar is becoming a currency for all Europe, and the idea of raising money through a market that is physically located in one place is being steadily eroded by the traffic in Eurodollars and Eurobonds, which belong to nowhere in particular. Whether in short- or long-term lending, any extrapolation of London's place in tomorrow's Europe from the evidence now available is likely to look wrong in another twenty years. But at least the City is likely to be making money and exercising its peculiar hold on people.

Bitterly criticised by Left-wing politicians over the years for naked self-interest, the City has survived with little intervention from governments, though more is likely over the next decade. The Governor raises his eyebrows; the bankers doff their hats; there is a discussion in a cosy parlour, and a formula is arrived at. The Stock Exchange sets standards of disclosure and behaviour for companies that want to issue securities, and in general has managed to fend off demands for an official supervisory body on the lines of the American Securities and Exchange Commission—set up after the Wall Street crash of 1929 to regulate the market there. Both the new Companies Act of 1967, and the growing power of the institutions, have helped maintain pressure on the London Stock Exchange, which can make a convincing case against official intervention simply because it has shown itself susceptible to unofficial pressures in the past. A revised and tougher 'code of conduct' for take-overs and mergers, agreed by the leading City organisations in 1968, may well have forestalled attempts by the Government to impose an S.E.C. type of body.

In a public-relations sense, the City's nastiest moment since the war came years ago, in 1957. In September that year, sterling was enduring one of its recurrent crises. Bank Rate was raised as a defensive measure, and this was preceded by some selling of Government securities, which automatically fall in price when Bank Rate goes up. A rumour got about that news of the rise had leaked out in advance, and had been the basis for the selling; to investigate the matter, a full-scale Government inquiry was set up, the 'Bank Rate Tribunal'. It found that there had been no leak, but the evidence it heard, and later published, gave a more detailed account of everyday behaviour than most people would care to give of themselves. Everyone had acted properly but they had been shown in action, making money and enjoying it. A number of M.P.s (including Harold Wilson, then a member of the Labour Opposition) tried to make capital from the 'old-boy' atmosphere that they detected. Some of the participants had been shooting grouse in Yorkshire, and this branded them as pleasure-seeking reactionaries in the eyes of the Left.

But the fact was that apart from embarrassment all round and a convenient focus for jokes about grouse moors, the tribunal produced nothing at all. Anyone who doubts that the City has an elaborate old-boy system has only to read the volume of evidence, but there was no suggestion that it was sinister. In retrospect it strengthened the City's right to manage its own affairs, since a long public inquiry had failed to turn up anything nasty.

The City's freedom from formal controls is one of the attractions that has brought the world's money-men there in force. The foreign invasion, in turn, helps to energise the natives. Many of the famous names originally came from somewhere else—Rothschilds from Frankfurt, Hambros from Norway, Lazards from New Orleans, Barings from Bremen; the City has a long tradition of making the most of new talents. However it emerges from the present state of flux, it will have learnt some fresh tricks.

The process works both ways. Merrill Lynch, Pierce, Fenner and Smith, the New York stockbroking firm, has been in the City since 1960, advertising its services and doing good business. Lacking a City tradition, it has to acquire one. The London staff once sent a joke photograph of themselves, with bowler hats and tight-furled umbrellas, to New York. It was promptly printed in the annual report.

6 City Mechanism

Visiting Europeans who don't know the City are sometimes overawed by the conglomeration of brass plaques, front doors, frosted glass and barred windows. The banks run into hundreds, let alone the insurance companies and brokers, the gold and foreign exchange firms, the merchants and commodity dealers. The City has seventy or eighty British and British Commonwealth deposit and merchant banks, twelve discount houses, dozens of specialist banks in the fields of capital-raising and hire-purchase financing, and more than a hundred branches and representatives of foreign banks. There are Communist banks and Jewish banks; open-plan American banks and comfortable little English banks with a coal fire in the grate and a fortune in gold in the cellar. The National Provincial Bank is in a thirty-storey skyscraper where the rent is rumoured to be a million pounds a year. Barings has an old-fashioned partners' room that was once featured in the magazine *Country Life*, and a small neat room at the top of a staircase, with clean pink blotter and three telephones, where a partner (as directors are still called) can go if he wants to be on his own. At the Moscow Narodny Bank near London Bridge the chairman has the largest private office in the City.

The biggest staffs and the widest front doors belong to the clearing banks. Until 1967 there was a 'Big Five': Barclays, Midland, Lloyds, Westminster and National Provincial, in that order. Then the last two merged, and shortly afterwards Barclays, Lloyds and a smaller deposit bank, Martins, proposed to do the same. This left the Barclays group comfortably ahead, with more than £5,500 million in deposits, making it the world's largest bank outside the U.S.[1]

Although 'deposit' banks is what they are, they are called 'clearing' banks because their cheques are dealt with centrally at the Bankers' Clearing House in the City. Before the mergers there were eleven clearing banks, with more than 13,000 branches, and their cheques, apart from those sorted out locally in provincial cities, descend on the Bankers' Clearing House in a daily torrent of paper. Rows of girls with adding machines leaf through bundles of cheques for amounts that frequently run into hundreds of thousands of pounds; by centralising the process in this way, banks need transfer only the marginal balances owing to one another at the end of each afternoon —perhaps £40 or £50 million of a total of above £1,500 million. No one else in Europe uses cheques like the British, and at the Clearing House the great tides of City money are visible.

The clearing banks have about ninety branches in the City, apart from the head offices of the largest, many of them catering especially for some particular market or trade. Bank managers here are especially wily men, accustomed to handling other wily men. A manager at Eastcheap, dealing with importers, will be lending them money against the security of the goods when they arrive at the warehouse. 'I lend against canned goods, rice, flour in bags, canary seed, pulp in casks for jam-making and dried fruit—not fresh fruit, which can go bad. I'll lend against ginger and Chinese sprayed dried egg, though actually I don't know what that is. I'll lend to a company importing shoes but not against the security of the shoes themselves. It's easier to get rid of peaches in tins than shoes. The same is true of wool, tea and rubber. There's a market in these things, but not in shoes or paint or ladies' dresses. I've been asked to lend against plastic flowers but I've refused.'

A manager near the Stock Exchange will be lending large sums for short periods to stockbrokers, trying to make sure the money is used to finance the broker's day-to-day business and not lent on to clients

[1] Barclays had held this position before, but lost it when the pound was devalued in November 1967. Since the usual standard of comparison is the size of banks' deposits expressed in U.S. dollars, the 14 per cent devaluation reduced the British figures by one-seventh. Barclays sank from fifth to tenth, Lloyds from sixteenth to twenty-fifth. Bankers gnashed their teeth, until devaluation pushed them up the table again.

for them to speculate with. 'I have eight or nine hundred overdrafts and about a hundred of these are brokers and jobbers. It's nothing for a firm of stockjobbers in the gilt-edged market to ring up and ask for half a million pounds, just for the day. Jobbers are legitimately entitled to hold the stock, and they deal in very large amounts. One knows the customers one can trust. It's like a little intimate circle at the Stock Exchange. I know how many times they've been divorced. I know a lot about their private lives. I know the people who are willing to talk. I don't mind admitting that I have on occasion taken certain individuals out and plied them with drink, and I've always got my answer. It's rather like living in a small country town. You remember that last stockbroker who went bust? I could have told you about that before it happened.'

An insistence on the 'personal element' in banking runs through the profession, and one hears as exalted a person as the chief general manager at the head office of a clearing bank saying much the same thing as the manager of a little branch in the country who can lend no more than £2,000 on his own initiative: 'Banking is not in any sense a science, it is the art of understanding people.' This is only part of the truth. It's the kind of throw-away English attitude, accompanied by a twinkle in the eye, that has its counterpart in the casual contempt I heard from an American in the City for 'the old kind of grey-gloves banking.' Technical problems multiply. An American airline needn't buy a new plane direct; the bank will pay for it and lease it to the company. Computers are being used by American banks to envisage future situations in a particular industry or firm, and so make it possible to lend money safely over longer periods. It's true that computers don't remove the need to form a judgment of the borrower, and that bankers who talk about the art of measuring character are also going to use more scientific aids where they think it necessary. But when the chief general manager rubs his thumb and forefinger together and talks at length about 'the feel of things,' insisting that 'even with big companies one forms favourable or unfavourable impressions of the people who are running them,' it suggests that the English attitude goes deep.

Much of the lending at this and the other clearing banks is unsecured; the company is allowed to run an overdraft for a period of weeks or months on the strength of its management. Traditionally, this is what a clearing bank is for: short-term lending that the borrower agrees to pay back within a given period. The loan is usually made as an overdraft, the customer being allowed to spend money he hasn't got by writing cheques against his current account, up to an agreed figure. The interest he pays will be somewhere above the level of Bank Rate (the key interest rate, at which the Bank of England will lend to the money market), depending on whether he's a large industrial customer with a famous name, who will be paying Bank Rate plus one-half per cent, or a young doctor borrowing money to bridge the purchase of a house, who will probably have to pay Bank Rate plus 2 per cent.

It's essentially an informal system, perhaps because the English are natural bankers who lend money by intuition rather than by going through the administrative agonies of the Continental banker. A detailed survey by Glyn, Mills & Co., one of the smaller and more adventurous clearing banks, has shown that short-term lending in Britain is simpler and cheaper than it is anywhere else in Europe. Many European countries do most of their short-term lending against bills of exchange, a clumsier system; where overdrafts are available, there is more insistence on tangible securities that the banker can keep in his safe. The apparent advantages of the British method lead some City men to believe hopefully that if Britain enters the Common Market and there is a corresponding surge of British industry across the Channel, the clearing banks will be carried along (just as American banks have been carried into Europe by American companies and investments). Once arrived on the Continent, runs this theory, there will be rich pickings for these intuitive bankers with their greater flexibility, etc.

If events should turn out like this—and City bankers are going to have to run hard to keep up with the Americans in Europe, whether Britain enters the Market or not—then the clearing banks might find the outlet that so far has eluded them. They have a stately, ponderous air that isn't dispelled by the popular advertising they now use to brighten their image. As far as the public is concerned, they have, indeed, changed enormously. They want more deposits, and in order to get them from people at large they must appear as everybody's friend: jolly fellows, not only safe but helpful. Their head offices in the City epitomise the old image, usually with a huge marbled banking hall, overlaid with offices where the carpets grow thicker and the attendants more courteous as you approach the top management. A faint smell of soap blows along the panelled corridors from the wash-rooms as the managers go to lunch; a faint smell of cigars blows up from the lift-shafts as they return. I was once in a lift returning with some bowler-hatted bankers who had been to see a publicity film, in which a local manager was shown driving a Ford Anglia. It was rather a small, popular car for a manager, they agreed; it was hardly the thing; it was a bit infra-dig, said someone, and they were all nodding thoughtfully as they got out of the lift.

But the point of the advertising is to make people see bankers as smaller and more human. Banks have fallen over themselves to be agreeable, though there's often a great gulf between the agreeable advertising film in the cinema and the cold inhospitality of many branches. Personal-loan schemes have been introduced for small borrowers; credit cards and 'cheque cards'—which guarantee payment of cheques up to a fixed amount, usually £30—have appeared. The clearing banks scurried about in response to the national giro as soon as it was announced that the Post Office would introduce it in 1968. Some years previously the banks had introduced a 'direct-transfer' system by which customers could pay bills by instructing a bank direct to move money into the relevant account; this is done by filling in a form, and used to cost 6d. a time. When the banks saw the national giro coming, they improved the service, removed the charge for regular customers, and, nervous at the thought of competing with ever-open post offices, announced proudly that they, too, had a giro. Since a true giro not only uses direct-transfer, without cheques, but also holds all the users' accounts centrally, the banks were letting their enthusiasm run away with them. The same was true of the Post Office, which claimed to be offering 'a new current account banking facility,' but was, in fact, offering a money-transmission system without overdrafts and other basic banking services. Eighty-five years after the first giro, in Austria, the British public found itself hit by two at once; this is typical of the way things have gone in banking, where everyone needs to coax money from the newly affluent, and is perfectly willing to befuddle them if it seems likely to produce results.

Behind the scenes, the clearing banks improved their services with increased mechanisation and wide use of computers. Glyn, Mills, which handles officers' pay for the War Office and Air Ministry, began using a computer to process payments in 1959, and since then, coding-figures in magnetic ink have crept on to everyone's cheques.

The clearing banks look different and are different, yet in some respects they are stationary. They reacted with pain and indignation to a report of the Government's Prices and Incomes Board in 1967 which suggested that they should compete more among themselves, in particular by ending their private agreement to limit interest on deposits to 2 per cent below Bank Rate. The clearing banks deny themselves whole worlds of action because they believe they know their place in the system, and others (like the Prices and Incomes Board) don't. They are not meant, they insist, to lend money medium-term, for year and years, and they are not meant to pay for deposits at the higher rates of interest that would be practicable if they *were* going to lend for these longer periods. What they have done instead, though they were coy about it at first, is to set up subsidiaries, or employ existing ones, to scoop up money—sterling or dollars—by paying more for it; and then to lend this out to industry for years at a time. All of them are now deep in the Eurodollar market, where many of the deposits originate. It doesn't worry Continental lenders, who know when they lend to MAIBL, Midland and International Banks Ltd, that the Midland and three other large banks are behind it. MAIBL was set up for the purpose, as was a joint company owned by National Provincial and Rothschild (the French Rothschilds, Banque Lambert and Piersons of Amsterdam also joined in here). Other back-door subsidiaries were contrived from existing companies. Barclays Bank (France), based on Paris, with nineteen branches in the country, found itself with a London office, set up to bid for surplus dollars. The clearing banks had soon collected well over a billion dollars through these back doors.

Anything that smells of what they define as 'specialist banking' is kept at arm's length by the clearing banks; they hive it off in a subsidiary or don't do it at all. The distinction isn't always clear to outsiders. The clearing banks finance trade and deal extensively in foreign exchange, which are both specialist activities. A clearing bank is always involved in an issue of shares, but with rare exceptions it doesn't manage the issue itself; it leaves this to an 'issuing house.' Nor do clearing banks appear in the long lists of underwriters to issues of Eurobonds—the sole exception among deposit banks in Europe. But these things are beginning to change. Glyn, Mills is interesting itself in new issues and the Eurobond market. The sharp line between clearing and merchant banks is becoming blurred. Back-door subsidiaries are one sign; the alliances with European banks for medium-term lending are another. The first direct participation in a merchant bank was by National & Grindlays, an affiliate of Lloyds Bank, with a two-thirds stake in William Brandts'; the next was by the Midland, which paid more than £8 million to buy a third of the Montagu Trust.

Merchants, Bankers

It is always assumed, and is presumably true, that by edging towards the merchant-banking way of life, the clearing banks can do themselves nothing but good. The clearing banks are big and rich, yet people worry about their future. The merchant banks are smaller but livelier; no one worries about them, and clearing bankers have been known to complain angrily that they are sick and tired of hearing what clever fellows these famous bankers are. The famous bankers themselves have succeeded in getting the best of both worlds, as far as their public appearance is concerned. They brush aside the books and articles that describe their work as glamorous and mysterious, insist that they are just plain money-managers who bring a certain something to the business, but know that glossy references to super-bankers will continue to rub off on them to their benefit.

Because the label is attractive, many banks in the City call themselves merchant banks. In some cases they live up to the pretensions of the title, but the true merchant bank is still one of the sixteen members of the Accepting Houses Committee. The name goes back to the origins of their power, as houses that 'accepted' bills of exchange, thus guaranteeing to pay the owner of the bill if the person who issued it in the first instance defaulted. In the nineteenth century, when everyone used bills of exchange to finance trade, London's merchant bankers (who mostly began as merchants, before they realised that money was a more profitable commodity than cocoa) were key figures in world trading. They had to be well-connected and judge what risks to take; they knew about people, or had to make it look as if they did, and this is the basis of the legend. They are still in the accepting business, though bills are less important. What they never forget is the need to offer a cool personal service, whether they are hatching a take-over in the private dining room and the directors are serving lunch themselves to ensure privacy (as they do at Kleinwort Benson) or sending a brief Telex to a Norwegian shipowner to say that his loan of $7 million for ten years, requested a few hours before, has now been arranged (as I heard them doing at Hambros).

They are punctilious; a butler enters the waiting room and removes a milligram of ash from the ashtray, head inclined deferentially; executive directors will see journalists with less formality than their counterparts at clearing banks, presumably because they are endlessly optimistic about meeting people, *any* people. Their managing directorships have multiplied in recent years because as business expands they must have enough high-level personal contacts to go round. 'We will give you bad advice on *anything*,' said a merchant banker, self-deprecating in an absent-minded way, without meaning it. 'If a client wants long-term money or medium-term money, we know where to get it through the market. We have close contacts with the insurance companies, who always have lots of money. We'll introduce a man and say he's all right. We've even got a surveyor if he wants to sell his house.'

Much of their time these days is spent as advisers and father-figures to British industry. No industrial merger, take-over or issue of new shares is complete without its merchant bankers in the wings, though they may not always be as wise as they think; some of the more old-fashioned still rely heavily on charm and reputation. Taxation advice is an industry in itself, and all legal varieties are available. Some of the banks now have offices in provincial towns like Birmingham, Leeds and Manchester that were once more remote from the City in spirit than Timbuktu.

When the Government—intervening in the private sector more subtly than by the old route of nationalisation—set up an Industrial Reorganisation Corporation in 1966, a merchant banker (Ronald Grierson of Warburgs) was appointed as its first managing director. The corporation aims to promote mergers and modernisation in the national interest, making loans and taking participations where necessary, and in general behaving rather like a State-owned *banque d'affaires*. When Grierson left after eighteen months, his successor was another merchant banker, Charles Villiers of Schroder Wagg—at a salary of £20,000 a year, less than he earned in the City but more than the British Government is prepared to pay unless it wants someone badly.

Nearly forty years ago the official Macmillan Report on finance and industry was regretting the lack of contact between the two in Britain, comparing it unfavourably with the situation elsewhere in Europe. That was in 1931, when many countries were soon to find during the financial crisis that their banks and industries were all too close together. The City's merchant banks (and the clearing banks, for that matter) have narrowed the gap without becoming involved as large direct shareholders in industry, like the French *banques d'affaires* and the German deposit banks. They may have a banker on the board, but they shy away from the idea of owning too big a slice of any single company, feeling much the same as insurance companies and pension funds, which fear political criticism should they take more than a very few per cent of the equity in one firm. But as the managers of shareholdings on behalf of others—both by running unit and investment trusts, and by looking after private portfolios and pension funds—the banks do decide where a lot of money shall be invested. The merchant banks are thought to manage several thousand million pounds. A single bank, Kleinwort Benson, has advertised the fact that it manages portfolios worth £350 million, apart from a stake in a unit trust. The clearing banks have improved their investment services and they, too, manage fat portfolios running into hundreds of millions of pounds apiece.

As their investment business has grown, merchant bankers have been able to bypass the Stock Exchange with much of their buying and selling, because they can now match clients' orders in the office. Their new powers have caused alarm in the City, where stockbrokers, forbidden to advertise, are already watching the much-advertised unit trusts, some run by banks, pull in money that escapes the Stock Exchange. Even worse for the brokers, aggressive merchant banks have sometimes managed to edge them out when a Stock Exchange issue is being made, and take all the client's business for themselves. Some critics see it as the beginning of a German-type situation that could end with a market dominated by comparatively few powerful dealers at the banks. The truth is probably less exciting, but the City is no longer an orderly society where everyone knows his place; it's harsher and more predatory.

Organising international deals of one sort and another is still very much a merchant bankers' preserve. Kleinwort Benson have gone into aircraft leasing on the American pattern, buying, to begin with, three Boeing 707s (one new and two second-hand) at a cost of £6,500,000. If the Channel Tunnel is ever built, merchant banks will be hovering in the background, raising money, reconciling differences, and taking a tiny percentage of a large amount, which is how they first grew rich; at least nine of them are in various Tunnel groups. It could be steelworks plant for Yugoslavia or destroyers for Iran. The merchant bank itself won't be providing the money—the plant in this instance cost £30 million, the destroyers £14 million—but it will be organising the band of clearing banks and insurance companies that actually have the funds. In theory there is no reason why a clearing bank, with many times the resources of a merchant bank, shouldn't do the organising itself; in practice it either lacks the necessary staff of skilled negotiators, lawyers, accountants and tax experts, or, equally important, *feels* that it lacks them, and that it would be improper to seek the business for itself.

The Shift towards Dollars

The merchant banks will try their hand at most things, even at being merchants; Hambros Bank has a fund of funny stories, that only self-assured bankers would tell, about their mixed success in selling goods that ranged from cars to honey, direct to the United States after the second war. But probably the merchant bankers' most significant plunge in the last twenty years has been into the handling of other countries' currencies, especially the U.S. dollar. It's significant for the bankers and significant for the City. It's part of a process that is reshaping London's money markets, faintly shadowing the political readjustment of Britain to the world; and although the merchant banks have been closely involved, the changes reach far beyond them.

There are two main areas of upheaval. First, the City's mechanism for handling the fluctuating supply of short-term money—the discount market, the 'money market' of the orthodox text-books—is changing rapidly; the City is finding new ways of circulating surplus funds. Second, the City has become a large-scale dealer in another currency altogether, dollars. Thus it has the old money market in pounds, and alongside it a new money market in dollars. These are the famous Eurodollars—dollar claims in the hands of banks, industries and individuals outside the U.S. Some of the Eurodollars find their way into the British money market after being changed into sterling; most of them meet the needs of borrowers in Europe, Japan and other parts of the world, but the market stays firmly based on London. The City's history as a financial centre is largely its history as a lender of sterling to finance world trade and industry. It still has the expertise but it no longer has sufficient sterling. So, with merchant banks in the lead, the City has done the obvious thing, and started lending someone else's money—and, when not actually lending it, organising the flow of money between other borrowers and lenders.

From 1958, when certain controls were relaxed, dollars were able to move freely in and out of London, as long as they weren't owned by British residents. During the past ten years the world's surplus dollars have been organised into an international money market, with London at the centre of it. (The term 'Eurodollar' is used to include other currencies that are employed in the same way, but none approaches the U.S. dollar in importance). More than a hundred London banks take part, among them merchant banks, the 'back-door' subsidiaries of the clearing banks, and foreign banks. Over twenty U.S. banks and a dozen Japanese are in the City, all busily trading in Eurodollars. Inside London, most Eurodollar business goes through the existing foreign exchange brokers. The Russian-owned Moscow Narodny, where young Soviet bankers come to see how they do it in the West, is among the biggest dealers. Thousands of millions of dollars pass through London in a year, though no one knows the turnover: it might be a billion more or a billion less. The entire Eurodollar market suffers from this lack of self-knowledge, which arises because there is so much reborrowing and relending; not all the economists and computers can work it out.

A bank that borrows Eurodollars can do several things with them. It can lend them to other banks, usually dealing in such large amounts that a margin on the interest-rate of one-sixteenth per cent is enough to show a worthwhile profit; this is the most hectic part of the market, full of subtle distinctions between shades of reliability, since all the lending is unsecured. It is a question of reputation and estimates of reputation. A Deutsche Bank or a Chase Manhattan will be able to borrow more and command a better rate than the little-known Swindlebank. Other things being equal, a leading American bank may be able to pay fractionally less for its Eurodollars than a leading British one. The base of the British bank is sterling, and in the event of some cataclysm overtaking the pound, the bank's dollar balances might be frozen by order of the Government. This is unlikely, if only because of the damaging memories it would leave behind for the next century or so. But as a Chase man in London said, 'people with ten or twenty million dollars to place can't help worrying about these little nuances.'

Besides lending to its fellows, a bank with Eurodollars can change them into sterling and lend this to the new-type London money markets. If it's an American bank, it can send dollars back to its head office for them to use at home. Finally the bank can lend the dollars direct to industrial customers for months or years at a time. A reputable London bank can whistle up large sums of money from neighbouring banks and insurance companies faster than anywhere else in the world, New York included. Louis Franck, chairman of the Montagu Trust, says that 'if someone came here now and asked me for two hundred million dollars for a year, and he was a first-class chap, I could propably find it for him within an hour. I'm not saying for three years, but for six months or one year, I'd make three telephone calls, and he'd have it.' Borrowers who want long-term Eurodollars get them by floating a loan against the issue of securities—the Eurobond market, where an oil company or a nationalised railway might be issuing bonds to raise $20 million for fifteen years. The same Eurodollars are used to buy the bonds; the same smiling gentlemen, the City's merchant bankers, figure prominently.

To be a banker in someone else's currency isn't quite the same as being a banker in your own. But by looking for dollar business, the City is only acknowledging that the dollar is king. Even the clearing banks have their back-door subsidiaries to deal in dollars. The more adventurous it is nowadays, the less a British bank is tied to sterling. The sizeable Bank of London and South America, based in London but leaning towards Latin America, was among the first to deal heavily in Eurodollars. Bolsa's 'international banking division' makes dollar loans to industry, and aims to 'propagate the image of the bank as a purveyor of worldwide international financial services, those services being far from confined to operations in the countries in which, as the name of the bank indicates, it has its main physical investments.' This sums up the new tendency: banking services must be worldwide and at least some of them must be in dollars. 'We have made this into a dollar bank rather than a sterling bank,' said a Bolsa director.

In London itself, the use of dollars has penetrated the most traditional part of the merchant bankers' work, the accepting, or guaranteeing, of bills of exchange. London banks are now accepting bills made out in dollars, knowing they can borrow in the Eurodollar market to finance them if they are called on to do so.

Money Markets, Old and New

The dollar is beginning to change the City. It is one of the reasons the local money market is altering so rapidly, and this adaptability in turn makes the City more attractive for dollars. The money market was once a simple thing, to be studied in isolation—the reservoir of national cash, managed by the twelve discount houses. They borrow from banks that have a surplus, often for only a day at a time, then re-lend the money to the Government against Treasury bills and short term bonds, and to commercial firms against bills of exchange. If a bank or industrial company has a million pounds to spare overnight, it can lend it to the discount market and earn a couple of hundred pounds in twenty-four hours. Other centres have short-term money markets, but none combine London's size and efficiency at marrying the needs of those who have money with those who need it. The bill-brokers are a distinctly patrician band of men who manage the market with a flourish and still march up and down the City in top hats. The operations are intricate but the principle is straightforward: they are wholesale merchants in money whose private business, licensed and benevolently overseen by the Bank of England, has come to act as a mechanism for smoothing out shortages and surpluses in the flow of domestic funds.

But the discount market is no longer alone in this. Since the 1950s it has been paralleled by other markets in short-term money, which pay better rates of interest, and between them now handle more than the discount market itself. Finance companies seeking funds to run their hire-purchase business compete fiercely and effectively. But the biggest market of all exists to find money for local authorities in Britain, ranging from cities with annual budgets of tens of millions of pounds, down to small rural councils needing half a million to tide them over. Britain's local authorities spend more than £5 billion a year—a third of all public expenditure. They used to borrow heavily from a State agency, the Public Works Loan Board, but from about 1955 the Government virtually forced them to bid in the open market. Now they have at least £1,600 million of other people's money on loan, which means that a town of even modest size, with a blackened little Town Hall and nothing better than a two-star hotel, may have a couple of million pounds borrowed from a brewery, a pension fund, the Milk Marketing Board or a bank. If it's a large authority, like the Greater London Council, it will be sufficiently confident of its resources to borrow money overnight, without worrying that it may have to be paid back next morning. Little Muddlecombe Urban Council may come into the market for no more than £50,000. In either case, it's secured on the income from the rates.[2]

The City loves to have middle-men for everything, and inevitably it now has local-authority brokers. They, in turn, may deal direct with the lenders, or they may work through yet another group of brokers who work in yet another new market—the interbank market. This sounds as if it should have been there always, since it consists merely of deals between banks to dispose of short-term sterling. It's what the discount market is doing, but with two important differences. First, the loans are made without security—unlike the discount market, where the houses borrow money to buy bills which they use as collateral against more loans in an elegant juggling operation. Second, the borrowing is done direct between banks, with

[2] Another form of security that circulates in the City, short-term bonds issued by local authorities, are not acceptable at the Bank of England—it won't take them as security when it lends to the money market. They pay a slightly less attractive rate of interest than they would if the Bank did accept them, reflecting another of those fine shades of financial opinion. The Public Works Loan Board will act as lender of last resort, and no local authority would be allowed to default. But the shade of difference persists. 'I suppose, you see, the theory is that the local Treasurer might go beserk,' said a merchant banker, not really seriously, but not quite jokingly, either.

only a broker as intermediary—whereas discount houses, though intermediaries, aren't brokers, but deal on their own behalf.

Clearing banks keep away from the inter-bank market, as they do from all these new parallel markets which have attracted money by paying higher rates of interest. It began in a small way, with merchant banks borrowing among themselves in order to lend to local authorities when these started looking for money after 1955. Clearing banks go on lending their surpluses through the discount market, but nowadays the merchant banks often by-pass it and deal with one another. For one reputable bank to borrow half a million from its reputable neighbour round the corner may seem an obvious thing to do, but in the City it was fairly revolutionary. 'It used to be considered a terrible thing,' said a broker, 'but now that it's come to be accepted, no one thinks that when Bank A borrows from Bank B, it's about to go bust.' It was convenient enough to be worth it. It began tentatively, then developed quickly, a domestic equivalent of the Eurodollar market, and, like that market, a sign of a freer approach. It makes the same distinctions between good names and not-quite-so-good names. One interbank broker said that even he was sometimes baffled at the apparently arbitrary decisions of bank dealers on whether or not to lend to someone. But it wasn't his job to query these matters; as a broker it would hardly be sensible. He produced the dealing book, as big as an old family Bible, and pointed to the loans arranged, with the commission pencilled in at one side. The Bank of London and South America had taken a million pounds for a month: commission, £26. 10s. 9d. Samuel Montagu had taken £50,000 overnight: 'for which', said the broker 'we collect the princely sum of tenpence.'

What stimulated interbank lending was the flow of dollars into London that began when British controls were relaxed in 1958. Some of these Eurodollar funds were changed into sterling and lent to finance companies and local authorities, often via the interbank market. Foreign banks, in particular, were quick to use the new markets to dispose of the short-term money they wanted to keep in London. In the past it had usually gone into the discount market. Once new markets with higher interest rates opened up, it went there. The influx of money, mainly Eurodollars, grew enormously after about 1960. So did the scope for playing those sophisticated games with electric calculators beloved of foreign-exchange departments.

Arbitrage dealing, which exploits anomalies between the rates in different markets and in different currencies, has thrived on Euro-dollars in general, and two of the most important fixed points are the London rates for interbank and local-authority lending, after the dollars have been changed into sterling.

This is the area where the sudden shift of money out of sterling and away from London can contribute to a 'run on the pound' like the one that preceded devaluation in 1967. The money, perhaps a billion dollars or more, has been left in London for a fractional percentage, and if the rates move or there are fears that the pound is unsafe, dealers pick up their phones (on the initiative of their own banks or their clients or both) and begin to sell sterling. This is the dark side of being an international money-centre where the local currency is weak; other people's 'hot money' is always welcome, but when they take it away again, for reasons that are no better and no worse than brought it there in the first place, patriotic old gentlemen and cunning old politicians make outraged noises. The City is more phlegmatic as a rule; it doesn't have many illusions.

As far as the money markets are concerned, the traffic in dollars has helped to provide the funds that now roam the City, as they roam the world, in search of high interest rates. Internationally there is a breaking down of compartments; the world has shrunk for bankers and company treasurers and rich men, just as it has it has for British holiday-makers who used to spend a fortnight at the seaside and now think nothing of going to Spain. Inside the City, the classical money-market, paying rates of interest that are pegged to the clearing banks' London Deposit Rate, has been enlarged to take in parallel markets where rates reflect the international money position.

The discount houses have wriggled uncomfortably as they watched money passing them by, though it was some years before they did much about it. They haven't been anxious to talk about changes that might ruin them, and long after the discount market was becoming blurred at the edges, one still heard it being described in the old terms, as though the parallel markets were a temporary feature of little importance. The bill brokers now know better than this. What they have done in the last few years (apart from becoming more machine-age-minded, with economists in tow and closed-circuit television for all departments) is to get a foothold in the competition, either by buying their way into existing firms of local authority and interbank brokers, or by setting up their own departments. Some have linked up with foreign exchange brokers, a closed shop of only ten firms, so as to share in the Eurodollar business.

'They're getting the feel of borrowing and lending a foreign currency,' said an official at the Bank of England, which has sanctioned all the discount-market developments, as it had to if they were to proceed. He said the changes had been encouraged for reasons of flexibility, the inevitable City motive. 'We bent the structure,' he said, with pleasure.

The City (he seemed to be saying) was interested in dollars but it was also interested in orderly conduct. His remarks—issuing from behind a large desk with a tiny television screen, across which a hand came and went writing shakily and indecipherably—make a useful guide to City attitudes at a time of change. 'The Bank thought hard about letting discount houses go in for foreign-currency business,' he said. 'Before the war, London had about thirty-five foreign-exchange firms, and it was a pretty ropey market. After the war we decided to re-establish it with nine or ten good ones. They needed to be firms of substance. So some hard thinking was necessary if we were to allow these brokers to be bought up by people who were doing another sort of business. They might, for instance, concentrate on some other aspect of their business, such as handling Eurodollar deposits, then pay inadequate salaries to the foreign exchange dealer themselves, and lower the standards of the market.'

In the end, the Bank was satisfied. But what if the Bank hadn't been satisfied, and a discount house had tried to defy authority? 'Oh, we hold the whip hand,' he said, squinting down at the ridiculous blue screen. 'If they had insisted against the Bank's wishes, the Bank would have said, "You must decide to be one thing or the other, and if you're going to be foreign exchange dealers then we'll close your account as a discount house at the Bank".'

No such unthinkable conflict arose, and within a year or two, half a dozen bill brokers were established in the parallel markets. So far their contacts with dollars were limited, but they increased when a number of them were allowed to deal in a new line of business, the Eurodollar 'certificates of deposit', or CDs, that first appeared in the City in 1966. Dollar CDs are a kind of temporary Eurodollar bank-note, issued by banks against deposits made with them, their virtue being that they can be resold at any time. A CD may run for as little as a month or as much as a year. If the depositor wants to retrieve his dollars before the CD matures, he sells the certificate in the market that has grown up among a number of British and foreign banks, especially the Americans. With the CDs, Eurodollars were translated into negotiable pieces of paper instead of simple deposits. They can be for as little as $25,000, compared with the usual Eurodollar dealing unit of $1,000,000, and among others they have attracted the money-world's equivalent of the small depositor.

When CDs began to circulate in the City, some of the discount houses were given permission to deal in them—usually as 'principals', buying and selling them for their own account, using borrowed dollars to finance the business. 'It was a break with anything formerly known in London,' said the Bank of England man, 'because the discount houses were now going to borrow and hold foreign currencies. The logic of allowing this was that the American banks were doing it anyway. So we bent the structure again.'

The market had made an important change of direction, and City men began to contemplate a time when the discount houses might be helping to operate an international money market in dollars, as they have operated the national market in sterling. Bill brokers are already building up their contacts beyond the Channel; travelling (without top hats) to make their faces familiar to the world outside.

East Meets West

Foreign banks have been in the City for a hundred years, though never on the present scale, They aren't always easy to define, since they merge into the heterogeneous category of 'British overseas and Commonwealth banks.' This includes banks with their head offices in the City, such as Barclays DCO—a subsidiary of the clearing bank—and the Bank of London and South America; and others headquartered outside Britain, mainly in Australia and Canada. Some foreign banks, chiefly American, have entered the City obliquely, taking a stake in local houses (First National City has 10 per cent of Hill, Samuel; Mellon National Bank & Trust Co. has 10 per cent of the Bank of London and South America).

The number of outright foreign banks, represented by either full branches or affiliated companies, is above ninety and still growing. The French have nine banks in the City; they were the first to arrive. The office of the general manager at the Crédit Lyonnais, which set up during the Franco-Prussian war in 1871 as an insurance against hard times, contrives to look old-fashioned, yet not in the way of the shabby English banking parlour; it has a fire-screen and frosted glass, and lacks the comfortably lazy English atmosphere. The French in the City have been overtaken by the Japanese (eleven at the last count), who finance most of their national trade in dollars and so are heavy borrowers in the Eurodollar market; and the Americans, with more than twenty. The American branches not only do a roaring Eurodollar business but, to the dismay of the British clearing banks, are attracting hundreds of millions of pounds in domestic deposits. Next come the Swiss, with six banks, the Belgians, Indians and Pakistanis with three apiece, and at least twenty countries with one or two banks: Germany, Holland, Spain, Cyprus, Greece, Turkey, Iran, Iraq, Kuwait, Israel, Russia, Czechoslovakia, Nigeria, South Africa, Canada, Communist China, Malaysia, Korea, Singapore and Thailand. Banks from other countries have 'representative offices,' which act as listening posts and channels for business without being able to do the business themselves; among them Italy (eight banks), Yugoslavia, Sweden, Bermuda and Indonesia. Many of the foreign banks in the City have offices elsewhere—usually in the West End of London, occasionally in the provinces.

The foreign banks may be financing trade for their own or other countries; they deal in Eurodollars, and in general they can make use of London's markets—insurance, gold, foreign exchange, commodities and the rest, as well as the short-term money markets. It's all very cosmopolitan. There is, for instance, the Moscow Narodny, established in London in 1919—taken for granted as part of the City scene, but also a significant junction between East and West. Although the Narodny is run largely by Russians and owned by the Soviet Union, it doesn't appear to be at all isolated from the City; it's part of the machinery, and worth looking at if only for the way it illustrates the point that nothing is so international as money.

For its first forty years it was no more than a paying agent for Russia, until a former insurance man and banker in Moscow, A. I. Doubonossov, arrived as chairman in 1959. The Cold War was already less intense. After nine years of thaw the Socialist bank's assets had risen from £8 million to nearly £300 million, it was one of London's four or five biggest operators in Eurodollars, it had acquired a meaningful sub-title, 'the bank for East-West trade,' and the podgy-faced Doubonossov (who has since retired) had become a City character. He once walked round to the new Rothschild building with a camera and started filming in the courtyard, only to be sent away by an attendant who said that photographers weren't allowed. Back in his office, he telephoned one of the Rothschilds and said meekly that he hadn't meant to intrude. They were suitably shocked, and Doubonossov was promptly offered every facility for his photographs.

A former English member of the staff said it was impossible to tell whether the Russian authorities had realised how the bank would develop. 'Off the record,' he added, 'I sometimes wonder if Moscow think they've got a cuckoo.' If so, they seem content with it; before he retired, his Government awarded Doubonossov the high-ranking Soviet Order of the Red Banner for 'work in assisting the promotion and development of Anglo-Soviet financial and commercial relations.' But Russia is still a long way off. The Narodny once received a message from Moscow, inquiring whether a firm called Imperial Chemical Industries was safe for £1,000 of credit.

The bank originated with the Moskovskii Narodnyi, the people's bank of Moscow, and its shareholders are Russian banks and trading corporations. It was hopefully christened 'the bank for East-West trade' after Doubonossov took over, as a gesture rather than because it meant anything at the time, but within a few years it was financing trade not only with Russia but with other countries in Eastern Europe. It also acts for Cuba and arranges most of its payments for trade deals with Britain. By 1964 it was influential enough to organise a consortium of London banks at a couple of days' notice, to import £40 million worth of Australian wheat into Rumania. The State banks of most Soviet-bloc countries channel their sterling surpluses through the Moscow Narodny, which lends them to the money market. When Bulgaria earns pounds by selling a cargo of jam and tomatoes, the money goes to a British town council or hire-purchase company until Bulgaria needs the foreign exchange.

The Moscow Narodny has a branch in Beirut for Middle Eastern trade, controlled from London, and there are other Russian banks, Moscow-directed, in Paris (Banque Commerciale pour l'Europe du Nord) and Zurich (Wozchod Handelsbank). There has been talk of a Moscow Narodny branch in West Germany, with the Germans wanting an entirely new bank, and the Russians arguing stubbornly that it should be a branch of the London bank. Once, in the 1920s, the Russians had a banking agency in New York, and it wouldn't be surprising if they went back one day. To return would be a political act; but below the surface the dealers and money-traders provide a continuing commercial contact.

The Moscow Narodny and its fellow banks trade extensively in Eurodollars—it has been suggested that one of the pressures that helped the market to grow in its early days arose from the Russian reluctance to hold U.S. dollars in the ordinary way. The Soviet Union came to need dollars for international trading, but was afraid that in some cold-war crisis its holdings might be frozen by the U.S. Government. Ten years ago, when Russia was still only beginning to emerge from its isolation, it even crossed people's minds that creditors of Imperial Russia might resurrect their claims against the Soviet Government, and persuade someone to block dollar balances. The pool of Eurodollars, owned outside the U.S., provided a means of obtaining dollars anonymously and at several removes from the American authorities.

The Moscow Narodny serves as a training-ground in Western methods for young Soviet bankers. There are five resident Russian directors besides the chairman, and usually two or three younger men, graduates who spend a year or so studying capitalism in action. At home, they have a simpler system to compare with London's. A chain of more than 70,000 savings banks handles private accounts and domestic payments for electricity, rent and so on. Capital investment by industry is handled by the Stroibank, foreign trade by the Vneshtorgbank (probably one of the largest commercial banks in the world, though there are no figures), and short-term business credit by the Gosbank, which has 5,000 branches, and is also Russia's central bank.

Visiting Russians have to grasp the principle of dealing with private firms. 'In Russia,' said the Englishman who has worked there, 'to be a banker is to be an official. They don't find it easy to understand that you must have status information on your customer before you can give him an overdraft. A man comes to London fresh from the advances department of the Gosbank, and his whole experience has been of dealing with State organisations. As long as borrowers keep within the State plan, they can't go bankrupt. There are all sorts of little things. When a cheque comes in here, they don't understand that it might bounce—in Russia they wouldn't be using a cheque in any case.'

Whatever they need to learn, the Moscow Narodny's bankers have been good at keeping in with the City. They are enormously polite and anxious to acknowledge the local hospitality; in turn, City bankers say that the Russians are welcome because they follow the rules and act like any other God-fearing, profit-making institution. The Chinese, now, are a different matter. The Bank of China, in London since 1929, has a fair-sized staff of 110 (compare the National Bank of Greece with fifty and First National City with 500), and Chinese bankers can be seen in Cannon Street, dressed in blue overalls, among the dark suits and short skirts. The bank says guardedly that it behaves 'rather like all the foreign banks in London,' with special emphasis on trade, but declines to say more on the grounds that it doesn't want publicity. The bank has few or no direct dealings with the foreign-exchange and Eurodollar markets, though it uses two clearing banks as correspondents, and works through them when the occasion arises. From time to time it has substantial sterling balances, and the bill brokers include it in their rounds. One of them said he thought the Chinese made 'quite good dealers when you get down to it,' though it was a pity that they tended to move their money about for political rather than economic reasons. The interbank market also gets contributions from the Bank of China. (Sterling is an easy currency for the Chinese to obtain, since Hong Kong has a free market where they can buy large amounts of it in exchange for yen). But in general, the Bank of China is on the fringes of the City: an uneasy visitor in the capital of money.

7 *Switzerland, a Nice Safe Place*

Switzerland, a country with a population of five and three-quarter million, has more than 400 banks, and is proud of all but a few; it's rather ashamed of these, and would rather not discuss them. A leaflet distributed by the leading Swiss Credit Bank speaks of 'a network of nearly 4,300 banks,' but this is the total of branches, down to the man-and-a-boy level, not the number of banking firms. By taking the higher figure it is possible to say that Switzerland has more banks than dentists, and one hears it said with relish; somehow the comparison with dentists, solid and skilful men but a shade intimidating, is just right.

The Swiss will perform any conceivable service to do with finance, though if you say this to a Swiss banker, meaning to be polite, he is sure to bridle and begin to defend himself vigorously against the charges of dishonesty, sharp practice, speculation, coldness, greed and self-interest that he thinks you may be hinting at. The Swiss have made an international finance centre out of a small country that has comparatively little of the trading importance, and none of the political importance, that usually go with financial power, and in order to do it they have had to acquire an almost magical reputation. It is fear of seeing this reputation damaged that makes them so anxious to pass over their bad banks, so touchy at visitors' remarks.

They not only want to appear perfect; in a hotly competitive Europe, perhaps they need to appear perfect as well. Bankers in Beirut, where governments have tried to foster a liberal financial climate, talk of making the Lebanon into 'the Switzerland of the Middle East.' One enthusiastic member of the staff of Intra, Beirut's leading bank at the time, wrote glowingly in 1965 about 'this curious Zurich of the East.' But Intra crashed spectacularly the following year, making Beirut look altogether too curious to people in search of a haven for their money. What bothers Swiss bankers is the awful possibility that anyone should hint or think, just for a second, that Switzerland is the Beirut of Europe. Pointing out that the country lacks a large trade of its own, the chief general manager of the Swiss Credit Bank, Mr Eberhard Reinhardt, writing about Switzerland as a financial centre, says that '*its main support are moral factors*'; the italics are his.

The Swiss take themselves seriously. Another leading banker, Dr Alfred Schaefer, president of the Union Bank, calls Switzerland the 'prototype of an internationally-oriented nation,' and to some extent the country's complex web of relationships with the rest of the world bears him out. Because of its agreeable attitude to taxation, thousands of holding companies have been established in Switzerland; a Swiss holding company can be fitted into a multi-national trading enterprise, for example as the distributor of products that are made elsewhere, and save the parent organisation tax that would have to be paid if the operation were conducted entirely from the country of manufacture.

As bankers, the Swiss do business with the rest of the world on a formidable scale. The majority of the country's hundreds of banks are small, local and purely domestic, but a handful of big commercial banks, and a few dozen private houses, look outward. These are the core of Switzerland as a financial centre. They handle payments between international clients, both companies and individuals, and as a result they do a roaring business in foreign exchange. They accept deposits from the same sort of clients, and immediately have to reinvest the money outside Switzerland because the country has no short-term money market to absorb it. Not only is Switzerland too small to have one like London's, but Swiss governments, perenially prudent, pay as they go, without the regular large-scale borrowing against Treasury bills and the like that helps to create money markets in less conservative lands. So the money has to be placed outside Switzerland, usually in London or New York. Swiss banks also deal extensively in gold, both as bullion and as coins, and run the biggest market in Europe for exchanging banknotes.

Switzerland is an attractive market for foreign borrowers who want to raise capital, because so much spare money is available, and the country can afford to have low interest rates. As with all Swiss funds, some of the money comes from the Swiss themselves, who are assiduous savers, and some from outside the country. There are no stockbrokers: the banks do it all, looking after their clients' securities on a grand scale. The fireproof vaults[1] of a big Swiss bank are stuffed with a range of paper that leaves few if any of the world's leading companies unrepresented; since in this case the banks are handling securities and not cash for their customers, the amounts involved, perhaps a total of $30 or $40 billion for all the banks in the country, don't appear in balance sheets or anywhere else.

Of all the Swiss banks' activities, their handling of deposits for foreigners is the one that attracts most publicity and touches the rawest nerves. As far as the Swiss are concerned, funds owned by firms, trusts, banks and individuals anywhere in the world can flow unhindered into Switzerland and be re-deposited elsewhere. The latest figure available is for the end of 1966, and was calculated by the Swiss National Bank from balance sheets (which means that the private banks, which publish no balance sheets, are not included).

At that time, over $4 billion of the world's money was known to have been deposited with Swiss banks.[2] The largest slice (undisclosed, but probably a sixth) came from one country, Italy—much of it illegally, escaping as fast as it could from Italian taxes, aided and abetted by the geographical closeness of the two countries, and by the cheerfully amoral Latin attitude to fiscal matters. About $350 million apiece stemmed from Britain, the United States, France,

[1] I was shown a private banker's vault in Basle, built in a hole newly escavated under the bank, and lined with armoured steel from an old battleship. Reached through a solid outer door and a barred inner one, it contained nothing more exciting to look at than rows of clients' safe-deposit boxes, and tall grey cabinets containing share certificates. The clients hold the only keys to the boxes; they have a table and chairs where they can sit and make sure it's all there. 'I hover in the background and try to see what they've got,' said the banker.

[2] The 1967 total, not yet broken down country by country, shows an enormous jump, to $5·4 billion: a year of monetary crises had pumped another billion dollars or so of the world's money into Switzerland.

Germany and, an odd name in such company, Liechtenstein. This is the little Ruritanian State between Switzerland and Austria, and the large sums of money that are deposited with its neighbours' banks are the lovely, more-or-less-tax-free income of holding companies set up in Liechtenstein by manufacturers, pop singers and pension funds elsewhere in the world, anxious to avail themselves of the tolerant climate that flourishes under Crown Prince Franz Josef the Second, last of the Hapsburgs with a throne.

Central and South America between them had roughly $450 million in Switzerland. Altogether money from twenty countries had gone into the commercial banks, plus unknown sums into the others, and found its way out again to the world's money markets. One begins to see why moral factors loom so large, since any country that sits at the junction of such flows of money is going to be constantly scrutinised and often criticised by the rest of the world, and come to need a *raison d'etre* beyond mere convenience. The Swiss are in an obvious position to be envied, feared a little, seen as faceless men with endless schemes for managing things to suit themselves. The Union Bank has estimated that Swiss banks are paying an average of just under 3 per cent on the money deposited with them, and collecting about 4·5 per cent on the same money when it's invested elsewhere. A profit of 1·5 per cent on $4 billion is about $60 million—and this is just one side of the business. It's impossible to make profits of this order and then expect to be congratulated by bankers and other governments for doing such a good job.

So even if there were no other grounds for needing to insist on moral factors, the well publicised position of the Swiss banks would make a high-sounding attitude desirable; it sounds so much better to describe oneself as a custodian. Here is Mr Reinhardt again, this time in conversation: 'We deal with money and so we deal with public responsibility. There is good money and bad money. It must be handled carefully. It is not like selling shoes or radios.'

The point of view is common to bankers everywhere, but only the Swiss, who are super-bankers, say it so often and with such conviction. Because their dearest asset is their reputation, they must keep emphasising the fact that they are so reputable.

This causes much irritation among financiers in other countries. 'They are the centre for the international savers of the world,' said an American investment banker. 'No one can match their secretiveness. No one can match their basic dullness, either. They're so dull, in fact, that it would never cross their minds to put the money in their pockets and catch a plane to Brazil. In fact, one wonders if it *is* honesty with the Swiss or just plain dullness.' A young Swiss banker who has shaken the dust of Basle, a particularly virtuous city, off his feet, and gone to work in London, said much the same thing, and added some rude jokes about his country ('Give a Swiss a crutch and he'll break his leg to use it', etc.)

Yet all that the Swiss have done is to be explicit about things that concern bankers everywhere. They see themselves as sober, prudent men, keepers of secrets, rocklike in their discretion. Most bankers have this flattering self-regard, but the Swiss need to take it a little further. When I was at a private bank in Basle, I noticed a large iron machine, like a cross between an old-fashioned mangle and a photocopier, by the porter's desk. I asked the partner who was with me. Ah, he said, that is a paper-shredding machine, and every night we empty the contents of the wastepaper baskets into it, and it shreds up the paper so that nothing readable is left. He demonstrated with a sheet of foolscap, which emerged as little crinkly paper worms. He didn't smile, because it was, after all, a serious demonstration.

All banks keep secrets, but few countries make banking secrecy part of the law, as they do in Switzerland. It is one of the few aspects of Swiss banking where the rules are laid down by the State—and these particular rules were made because they were good for the country's reputation and so, ultimately, for business. Jocelyn Hambro, the chairman of Hambros Bank, once said that he wished there was more privacy for British bank customers, and there's no doubt that Switzerland is the sort of place that bankers dream about. The 'numbered accounts', where only two or three people at the bank know the identity of the person behind the code-number, is an indispensable part of the Swiss legend.

Privacy has become a cardinal virtue, which is perhaps unavoidable when a country is as small and intensely commercial as Switzerland. An executive at the Swiss Credit Bank said that it wasn't just a banker's preference but a way of life: 'In an overpopulated area, you make people unhappy if you ask them to compare everything—

what they earn and what they have.' He added, inelegantly but earnestly: 'If someone is going to the toilet, you know what is happening, but you don't go and look.'

It's not only Swiss privacy that other bankers enjoy but Swiss political stability. Both the privacy and the stability are part of that same prudent approach to life—so easy to laugh at, so useful when it comes to soothing nervous customers. All the jokes about a land of cuckoo-clocks and milk chocolate fall flat when a man with a million dollars in his pocket hurries off with it to Zurich because he knows, or thinks he knows, that it will be safer there. Once again, it is a matter of reputation.

Locked away behind mountains in the middle of Europe, near to many countries but long remaining aloof from them, Switzerland has been inward-looking and slow to change. Strikes are regarded as instruments of the devil; women don't have the vote. Someone suggested that Switzerland's telephones reflect a lingering insularity—the internal service is highly efficient, with trunk-dialling throughout the country, but an outward-dialling system, into the rest of Europe, is taking a long time to install. Certainly the country has kept itself to itself, and found that it pays not to get involved. When the first world war and its aftermath put an end to the free movement of capital in Europe, Switzerland was left as the one place that people could trust to let funds move in and out at will. Invaders and revolutions have missed it, and so have crippling slumps and disastrous inflation. Only someone who has seen his currency crumble and his banks go down like ninepins, as so aften in Europe in the last half-century, can appreciate the safe, warm feeling that Switzerland provides.

Two Swiss people in two days, one a banker and the other an economist, looked through their loose change and found a 1 franc piece dated eighteen-hundred and something so as to impress me with the stability of the country. 'I showed a nineteenth-century coin to a Greek gentleman who was on holiday in Geneva,' said the banker. 'He said he just couldn't believe it.' The demonstration doesn't work with Englishmen, who see plenty of black Victorian pennies; but to Greeks, Germans, Belgians, Dutch and many others whose countries have been more exposed to violence, an old coin still in circulation is reassuring.

Inside their own country the Swiss have an old-fashioned attitude to hard cash. The banks hold a higher proportion of their assets in the form of banknotes than is customary—half as much again as in London and New York. Cheques are little used in everyday life, and even senior officials and executives are likely to be paid in cash, or to have their salaries credited to giro accounts. Many commercial payments are made in banknotes. This is not unusual in Europe, but one might expect the Swiss, of all people, to have moved further towards the cashless society of cheques and credit cards. However, it might be rash, or it might *look* rash; it might be noticed. Clever as they are at finance, the Swiss are not primarily selling expertise and sophistication. At the heart of their reputation is the feeling that they are safe, and nothing must be allowed to diminish it.

They have a lot of gold about the place, and the National Bank's reserves cover the paper money in circulation one and one-third times; the Swiss franc is the only domestic currency in the world that is backed up by more than enough gold to, in theory, swap all the citizens' bits of paper for bars of precious metal. I asked a manager at the National Bank if they kept their gold in vaults underneath the building, as they do at the Bank of England, but he pretended not to hear. I felt I had been disrespectful; I mentioned it to a commercial banker, who said that of course, it was perfectly natural to ignore a question like that. He himself had no idea where the nation's gold was kept, though, since the banking law decreed that the minimum gold-cover for the notes, which is 40 per cent, must be retained within the territorial limits, there must be a lot of it around somewhere, apart from the amounts deposited overseas, in London and Fort Knox. He supposed that some of it was in Berne, the capital, and the rest was perhaps cached away in the mountains, where it was hidden during the war. As a Swiss banker once reminded the *New York Times*, after some indiscreet American comments had caused a flurry in the world's gold markets: 'Monetary affairs are a delicate flower.'

The Swiss do everything they can to keep the flower in bloom. The State and the banking system agree about most things, and relations between bankers and the Government are easy-going, with few of the tensions that arise in so many countries. The idea of the Government owning banks is ridiculous. Even the National Bank plays a smaller part in the domestic scene than most central banks in Europe, and the official Banking Commission, while it supervises the annual auditing of banks from a distance, is not regarded as an inquisitor. Privacy and stability, in the Swiss view, are virtues that won't benefit from interference by the State; the banks can be trusted to know what's best, and so the rules are kept to a minimum. It's easy to set up a bank in Switzerland, so easy and potentially so profitable that a few rogues have done it without hindrance. Some have come unstuck; some are still in business; all strike at the root of Swiss sensitivity, by reminding people that freedom has its disadvantages.

Switzerland is certainly money-oriented. It must be nice for the Swiss to think it is more than this, that they have found a reliable blueprint for some splendidly global society of the future, and that their fat little land really is the 'prototype of an internationally-oriented nation', as Dr Schaefer suggests. The trouble is that for all its links with the rest of the world, Switzerland remains idiosyncratic: there is nowhere else like it, which is why it has proved to be so successful. It is a retreat, a haven, a safe place in an uncertain world. This is its charm—and its weakness.

Well-oiled Machinery

So much has been written about Swiss banks that it's not easy to regard them merely as pieces of well-oiled machinery, humming discreetly in Zurich, Basle and Geneva. In particular, they have been attacked for letting crooks and tax evaders hide behind numbered accounts, and for speculating against the pound in time of crisis—now more or less an annual event. Words are loaded; bankers smile coldly and present the visiting journalist with reprinted articles headed 'Unfounded Criticism of the Swiss Bank Secret' and 'A Distorted Portrait of Switzerland'; questions about tax evasion are answered before he has time to ask them.

Before I went to Zurich, a Swiss banker in London advised me to use cunning when inquiring about numbered accounts. 'Their hair will stand on end,' he said. 'But tell them you realise that numbered accounts didn't arise as a swindle, as some people imagine, but to protect the Jews. In the thirties, German Jews wanted to open accounts without the Nazis finding out. I'd make that point to them, if I were you.' As I was leaving he shook hands and said, 'Best of luck. Lots of courage,' as if I were going to a battle.

In the event, most of them talked non-stop about secrecy and speculation. First, though, some facts about the well-oiled machinery. There are three main financial centres, and at least three other cities of some importance. Switzerland is a decentralised country, a federation of cantons, each with its own flavour. (When an international firm sets up a holding company in Switzerland, it will choose its canton carefully so as to ensure the maximum tax advantage; some cantons are more obliging than others). So although Zurich is the most important centre, it has only two of the three largest banks; the third is Basle, which also has private banks. But the private banking centre is Geneva, though foreign banks have mushroomed there in recent years, giving the place a raffish air that hurts the feelings of the proud old Protestant bankers. These three cities are followed by Berne, the federal capital; Lausanne, which has a hinterland of expensive villas along Lake Geneva; and Lugano, near the Italian border, where banks have sprung up to service the brisk and sometimes shady business in funds coming in from Italy.

Zurich, which now has a population of half a million, more than sixty banks, and much industry in the area, was a late starter. Geneva and Basle had a few bankers of substance in the eighteenth century, but it wasn't until late in the nineteenth that Zurich came to life. As the economy developed, changing Switzerland from a poor country with no natural wealth to a rich one with thriving industries, Zurich's position turned out to be the most convenient for a commercial capital.

The Union Bank and the Swiss Credit Bank have their headquarters there. The third of the Big Three, the Swiss Bank Corporation, has remained in Basle, where it was founded, but has to run a second headquarters in Zurich so that it can keep up appearances and services. None of these three banks is a giant by world standards. But all three would rank higher in a league-table that measured international standing instead of deposits, if one could be devised.

Of the three, the Swiss Credit Bank is the oldest, the Swiss Bank Corporation is the biggest and the Union Bank is the most aggressive. In a banking community that is still desperately conservative about its advertising, the Union Bank has daringly gone in for ads that show a man with a badge in his lapel, announcing *I like Women* (meaning they want women customers). Its most spectacular coup was to merge with a Swiss holding company called Interhandel, formerly part of the German I.G.Farben chemical group, whose assets were blocked in the United States in 1942, and released only after years of wrangling.

The three banks, and most of the others in Zurich, are on or near the Bahnhofstrasse, a long and grimly elegant avenue that runs between the railway station and the lake. There is no banking quarter as such, and the stony facades with gold coins and stock-market prices in the window are interspersed with fashionable shops. It is probably the third financial city of the world, after New York and London, and certainly the most important on the continent of Europe as regards the weight of money that passes through it; though like most such centres, it doesn't present much of a picture from the outside. About a quarter of Switzerland's 30,000 bank employees work there, and at 7.30 in the morning the big blue trams are arriving in the central Paradeplatz, which adjoins the Bahnhofstrasse, full of men with umbrellas and newspapers, who hurry across the square to the Swiss Credit Bank on one side, the Swiss Bank Corporation on another. They used to work from 7.45 until 5 p.m., with enough time to go home for lunch. Now that commuters have moved farther out of the city, the banks have opened their own canteens and dining rooms, and introduced what are laughably described as 'English hours', with three-quarters of an hour for lunch. 'You stuff yourself for forty-five minutes, then back to your desk,' said a banker.

Among the elite at Zurich's banks are the seventy or so members of the local Forex Club, affiliated to the worldwide organisation for foreign-exchange dealers. As well as the dealers themselves, sprawling in their shirt-sleeves, busy with telephones and electric calculators, the membership includes the senior managers who run these hectic departments. At the Union Bank, the man in charge was big, fortyish, with thinning hair and an amiable manner above an underlying tension. He gave a large smile and said, 'I am one of the super-gnomes,' conveniently pinning himself down for closer inspection.

'The Gnomes of Zurich' are supposed to be those Swiss bankers who feather their nest, in times of monetary crisis, by speculating against other people's currencies and especially sterling. The myth is convenient for a politician in London who wants a scapegoat at a safe distance, and some people imagine the gnomes to be a finite group, almost members of a gnome organisation, eight or ten strong, making private fortunes out of other people's misery, like the proprietors of blacking factories in Victorian London. Whatever they are (they reappear later on), the gnomes are more numerous and less autonomous than that—the servants of large and respectable banks, like Barclays and the Bank of America. In the flesh they have the grey suits and pale faces of salaried bankers everywhere.

With its preponderance of bankers in this anonymous, institutional class, Zurich is apt to be smiled at by the partners of smaller, older houses in snobbier places like Basle and Geneva. 'We understate here,' said a man in Basle, sitting amid old painted furniture, with a tram-free street framed in the window. 'But the Zurich people overstate. They have big mouths and they speak with a horrible dialect. If a Zuricher earns more money this year than last he'll buy a bigger car, but in Basle he'll buy a smaller one.' The Swiss have a strong sense of place and are given to unkind generalisations about towns and cantons other than their own. A man at Pictet & Co., founded 1805, one of the close inner circle of seven private banking houses in Geneva, said that the partners came to work by Mercedes but wouldn't dream of using anything grander. Whereas a friend of his, when he was promoted to manager with a firm in Zurich, was advised that it was time he stopped going in a Pegueot and took to a Rolls Royce.

About sixty private banks survive, of the several hundred that existed at the start of the century, and half of them arc tiny. It is assumed that their balance sheets, if published, would not look impressive besides those of the commercial banks, since their strength lies in the portfolios of bonds and shares that they hold for clients. Most of them are more broker than banker. They like to deal with the really rich. A leading private bank would not be much interested in a portfolio of less than around \$100,000 unless, as might happen, the client had other qualifications, such as the right friends or the right family connections.

Estimates of the total value of portfolios go as high as \$5 billion, and a cross-section through the vaults would reveal the financial strata of a century or two. Huguenots who went to Geneva at the end of the seventeenth century, when France was expelling Protestants, opened banks which later benefited from the fortunes that left Paris in the French Revolution. Geneva's banks still look to France for many of their clients, and have been handling some of the great French fortunes for well over a hundred years. They have done the same for rich Europeans in many countries, and the sons of these long lasting clients get to know the sons of bankers, generation after generation.

Eight or nine partners, two or three hundred employees, would be the maximum at one of the Geneva houses. The setting is what you'd expect. The square outside has trees and a church, or a stone bench and a fountain, with bicycles and bonnets glittering in the sun. The name appears, if at all, on a small plate. Sometimes only the initials appear. (In Basle, the house of Hans Seligman-Schürch has a brass plate that says 'H.S.-Sch. & Co.', like an advertisement for Schweppes. One of the partners says that the reason, *of course*, is to avoid publicity. He adds that a visiting Japanese journalist was so intrigued that he made a point of writing about it. (This seems to be getting the best of both worlds). Inside, the bank will be quiet and well carpeted, with pictures of dead partners on the walls, looking grimmer than the living partners below, who speak casually impeccable English and occasionally turn out to have been educated at English public schools and later done a stint in the City. Family names predominate, and when a new partner has no apparent family connection, an old partner has been known to search genealogical tables to see if he can find one. Bordier & Co. has six partners, all Bordiers. Thirty or so families dominate the scene.

Because they are responsible to no one but themselves, the Geneva bankers can afford to perpetuate traditions that seem meaningless, but perhaps are not, in terms of pleasing the customers—who, even though they may not be aware of the traditions, would be aware if they changed, and react uneasily, as to the sight of orange socks or spotted bow-ties. Customers' statements are often handwritten. Religion still matters, in that few if any of the old Geneva banks would have a Roman Catholic anywhere near the senior echelons. Within the last few years, a young man has been taken into one of the seven houses, with a view to becoming a partner, on condition that he doesn't marry a Catholic. A man who began his career at another of the seven was solemnly presented with a subscription to

La Vie Protestante as his Christmas bonus. (He's now the senior partner at a rival bank.)

Their attitude to clients has to be highly personal, and all of them claim this face-to-face relationship as their chief advantage over the commercial banks. When an unnamed 'international bank in Switzerland' advertised in the European *Herald Tribune* for an executive to deal with foreign clients, it asked applicants to send 'a recent snapshot'. Private bankers like to describe themselves as friends and trustees and, in particular, doctors. They take the rich man's pulse and prescribe massive injections of confidence to soothe his jangling nerves. 'At the big institutions', said a Basle banker, 'the stocks are put into the portfolios, let's say, without love. My view resembles that of a doctor. I see that such-and-such a share will do you good—you'll feel well with it. Then in comes an old lady, and she won't take to the medicine I've been giving you. I may say to her, I suggest that you invest in this American stock, a company that makes chewing gum with jokes on the wrapper. She may say, good gracious, who do you think I am? I want a dignified stock like Royal Dutch or Rio Tinto. You must understand that every portfolio has a face, a personality.'

The private bankers relish their place as confidants and old pals, hearing about wives and children, advising on education, even making appointments with the dentist. There's no end to the secrets they can enjoy having to keep. 'It's very much in our character,' said a partner in a Geneva bank. 'My father would have considered it highly impertinent if I'd asked him who he voted for. When someone like myself joins a bank in Switzerland, there's no certainty that my relations will put their money into it because I'm there—it's more likely that they'll take it out again so that I won't know what they've got. They will certainly have their money spread among several banks.'

No one questions their discretion, though many people have questioned their ability as investment bankers in recent years, when the decline in European stock markets caught some of them unawares, and lost large sums for customers. Their slowness in moving out of European securities and into the New York market is admitted by some of the Swiss themselves, though they tend to blame the investors themselves for being old fashioned, stubbornly resisting the go-go policies of their bankers. (It's hard to get it right. Having been criticised for moving too slowly in the past, they then find themselves criticised for moving too quickly, at, for instance, the time of the Middle East crisis in 1967, when they sold oil shares heavily and had to buy them back at a loss when the market made a rapid recovery. The *Economist* spoke crisply of 'Swiss-based investors with their usual exquisitely bad sense of timing.')

Among the other excuses I heard from private bankers was that information about American stocks was not always available in Europe in time for the dealer to act quickly and profitably. 'By the time it gets here, the cream is off,' said a securities manager in Geneva. 'Sometimes a stock is introduced very, very quietly in New York. By the time the analysis comes out, the price has gone right up, and it's a speculative long-term buy.' Coming from a senior executive at one of Geneva's inner seven, this was an interesting admission of the extent to which the experts can be left out in the cold. He rounded it off by saying that 'you can't expect a banker in Switzerland to have the same floor knowledge as a broker in New York or Boston.'

American stockbrokers are hard at work in Geneva and Zurich, trying to make the same point. They have descended in droves, offering their services as an alternative, but it is unlikely that so far they have done much to prise substantial investors away from the Swiss banks. They retain their magic. 'I always wanted an English Raleigh bicycle when I was a boy,' said a Geneva banker. 'I could have had others, but only a Raleigh would do. Looking back now, I realise that all bicycles are more or less the same, but I couldn't see it then. This is how people at large see the Swiss banks.'

They themselves were surprised, soon after the second world war, to see the way their traditional business came back. Many of them had written it off, assuming that post-war Europe would have no place for portfolio management on a large scale. With Germany in ruins and almost every national economy drained of energy, private bankers turned towards commercial business, then promptly turned back again when it became apparent, long before 1950, that the new Europe would have rich men, just like the old. In Zurich, the powerful private bank of Julius Bär & Co. retained its interest in the commercial side, so that it's now both kinds of institution. But most private houses still say they would find deposit-taking and trade-financing too hazardous for banks of their size.

Finally, among banks that are internationally important, come the foreign firms that have crowded into Switzerland, seeking a share of the profitable business to be had. There are dozens of them, mainly in Geneva; this is the city for private fortunes, and no questions asked; money is more volatile here than it is in the staider setting of Zurich. The foreign banks include many quite ordinary ones—Crédit Lyonnais and Banque de Paris et des Pays-Bas, Barclays and Lloyds, American Express and First National City. Non-Swiss banks accounted for 3·5 per cent of Swiss bank assets in 1955, and more than double this figure a few years later.

Not all the non-Swiss banks are above suspicion. About once a year a dubious bank collapses, making the Swiss wince and tell one another, yet again, that something must be done to tighten the regulations and keep out the cowboys. It's easier to open a bank than a chemist's shop in Switzerland. What regulations exist are easily sidestepped. 'A majority of the board must be Swiss,' said a National Bank executive, 'but you can always find Swiss lawyers to oblige.

The fringe of 'easy banks' that exploits this freedom from control attracts money by its willingness to take deposits without asking questions, perhaps also by paying higher interest rates, and recouping itself with high-risk investments. It's a situation that the Swiss dislike intensely, because it traps them with their own philosophy. 'There is no doubt that our banking system allows dishonesty,' said one of its senior operators, 'but it is a question of the price you have to pay for democracy and liberalism.'

This conflict runs through Swiss banking: one reason the system works so well and attracts so much business is because it's free, yet if the freedom lets in knavery, then reputations will suffer and business will fly away. The answer is to insist that the abuse is marginal, that only ignorance or envy could say otherwise, and that moral virtue will prevail. 'I may have a colleague who is not a ball of fire,' said a partner at one of Geneva's oldest banks, 'but who may be valuable by reason of his solidity. The credit of a bank such as this depends on the moral standing of the partners.'

It seems almost improper to criticise so upright a nation of bankers. They would very much like you to think so.

The Gnomes of Zurich

One criticism that the Swiss have little difficulty in refuting is that they emerge from their caves in time of crisis to speculate against the pound. The phrase 'Gnomes of Zurich' is attributed to Mr. George Brown, who is said to have produced it in 1964 when he was in charge of economic affairs in Mr Wilson's new Labour Government. This Government inherited an economic crisis which promptly got worse, a situation calculated to cause maximum bitterness among Labour Ministers. They saw the old bogy of an international conspiracy among hard-hearted bankers anxious to see the workers kept in their place, not given more welfare benefits.

The Ministers probably had grounds for worrying. A suspicion that any Labour Government will be soft-hearted and muddle-headed in its economic policies lurks at the back of the collective business mind, and the Swiss business mind is more suspicious than most. Speaking to the Economic Research Council in London in 1966, Hans J. Bär of the Zurich bank spelt out the orthodox anxiety of the Swiss—commonplace to them but vinegar and ashes to a Socialist. Mr. Bär pointed out that 'a country where social welfare is still to a large extent within the sphere of the individual and his employer [Switzerland] cannot help but look with suspicion and perhaps a little bit of envy upon a country [Britain] where the Welfare State is written with capital letters at the expense of an almost permanent budgetary deficit, which means offering welfare on borrowed money. Can it not be understood that a country which in general does not accept the strike as a suitable instrument to settle labour disputes, regards with misgivings a situation where strikes—even against the general interest—are condoned?'

Harold Wilson is reported to have said once that foreign bankers took a view of Labour that could be measured as a drop in confidence of several hundred million pounds, compared with the banker's view of the Conservatives. Yet whatever the loss of confidence, the process involved is much vaguer than a phrase like 'Gnomes of Zurich' suggests, with its hint of malicious speculators whispering into telephones. Mr. Wilson even relented (in 1966) to the point of telling Parliament that he didn't believe in 'bearded troglodytes deep below ground'. The idea of a bankers' conspiracy is really an attempt to pin the general unease of business interests on to an identifiable group; and the idea of a Swiss bankers' conspiracy is a slightly paranoiac refinement of the process. As the chairman of the Swiss Credit Bank, Mr. F. W. Schulthess, told his shareholders: 'Nobody cares to admit that confidence is waning at home, and so to many abroad it seems preferable to lay the blame on Swiss bankers.'

It was not only bankers who turned against the pound in 1964 but industrialists, not only Swiss but Belgians, Americans and Britons, and what most of them were doing was protecting their interests rather than setting out to make a killing at the expense of someone else's currency. If the pound had been devalued, as it was three years later, those who held sterling would have had their holdings reduced by the amount of the devaluation; so they sold their sterling and bought something else that looked safer. There was a run on the pound, and in the end it was saved from what might have been total collapse by an enormous propping-up operation among Western governments to the tune of $4,000 million.

The Swiss helped in the run on the pound but they also helped to prop it up again; and they like to point out that they have been among the prime movers in organising the central-bank cooperation that has grown up in the 1960s, to cope with fierce attacks on currencies. Stability, as they point out time and again, is what they want; chaos would ruin them.

This doesn't stop the Swiss from being involved in the mechanics of selling sterling. If their clients want to sell, then they must act on their behalf. Whenever there's a sterling crisis, international corporations hurry to sell their pounds for forward delivery, ensuring that at a date in the not-too-distant future they will get a guaranteed price for the currency they need for everyday commercial business. Others —individuals or firms—with strong nerves may be joining in as pure speculators, playing the old game of selling for forward delivery in the hope that by the time they have to produce the sterling it will have been devalued, enabling them to buy it cheaply.

The big Swiss banks deny flatly that they ever do this with their own money, and suggest they aren't keen to do too much of it for others. The foreign-exchange manager at the Union Bank (the super-gnome) said categorically that 'the Union Bank of Switzerland has never been short of sterling as a bank. [i.e. it has never sold sterling it hasn't got in order to buy back sterling it doesn't want at a profit]. Of course, there are customers who may have been. But I can also tell you that there have been international customers whose orders were refused. We said, all right, if you want to sell sterling short, you go to London and do it direct. Don't do it under the cover of Swiss banks.'

More subtly, the Swiss can influence events by their day-by-day, hour-by-hour approach to the foreign-exchange market. When a commercial client sells because he fears devaluation, his banker may have helped to instil the fear. And though it may not be 'speculating', a bank has to take hour-by-hour positions in a currency, perhaps buying what it's offered before any purchaser is in sight; the way it behaves may reflect its natural reluctance to go on holding a weak currency. Foreign-exchange operators are sensitive creatures, and when pressed for advice and decisions, they tread carefully, all their bankers' alarm-bells ringing, and naturally shrink from advocating support of a currency that was in trouble half an hour before—since when things may have got worse, if only they knew. Rumours can sweep across Europe in five minutes through a chain of hurried phone conversations between dealers who are making highly technical decisions amid a perpetual cloud of gossip, rather like City stockbrokers, except that the exchange dealer is more isolated and more subject to attacks of nerves.

I was in Zurich during the 1967 Middle East crisis, when money was pouring into Switzerland, much of it switched out of London by Arab depositors (Swiss banks immediately returned some of it to the City). Dealing rooms were hectic. There was a rumour that the Suez Canal had been blocked, which turned out to be true, and a rumour that Nasser had fled Egypt, which wasn't. One Thursday afternoon the word went round that the United States was about to suspend all sales of gold, which would mean that dollars couldn't be turned into metal. If this happened it would remove the stabilising effect of a fixed gold price and have enormous repercussions. Dealers phoned one another, Zurich to London, London to Amsterdam, Amsterdam to Frankfurt, trying to trace the story.

At one of the Big Three, a manager in his shirt-sleeves said it was the most fantastic afternoon he'd ever known in the market. Between going to lunch and coming back, the price of U.S. dollars had slipped sharply; the Arabs were selling, the gold-embargo rumours were circulating. They had traced them back to Paris, then lost the trail. In the next room the telephone lights at the dealing positions didn't stop flashing. On top of everything, said the manager, the annual meeting of Forex, the international club for foreign-exchange men, was about to start in Amsterdam, and dealers were anxious to get away. 'I was supposed to go tonight,' he said, 'but I'll wait till Friday now. I don't want to be left holding the baby. I've got a position of ten million dollars at the moment and I'm being offered more and more dollars all the time. So what do I do? I say, Hell, sell the lot. I want to sleep easy in Amsterdam.'

He said that oddly enough, he had noticed before that the eve of the annual Forex get-together exaggerated any air of crisis that happened to prevail at the time, presumably because dealers wanted to straighten out their balances before leaving. He made the market sound a personal affair. Next morning the airmail edition of *The Times* reported that 'world foreign exchange markets continue to be sensitive to events in the Middle East' without actually saying that there had never been a day like Thursday. I telephoned the manager before he left for Amsterdam, to see if another fantastic session was forecast, but he seemed to have forgotten what he had said the previous afternoon. He seemed puzzled at the question. 'We have busy days and hectic days,' he said. 'I couldn't tell you it was more active than the others. It was filled up with uncertainties, that was the unusual feature.' So it all came back to rumours, a lot of business, and the mild hysteria of the moment.

The gnomes resent their label. 'We have mixed feelings of amusement on one side and bitterness on the other,' said the super-gnome. 'We do what we can. Then to be branded as mischievous is not very nice.' The phrase isn't always taken to imply malice. A spokesman for the Swiss Bankers' Association thought a gnome was 'a busy little person'; a private banker, who kept insisting that the 1964 crisis was brought about entirely by the welfare-happy presence of Mr. Wilson, took gnomes to be 'funny little people who run around looking picturesque,' though this may have been wishful thinking.

A book called 'The Gnomes of Zurich' upset the Swiss terribly when it came out a few years ago. Written by an American of Swiss ancestry, T. R. Fehrenbach, this made them seem more hypocritical than picturesque. In private many of them admitted that it was fair if unwelcome, but the public response was horrified. A Swiss in London said he had it on good authority that non-Swiss bankers in Europe, anxious to see such a damaging book widely circulated, were thinking of buying hundreds of copies and circulating them to clients. The author says the Swiss reactions were 'hurt, angry and icy;' he heard from an incensed banker in Berne who said that 200 years ago he would have been publicly hanged, and good riddance, if ever he re-entered Swiss jurisdiction. Sensitivity among business men in Switzerland, as Fehrenbach noted afterwards, is much greater than it is in Britain and the U.S.

Mr. Schulthess of the Swiss Credit Bank has not only talked about 'scurrilous publicity' and 'pseudo-expert books' from abroad but has suggested darkly that the recurrence of these 'literary concoctions of dubious standard' is 'almost systematically arranged.' His conclusion is that 'fundamentally the attacks aim at a broader target, namely at the efficient Swiss economy as a whole. Economic competition—both national and worldwide—sometimes employs strange weapons.' In other words, those who criticise Swiss banking habits are really engaged in an economic cold war against the prosperous Swiss. 'Conspiracy' theories are not confined to the anti-gnome camp.

Numbered Accounts, Bankers' Secrets

Perhaps they are sensitive because they know there are skeletons in the cupboard. They can answer the gnome-and-speculation charges without much trouble; where some of them grow uneasy is in the field of secrecy, numbered accounts and tax evasion: the by-products of freedom. It is not that they are doing anything wrong on Swiss territory, but that they are providing services that can be used legally by operators who may not be entirely clean in the eyes of their own governments. This isn't a question of crooks concealing illicit fortunes, though that happens too, at the shady banks that will take money from anyone. The routine Swiss response to the critic who cites numbered accounts is to admit that the occasional bank will have the occasional crooked client, then to add that this is hardly a reason to condemn the whole system. This pained reaction conceals the real point, which is simply that Switzerland is a good place for fiddles, big and small, not by international criminals but by jolly business men playing their endless game of financial hide and seek with the authorities.

The point about Switzerland is that the authorities are on the side of the business man. Privacy and secrecy are the right of the citizen: property and the profit-motive are respected: the State is kept in its place. 'There is nothing extraordinary about banking secrecy in itself,' said the President of the Swiss Confederation, Mr. Roger Bonvin, in a speech to foreign journalists. Inevitably he made it appear a moral question: 'It takes some strength of character not to spend everything one earns, and nothing is more natural than a modest reticence about one's savings.'

Put like that it sounds reasonable, if a trifle priggish. It is what the world was like, once upon a time. A man's life is his own—not the State's, not even his wife's. In their hearts, many Americans and Britons may feel the same, especially where wives are concerned. If they do, they know they are hankering for a past that's gone. But the Swiss can still get away with it. Women don't have the vote so why should men pretend to treat them as equals? 'What I do with my money is an expression of my fundamental ideas of liberty,' said a private banker. 'It's like going to see my doctor—the reason doesn't concern my wife or my children.' The law lays down that in general, a husband can ask his banker for information about his wife's affairs; but she can't ask about his affairs under any circumstances unless he gives her specific authority to do so.

With such ingrained assumptions, the Swiss have found little difficulty in building up a system where secrecy is made to seem as honourable as it's useful. The numbered account is known in other countries, but no one else has developed it on the same scale. A numbered account means that the client is allocated a unique number and that this, not his name, is used internally at the bank. No more than two or three senior officials or partners of the bank will know the identity behind the number. Such an account is unlikely to bear any interest and may actually cost the depositor a quarter or a half per cent for the privilege of having it.

The numbered account is a refinement, and in theory a customer is fully protected even without one. But it adds a feeling of security. In the same way, Swiss banking law on the subject of secrecy is reassuring, although it does no more than specify penalties for a breach of what is supposed to be banking practice everywhere. The law was passed in 1934, at a time when money, much of it Jewish, was beginning to leave Germany, and Nazi agents were trying to find where it was going. (This is the point I was advised to make, so as to show the Swiss I was on their side. They never fail to make the point themselves). It says that any bank employee who 'violates the professional secret' can be fined up to 20,000 francs (about $4,800) and go to prison for six months. It doesn't say what it means by professional secrecy, though some of the cantons have their own laws which say expressly that no bank may divulge information to the tax or exchange-control authorities. The law applies equally to all banks on Swiss soil, so that the Swiss branch of a foreign-owned bank is not allowed to pass information about customers to its own top management. A man at the Banque de Paris et des Pays-Bas described how an inspector from head office in Paris would come to the Swiss branch and be installed in a room, where he would be allowed to inspect selected information. He couldn't call for customers' statements: that would have been a breach of confidence.

This respect for secrecy may be obsessive, but it's pleasing to those who happen to have secrets. What matters is not that Swiss banks respect secrecy—all banks everywhere claim to do the same—but that they extend their discretion beyond the point that other countries might consider reasonable. British and American bankers will talk only when they have to—but they have to talk more often than bankers in Switzerland. In Britain, where the law rests on a case of 1924, banks will disclose details of a customer's account to the police and other authorities when directed by a court order or subpoena, or when the bank decides that it's 'in the public interest' to do so.[3] A man who is being divorced by his wife can have his bank statement called for if the court suspects he can afford to pay more alimony than he's willing to admit. Tribunals and official inquiries are often licensed to issue subpoenas. In Switzerland,

[3] As a British bank security officer pointed out, this doesn't mean the interests of a member of the public. An important customer at a branch was owed money by an associate who kept his account at the same branch. The first customer asked the manager to let him see the second customer's bank statement. The manager, under pressure from a valuable customer, referred the case to a local director, who referred it to head office, who said no.

criminal and civil courts can order a bank to disclose; but in practice it's a rare event.

Swiss bank secrecy means, in particular, not giving information to the income-tax collector. It's easier to prise the information from a British bank, not through any weakness in the bankers but because the system allows it; the public attitude towards tax dodging is harsher. The Inland Revenue may first approach the bank and plead 'public interest' as a reason for seeing a customer's account. When this fails, as it probably will, the Revenue can assess the unco-operative citizen for a crippling sum. He can appeal to a body called the Special Commissioners; but once he does this, the Special Commissioners can issue a subpoena, ordering the bank to disclose.

Similarly in the United States, the Inland Revenue Service can use subpoenas as an effective means of breaking bank secrecy. The threat of a subpoena is often enough. 'There is not the same feeling as there is in Switzerland,' said a New York banker, adding that 'the occasional bank official might reveal things informally to a tax inspector because the psychological climate is so different.'

All this confirms the worst fears of the Anglo-Saxon taxpayer, and makes the attractions of Switzerland obvious. As the Swiss put it blandly, it isn't that we condone crime, it's simply that we take a milder view of tax-paying. Tax legislation lays down that banks are under no obligation to tell the authorities anything about their customers' accounts. The customer himself can be asked, and he must then get the information from his bank. But the taxmen are forbidden to make 'fishing expeditions'—demanding that the citizen produce statements from a variety of banks, without concrete evidence that he has money in any of them. In criminal cases, a court can order the bank to disclose; but tax affairs rarely come within the Swiss definition of crime.

It is a liberal system of tax collection but for the Swiss themselves it usually means paying up and looking happy, as it does for tax-payers everywhere. It is the non-Swiss who stands to benefit most. He is covered by the laws on bank secrecy and tax disclosure, and the only authorities who might intervene in a limited way—the Swiss—have no interest in doing so. Not only the secrecy is attractive. Money can enter Switzerland because there are no exchange controls to stop it. Once there, it can be invested by the non-resident without any tax being claimed by the Swiss authorities from the income—'this fantastic thing that we can still afford to do,' as a glowing banker described it. But secrecy is what gilds the whole machine.

Speeches and articles by the Swiss step gingerly in this area. The problem, they suggest, belongs to the countries with the penal rates of taxation, rather than to Switzerland, which is providing a service and not entering into the rights and wrongs of such complicated matters. In private they sound different, admitting what is obvious, that the assurance of complete secrecy, with or without a numbered account, helps to bring tax-evasion money into Switzerland. 'Our banks are extensively used for evasion,' said an executive at one of Geneva's inner seven. The money that comes in may have been earned by a company or an individual outside the country of residence where tax should be paid, and transferred quietly to Switzerland. It may represent profits on deals in shares or property, legitimately acquired in the first place by (for instance) an American in Europe, who for obvious reasons prefers not to report the profits to his tax authorities. It may enter Switzerland as suitcases full of banknotes, which is the old-fashioned method used by many Italians.

However it arrives, it obviously wants to remain hidden from someone. I asked a banker in Basle about double-taxation agreements; these exist between many countries, and enable someone who has tax deducted from his income in two countries eventually to get his money back from one of them. The banker didn't know the answer because, as he said, 'to tell the truth I don't have any clients who make use of double-taxation agreements—it wouldn't be worth their while.' The reason it wouldn't be worth their while is that in order to invoke an agreement, a client would have to declare his identity. Interest paid on U.S. securities has a 30 per cent withholding tax deducted at source. A Swiss bank collects $70 for every $100 gross that's due to its client, without saying who the client is. He may be an American citizen, resident in Switzerland, who then has to pay Swiss taxes on the $70. But if his income is high, it will be more profitable for him to pay twice than it would be to invoke the double-taxation treaty, declare his income to the U.S. authorities, and pay a single tax bill at a harsher rate. If the customer doesn't live in Switzerland, but only uses a bank there, he isn't liable for Swiss income tax at all. He pays his 30 per cent and shuts up.

It's less than he would pay in U.S. taxes if he were assessed on his true income, but it's clearly tax he would rather avoid if he can. This is why Eurobonds issued via Luxembourg and Delaware have been so successful, because interest is paid net without tax deducted at source. This is a conscious effort to attract money from tax-evading sources like Switzerland, and it's generally thought that well over half the bonds end up in the vaults of Swiss banks, held on behalf of anonymous tax-evaders all over the world. Not 30 per cent, not even 3 per cent, is deducted: they get the lot.

Another device to help the wealthy collect their interest free of tax is used when Swiss banks invest their customers' funds in overseas money markets. The straightforward method would be for a customer to request his bank to place money in, say, the Eurodollar market, and pay him the interest. But under Swiss tax law, the bank has to withhold some of the interest before passing it on to the client. If he is non-resident, he can claim it back via a double-tax treaty; if he is a resident, it counts as an instalment against his final tax demand. In either case he would prefer to lay hands on the gross amount. So the bank will thoughtfully draw up a 'fiduciary contract', by which the money remains the client's and is lent on his behalf by the bank, which acts as an intermediary without taking responsibility for the loan. It will cost him a commission, probably a quarter per cent on the sum involved. But whoever borrows the money—say, a bank in Belgium—pays the interest direct to the client, so that there is no deduction. The interest arrives in exactly the way it would in any case: through the customer's bank in Switzerland. But when there's a fiduciary contract, the Swiss bank is collecting the interest on the client's behalf and not on its own. This is the sort of splendid idea that justifies the large amounts of money that tax lawyers get paid. There is a snag, as always, in that the client not only has to pay a commission, but is lending the money at his own risk. If the Belgian bank disappears with the cash, then he and not his Swiss bank is the loser. Devaluation of a currency is also a risk that he personally has to take. But with short-term lending the risks are modest, and well worth taking to avoid the tax. A partner of a medium-sized private bank told me that they had 141 such contracts outstanding with clients, all of them for deposits in the Eurodollar market.

For many people, Switzerland is synonymous with tax avoidance. The National Bank has estimated that of the country's 6,000 holding companies, with a total capital of $1,500 million, two-thirds are in foreign hands. Most of these have been set up by firms and individuals whose affairs need (or justify) an office outside their own country, and who have chosen a place where taxes are light. The Swiss are not greedy, and some cantons have gone out of their way to give tax privileges to foreign holding companies. A firm selling its products throughout Europe may use its Swiss office as a collecting point. Whatever income can be channelled through a Dutch cigar manufacturer's office in Lausanne will attract less tax than it would in Holland. It's all perfectly legal, but annoying for countries that lose tax revenue as a result. The Swiss worry about this. Dr. F. Aschinger, a leading Zurich journalist, talks about 'a kind of tax dumping that does the Swiss image no good.' But the practice is wholly in character.

The same is true of the tax concessions extended to foreigners who go to live in Switzerland. As residents they are liable to Swiss taxes, but as non-Swiss they may be able to get of lightly. It's an effective way of attracting film stars and ex-company chairman, but the implied picture of a taxation paradise, a sort of financial Riviera where the privileged few can retire, makes the Swiss uneasy and inclined to deny everything. They admit that at one time it was possible for foreigners to negotiate a tax deal with the cantonal authorities, but say that this no longer happens. 'Pure fiction', says a Swiss Credit Bank booklet. 'Existing tax agreements may be continued,' says Dr Aschinger, in a 1966 review of Fehrenbach's 'Gnomes of Zurich' book, 'but no new arrangements of that kind may be made, except by certain economically backward cantons for the purpose of attracting new industry.'

That sounds conclusive. However, what they mean when they deny that foreigners can negotiate their tax is not entirely what you might think they mean. An *ad hoc* arrangement between Mr. Big and a Swiss tax collector, negotiated without reference to established principles, is no longer possible. Special concessions, specifically catered for in cantonal laws, are very possible indeed.

Daunted by the evidence, I went to see an official of the Swiss Credit Bank. He began by saying firmly that one shouldn't talk of 'private tax arrangements' between cantons and foreigners. It was totally untrue. I mentioned a story I had heard in Geneva, that a foreigner might be assessed on the basis of how much it cost him to live *en pension* at an hotel; I said I supposed that this was another of those canards against the Swiss, but the official said no, no, it was perfectly true. But it was nothing to do with a private arrangement. 'It is a special tax feature for foreigners not earning their living in Switzerland,' he said. 'Instead of being taxed on their income they can be taxed on the basis of their living expenses.' At least two cantons, Vaud and Geneva, had such a law. The living expenses were calculated as five times the rent of the apartment where the taxpayer lived, or one and a half times the cost of the hotel. 'Of course,' he added, 'if someone has a Cadillac, a driver and two servants, the authorities will make a small addition.'

Switzerland is firmly on the side of people who have Cadillacs, who are entitled to have Cadillacs, who are thrifty or tough or clever enough to pay for Cadillacs. In a world that seems increasingly anxious to grind the faces of the rich, Switzerland is determinedly out of step. 'Personally,' said a Geneva banker, 'I feel willing to help when I see someone in another country paying 90 per cent of his income to the tax authorities.' 'The Swiss look at it like this,' said a colleague. 'They insist they have nothing to do with the tax systems of other countries. But if someone of good repute and with money comes to us and says, "I am paying too much in taxes at home," the Swiss will say, "All right, we will help you to avoid the greed of your tax inspector".'

Mr. Schulthess has said publicly that 'in the discussions between the Government and the individual, it is by no means always obvious on which side justice lies: too many tax laws are introduced into this world without having the morale (*sic*) of a just balance between governmental and individual right.' He added: 'Please do not misunderstand this statement: the refusal to act as judge does not mean that we facilitate or acquiesce in violations of the tax laws.' But although the majority of Swiss banks (and certainly one of the standing of Mr. Schulthess's Swiss Credit Bank) may not intend to violate anyone's laws, they can't help having customers who do. A few years ago a clerk who worked for one of the Big Three was goaled after he photocopied the names of numbered-account holders and sold them to blackmailers. The customers must have had something to hide, or they wouldn't have been susceptible to blackmail.

How banks say they behave when they think a customer is evading tax is instructive. A tax expert at a bank in Geneva, one of the leading seven, began with the ritual washing of hands: 'Whether our clients do or do not declare their income is no concern of ours. It is a question of personal habits.' Later he said that 'we do not accept American clients who have not declared their income,' but admitted that this happened only if the client brought it to his notice, which he would hardly be likely to do. 'I won't ask him, Do you declare or do you not declare? This is his own business.'

Criminal money is another matter. The Swiss will point out that a bandit or a blackmailer would not have his money accepted in the first place if a reputable bank had an inkling of its origin, and that criminal charges override banking secrecy; a numbered account can be opened up by court order. But *political* money is all right, because who is to pass judgment? Batista of Cuba and the Perons of the Argentine are said to have had millions of dollars in Switzerland before they were overthrown. Tshombe of Katanga side-tracked national revenue into Swiss accounts. The family of Rafael Trujillo, dictator of Santa Domingo till he was murdered some years ago, put their fortune there. One is usually given to understand that the more respectable banks decline money from the more blatant dictators—Fehrenbach says that Pictet & Co. in Geneva turned down Trujillo's—but, again, to decline money from some wicked prince or president means making a value judgment about his methods, his politics, his conscience—it's usually too emotive for a banker. A partner at Hentsch & Co. in Geneva agreed that the old-guard bankers turned down money like Trujillo's, but said it was quite illogical to do so, since it implied an absolute standard that didn't exist. 'How can you set up as an authority on what's honest?' he asked.

They are not their brothers' keepers—this is another phrase one hears. The private banker who talked to me about vanloads of smuggled lire coming north from Italy shook his head when I asked if this didn't create problems for the Swiss banks that accepted the money. 'You see,' he said patiently, 'it's legal once it crosses the border.' At the Union Bank, an official was talking about the many

Italian accounts held in Switzerland. I said I supposed that a lot of this was smuggled money, but he held up his hand like a policeman stopping traffic and said, 'It's no concern of ours.'

They are, in the end, realists. 'If you come to Switzerland with a lot of money,' said a Genevan, 'you have to prove, not that the money has been honestly earned, because that is a subjective judgment, but that you are an honest business man who wants to protect his family from the effects of harsh taxation.'

That seems to sum it up, though there are further distinctions to be made, depending on whether the customers are Anglo-Saxons or Others. Swiss bankers imply and sometimes say openly that they don't expect the French or Italians to be particularly honest about tax or currency-smuggling. But Anglo-Saxons are different. 'The English are basically honest,' said Dr Nicolas Bär, another of the family. 'They do not smuggle out large amounts of money.' A few yards down the Bahnhofstrasse a fellow banker said he wouldn't dream of opening an account for a British or American citizen if he thought he wanted to cheat the tax authorities. But it was different with an Italian, who didn't have the same standards.

I asked an American executive at a non-Swiss bank in Switzerland how he coped with all this. He winked and said, 'Here comes the ethical problem, and boy, it's a tough one. The attitude of Swiss banks is that they aren't tax collectors. That's fine, but—and here you become schizophrenic as a person—in countries like France and Italy, taxes are more a matter of negotiation or of games being played. With a customer from those countries I wouldn't hesitate if he was a guy who wanted to preserve his capital by dodging taxes. But say an American citizen wants to do it, under penalty of criminal law. If he dies and it comes out in his estate, then his children are going to suffer. I personally try to discourage him.' I asked what happened if he failed. He winked again and said, 'I pass him on to S., my Swiss colleague here, and leave it all to him.'

It's not difficult to see why the Swiss get so angry when they are criticised. What they are doing is perfectly straightforward, so why, they ask, should foreigners keep on at them? It must be ignorance and envy. But at the root of their anger is a degree of duplicity. If Swiss bankers could come into the open and say publicly that they are defending an old order, fighting a rearguard action on behalf of free enterprise, they would feel much better about it. Unfortunately they can't; it would sound too reactionary. So they are stuck with their dilemma—in private they are on the side of the old-fashioned financial swashbuckler who is fighting greedy governments and sailing as near the wind as he can; in public they must pay lip-service to the egalitarian rules that are prevailing in the West, where governments put increasingly powerful curbs on bankers and business men. Switzerland's *laissez-faire* way of banking is what makes it so attractive to other business men, yet the Swiss can never advertise the fact without apologising for it at the same time. Instead of saying bluntly that secrecy and freedom from prying governments are what business men everywhere would like to enjoy, they have to stress how morally upright they are. Instead of saying 'Look, numbered accounts!' they have to think about their public relations.

A Zurich banker told me regretfully that he gave the Swiss type of banking secrecy another twenty years at most. Switzerland would have to conform with 'the general attack against capitalism.' Its laws would become less liberal, its tax treaties with other countries more oppressive to the dodgers. 'But we shall make an effort to survive,' he said bleakly; and no doubt he and the rest of them will still be there in twenty years, even if things have changed. Zurich, Basle and Geneva will still have paper-shredding machines and numbered accounts, gnomes and reassurance. Switzerland is too useful not to last.

Liechtenstein, pop. 20,000

The difference between Switzerland, Luxembourg and Liechtenstein, which are all tax havens, is a matter of psychology. Switzerland is small but invaluable to world business; it is a tax haven, but it's other things as well. Luxembourg is smaller still, Liechtenstein is little to the point of scarcely being there at all. Luxembourg covers a thousand square miles and has a third of a million people, Liechtenstein covers sixty-odd square miles, a lot of them Alps, and has 20,000. Luxembourg has appeared intermittently in European history, owns a major steel industry, and is one of the Common Market's Six; Liechtenstein is a village-State between Austria and Switzerland with a prince, eighteen policeman, and a main street in Vaduz, the capital, which echoes each morning with cow-bells as the herds make for the meadows. The rest of Europe would long since have forgotten it existed if it weren't for its export trade in postage stamps and its policy towards other people's money. Liechtenstein is so small that it's below the point at which bad publicity matters, and its approach to tax-avoidance is shaped accordingly. Luxembourg can be mentioned to a banker without causing him to wink, but Liechtenstein is liable to produce broad smiles, as with the merchant banker in Hamburg who said, 'That's not a country, it's a foreign-exchange offence.'

This isn't to say that the 16,000 Liechtensteiners (the rest are foreigners) find such comments anything but offensive: they don't laugh at the jokes: what they do is to go on acting in a way that makes the jokes unavoidable.

There is nothing illegal about Liechtenstein's laws on holding companies for use by foreigners. The most popular kind, the 'establishment' or 'anstalt', may not be set up for an illegal or immoral purpose, and since 1963, one of its directors (usually the sole director) must live in Liechtenstein. However, the establishment isn't controlled by its director but by its founder, who can live anywhere he likes, and who has absolute freedom to do what he chooses with his company, including giving it away without telling the Liechtenstein director. This splendid apparatus, so vague and yet so legal, can be used by a company or a person as a channel through which money can be passed without paying tax. An ordinary citizen of any country, paying taxes in the ordinary way, is taxed on his earnings in that country; an Englishman isn't even allowed to export the money that is left after tax has been paid. But if the money earned outside the taxpayer's own country is sent direct to the company in Liechtenstein, it may well evade all tax. The growing number of companies that do business in more than one country has made it natural for people to seek collecting points where taxes are low. The Eurodollar market helps to increase the flow of stateless money that can avoid taxation as it moves around the world. Luxembourg exploits this situation and so does Switzerland. A holding company in a low-tax area can purchase raw materials at the market price, then sell them at an artificially high price to the parent company in a high-tax area. This reduces profits in the high-tax area and increases them in the low-tax area. But in Liechtenstein the rules are laxer, and the effrontery of having so many holding companies, perhaps twice as many as Switzerland's 6,000, lowers the tone of the place.

A banker at one of Liechtenstein's three banks said that he had recently returned from a trip to the Middle East, where 'the first thing they all said was, "Ah, you come from the place for evading taxes".' He regretted this very much, especially since the country had followed a more prudent policy than, for instance, Luxembourg. Foreign banks had tried to enter Liechtenstein in recent years, but the Government had stopped them; Prince Franz Josef hadn't liked the idea.

The banker made the absence of foreign banks sound a virtue, though one of Luxembourg's strong points is that so many reputable outsiders have gone there—banks, investment trusts, and holding companies formed by oil corporations and drug manufacturers. Most of them are there for reasons connected with tax, but there's nothing underhand about it, at least at the better end of the business. Everyone knows what's happening, and the illegality (if any) is committed only by whoever receives money that he doesn't declare to his tax authorities. Liechtenstein argues that its own position is similar—it provides the facilities, and can't be blamed if rogues abuse them. Unfortunately most of the companies that use Liechtenstein are reticent; whether they have been formed by manufacturers, patent-holders or celebrities, the names are difficult to obtain and rarely publicised. No doubt many of them are operated with perfect legality, but most of the affairs one hears about seem to include a rogue or two.

A shiver must have run through U.S. boardrooms when word got out in 1968 that a grand jury in New York had been investigating evidence of alleged tax-dodging by fifty American firms, using Liechtenstein holding companies. A Government official said they had the names of fifty corporations which had paid $2 million into Liechtenstein companies as 'commissions,' but which were thought to be unreported profits. None of the firms was named.

Government officials in Liechtenstein would rather discuss their industry than their holding companies. Postage stamps, which find their way into cheap packets for schoolboys all over the world, bring an income of more than $2 million a year, but the principality does produce more orthodox things, including stoves, cough medicine, false teeth, canned fruit, fabrics, ceramics and sausage skins.

For its size it's a highly industrialised country, and no doubt would continue to be comfortably off even without its tax-haven income.

This income comes chiefly from a small annual tax levied on the capital of each company. The capital can be as little as 50,000 Swiss francs, about $12,000, and the banker said that although at one time the founder could merely show the registrar of companies his 50,000 francs and then take it away again, he now had to pay the money into an account at a bank. Did the money have to stay there? Not exactly, said the banker—'as is the case all over the world, a company can do what it likes with its capital.' So the money could be borrowed, paid in, looked at, withdrawn and repaid. Everything about Liechtenstein is accommodating.

About ten lawyers and some professional company directors get most of the business, together with the banks. 'In reality,' said the banker, 'we do not have much importance in international financial matters,' and on a wide view this is true enough. But it's a reasonable guess that quantities of Eurodollars which have never been near a tax inspector reach the market via Liechtenstein. And $350 million of somebody's money, accumulated in Liechtenstein, is deposited with Swiss banks alone, according to Swiss official statistics. The banker thought this figure high; he couldn't understand it; but since the money was only passing through, it wasn't, he said, looking pleased at the formula, Liechtenstein's responsibility.

8 *The Unstoppable Americans*

The American managers and bankers who come to Europe have a habit of referring to it as one place. Europeans are sometimes amused or irritated at what they regard as ignorance, failing to see that for the newcomer it's a strength, giving him an advantage that is denied to them. They are only too aware of their history, but when an American looks at the map, what he sees is a thickly populated peninsula at the far end of a continent. Tell an American business man that from Stockholm in the north to Rome in the south is 1,200 miles and he'll probably say, 'Is that all?'

I was with a Zurich banker who had just been telephoned from New York, by a man about to leave for Paris who had asked, 'How is the weather in Europe?' The Swiss shook his head tolerantly, saying what funny fellows they were. 'I don't even know what the weather's like at the other end of Switzerland,' he said. But the question had made him uneasy. He talked about the importance for Europe of possessing many cultures, and how the differences between nations could enrich life even if they complicated it at the same time. He praised Europe but suddenly he said, 'Shall we be like Greece? Shall we try to stay the same and not realise it's time for Rome?'

This feeling that events are fast overtaking them was crystallised for many Europeans in Jean-Jacques Servan-Schreiber's book, 'Le Défi Americain,' with its celebrated proposition that by the 1980s, American industry in Europe could be the third industrial power in the world, after the United States itself and Russia. A new and alarming kind of European unity has loomed up, one that would not be neatly managed from inside but imposed more brutally to suit the newcomers. It would be the unity of American companies, operating in many countries but responsible to their parents across the Atlantic; financed by dollars (including dollars conveniently borrowed from the Europeans who own them) and attended by American banks.

Only the extent to which this will happen is arguable, since American business is already embedded in Europe and behaving in a way that diminishes frontiers by ignoring them. In this strange economic invasion, the bankers have followed where circumstances have led them. They have a firm hold on Europe, and because they deal in the most volatile and important commodity of all, they make it easier to see the process of penetration at work.

When a country is expanding its influence in the world it's natural for it to scatter banks in every continent. Even the Russians, politically isolated and comparatively self-sufficient, have them in Britain, France, Switzerland and the Lebanon. Until recently the last big international banking expansion was Britain's in the second half of the nineteenth century, when British money was being used to open up new countries. A chain of 4,500 branches in Africa, Asia, Australia and South America survives from this heyday, and is still the City's most important single source of foreign currency earnings. But these overseas banks are having to fight to hold their own, let alone expand. British trade with the areas has declined, and countries that were under-developed when the bankers went there are now well on the way to power, touchy about imperialism and apt to nationalise or at least interfere with institutions that remind them of the past. (The full title of Barclays DCO, which has 1,600 branches, most of them in Africa, used to be 'Barclays Dominion, Colonial and Overseas'. This was felt to have an unfortunate imperial ring, so in the 1950s the initials were made the official title. 'A bit stupid, actually,' said a Barclays man, 'because people ask what the D.C.O. stands for, and then you explain it to them, and then they laugh.')

The world's new travelling bankers, hungry for business and ruthlessly acquiring it, are the Americans. They were late starting and they are unlikely ever to open multitudes of branches as the British did. The days of such simple economic imperialism have gone, and the Americans move carefully, choosing their countries and their strategies, often buying their way into existing networks. Money is usually available, though rising debts to other countries have caused difficulties, especially since 1968, when President Johnson cut back overseas spending. In 1953, American banks had barely 100 branches overseas. By 1966 they had 250. The thickest cluster is in South America, one of the few areas where American banks have been operating for a long time. Another large group is in the Far East, and a third concentration is in Europe, where Continental branches have blossomed faster than anywhere else.

By the middle of 1968, at least twenty-three U.S. banks had fifty-five branches and twenty-seven representative offices in the E.E.C., Britain and Switzerland. They also had investments in more than forty European banks and finance organisations. Of the total, Britain had approximately forty, France twenty-one, Germany sixteen, Belgium and Italy twelve each, Switzerland ten, Netherlands six and Luxembourg five. Elsewhere in Europe, Spain had about a dozen offices and subsidiaries, and a few more were in Greece, Austria and Ireland.

Europe is a rich, dense market that is only beginning to break out of its parochial attitudes and see itself as a whole. Europeans are edging towards a frame of mind that the Americans arrive with. 'We are in Europe to stay, and we see Europe as an entity,' said one of them. 'But we find that Europeans often don't do this. They talk about the Common Market, but there's been no real homogenisation of the financial markets. Each country is still separate.'

Caught between his desire to beat the opposition and his anxiety to keep up good relations, the invading banker sometimes has the uncomfortable look of a man trying to go two ways at the same time. A branch manager at First National City Bank of New York, one of the two or three most active newcomers, described the policy as being 'aggressively friendly'. An officer of the equally active Chase Manhattan, working in a Dutch bank that is part-owned by Chase, explained proudly that he was busy building up files on the 500 indentifiable American companies in Holland, because 'it's the guy who does his homework who survives.' I murmured something about the healthy effect of aggressive techniques on sedate old Europe, but the banker got quite agitated and said the word was not *aggressive*, please, it was *vigorous*.

British bankers have glared at the Chase advertisements which suggest calling in the American bank to help the business man find new markets. The series of ads, showing banker and customer above a headline reading, 'In West Germany [or Belgium, or Mexico] too, you have a friend at Chase Manhattan,' was bearable, but the bold leading question in the later series, 'When you already have one bank, why call in Chase as well?' brought a sharp clicking of teeth. Yet it's inevitable that American banks, working with their own international clients, should want to offer their services to the growing band of European internationals.

'International' has become the most over-used word in business, a bogy-word to frighten people into believing that every company in the world must soon become a globe-straddling giant or die. This is nonsense; what is true is that at the top of the industrial community there is now developing a thick layer of companies that *are* international, operating in many countries at once, and requiring the services of money-men in each place. It's only natural for these companies to use people they know, as well as local institutions. Local banks are necessary for various reasons. They know the politicians. They have the deposits of local currency, so that loans can be made in guilders or francs or whatever it is, without having to bring in dollars and then convert them—which may be more expensive, and involves an 'exchange risk', that one currency may depreciate in terms of another. They may be old friends of the U.S. bank, which doesn't want to alienate them. Nevertheless, it is not difficult for an American bank to make its own services sound desirable, if not indispensable.

For many U.S. companies, venturing into the world for the first time, it is good for their morale when the bank they know at home is on the spot. The house flag uncurls in the sunlight; the blown-up picture of a traveller's cheque fills the window; the strange city becomes a little less strange. I was with an American banker in Germany, listening to him talk about the importance of trust, especially in a country where banks and industries are so close to one another ('A U.S. company goes and talks to a German bank,' he said, making it sound worse than it really is, 'and the next thing they know is that the bank turns out to be a major shareholder in the company's biggest competitor'). The phone rang and he had a long polite conversation, lasting nearly ten minutes. When it was over he banged the receiver down, breathed hard, looked out of the window, and said it was a man in Dusseldorf who kept pestering him to help get a telephone installed. It was wasting his time, he said, but unfortunately the man represented a 'valued corporate client' from back home, and so it was necessary to help him with his problems. On another occasion an American in Amsterdam explained that it had been a hell of a week because it was tulip time. Forty or fifty senior executives of American corporations, visiting their European subsidiaries, had arranged to travel via Amsterdam and see the flowers. 'They ask me what The Situation is,' he said wanly. 'So I come out from under my pile of papers and I tell them.'

The masks slips for a moment, but not in the presence of important visitors, who are greeted with fierce transatlantic handshakes and primed with masses of detail. Time after time I was with American bankers who had to break off the interview because Mr X from Milwaukee or Baltimore had stopped by.

The American bank is selling friendliness and good will; it's also selling pure service, always emphasising the magic word *international*. Money, they all claim, moves faster within the same bank than if it goes through the hands of several. The slanderous charge that money travels at a snail's pace between Continental banks—not only because of administrative complexity but because the banks want to hang on to the cash for a few days longer—is frequently made though difficult to prove. An American in Frankfurt said it could take a week or longer to transfer funds between Germany and Italy, because, as he put it, 'everyone warms their hands on it a bit.' Down the road, a rival American said, 'My friend, money sticks to people's fingers in the European banking system. I've known it take ten days to transfer money from Paris to Frankfurt. I don't say this is normal. The normal time is five to seven days.'

The 'hard-nosed corporate treasurer', a man one often hears about in American industry, won't take kindly to the idea of losing a week's interest on his money while it creeps across Europe; and the reputation for tardiness lingers, though it's probably less deserved than it was. Rapid transfers and multi-national lines of credit, so that a company can borrow up to prearranged amounts in a number of countries, are what the treasurer wants. The business man who thinks of Europe as one place will continually be reminded that it isn't, but the fewer the reminders, the better he'll be pleased. Large American companies tend to set up Europe-wide subsidiaries with a central headquarters as a matter of course. Oil companies, which are multi-national by nature (production, refining, transportation, marketing), illustrate the point, with managements who begin with the assumptions that many European companies have so far failed to make. Esso (in the U.S., Standard Oil of New Jersey), Mobil, Gulf and Continental base their European operations on London, which, since half of Shell and all B.P. are also there, is now Europe's oil capital. Marathon is in Geneva, Texaco and Phillips in Brussels, Signal in Paris.

Oil's appetite for daily working capital is immense, and so is its turnover of cash. Both as short-term borrower and short-term lender, it shuttles money between many countries. A difference of one-quarter per cent in a rate of interest is significant; one eighth is worth taking advantage of; even one-sixteenth can move spare money. The industry's long-term needs are also enormous, and oil companies are forever raising capital. They have been voracious borrowers in the Eurobond market, raising hundreds of millions of dollars between them to spend as and when they decide, in their operations outside the U.S.

All these activities seem to cry out for the 'international banker'. In addition, oil companies have to know the financial and political situation in many countries at once. They're astonishingly expert about taxation, since governments traditionally bleed oil companies whenever they can. Again, the cosmopolitan banker can add his knowledge to theirs.

This desirable breed of banker is wise and far-seeing and perhaps too good to be true. He pops up in advertisements, the answer to every business man's prayer, breathing 'international expertise' like a password. A senior finance officer of the Royal Dutch/Shell group said that as far as he was concerned, a lot of the talk about international giants of industry needing international giants of banking was rubbish. 'One American bank sends us a list of worldwide facilities every year,' he said. 'They seem to regard it as being of great importance. I scratch my head and wonder what I'm supposed to do with it.'

At any given moment, Shell has more than a billion dollars in cash and securities throughout the world. It has to spread its favours, partly because of its size, partly to make itself politically agreeable to as many countries as possible, and so it uses dozens of banks. 'When I see an American bank has opened a new branch in Yokohama or somewhere,' said the Shell man, 'my heart sinks because I know we'll get a letter asking if we'd like to open an account with them. But we prefer to do business with the banks on the spot. When an American bank solicits business like that, it's an embarrassment for us. As an international organisation, you can only operate as a good careful citizen.'

But Royal Dutch/Shell has been a genuinely international group for a long time; in many countries it is almost part of the social structure. Hundreds of companies, especially American, have grown up and outwards only in recent years, with their tireless fellow-bankers in attendance; the companies may use a variety of banks, but they are often major clients of the same American banks in many countries. The fact is that only American banks (and only a handful of these) are international in this sense, with branches staffed by competent officers in every continent. As yet, no one else can offer so much.

U.S. corporations are so fond of big multi-national money schemes that one chemical company formed its own bank. This is Dow Chemical, the fourth largest in the industry in the U.S., which for years after the second war remained in the Midwest, but rapidly became overseas-minded after about 1959, and now operates in Europe through Dow Chemicals Europe, based in Zurich. Dow went into European banking in 1963, buying a forty per cent share of a small Amsterdam bank, Mendes Gans, then two years later put down $23 million to found the Dow Banking Corporation in Switzerland. This wasn't to finance Dow's operations in Europe, but Dow's customers in the U.S., and especially the medium-sized company in search of medium-term loans. The bank makes profits of its own ('Dow doesn't touch anything that doesn't make money,' said a director, not smiling), but by serving clients and potential clients of the chemical business, it can bind them closer to the Dow empire. A firm that wants to borrow from Dow Banking might become a customer of Dow Chemicals in the process.

Dow Banking has a service contract with a Swiss bank in Zurich which does most of the paperwork, and it uses Mendes Gans in Amsterdam as a clearing house for money, enabling the Dow group to keep tighter control of its funds, and so reduce its cash requirements in Europe by several million dollars. As well as the bank, Dow has a Swiss holding company to look after its overseas investments; and when it wanted to borrow long-term money in Europe, it did the usual thing and formed a subsidiary, Dow Chemical Overseas Capital Corporation, to issue the bonds. One would expect a group as large as Dow to be clever with money, but the point here is that in Europe its financial strategy is based on the assumption that it is dealing with a single region.

The Americans arrived when Europe was in any case questioning and revising its financial strategies. Industry must run faster to stay in the same place; it has to be socially respectable (benefits for the workers) and technologically progressive; it faces hard, expensive opposition in a hard, expensive world, selling in open markets against international competitors. European companies have become more demanding of their bankers and stock exchanges, and the strain has shown up weaknesses in local systems, both for raising long-term money (hence the endless complaints about and inquiries into 'Europe's capital market') and for borrowing cash over shorter periods. Either the money isn't readily available via the stock exchanges and banks, or the machinery for passing it on to the borrower turns out to be defective.

A different Britain might have been able to exploit this situation, to its own and Europe's advantage. Frustration still nags some City men because they know that London has efficient money-raising machinery but not the money to go with it. Britain isn't wealthy enough to lend to Europe; if it was, then the London Stock Exchange would be open to long-term borrowers all over the continent. Similarly, a rich and expansionist Britain might have peppered the Continent with banks, whose resources and experience would have helped to find short-term finance for industry as it flowered again after the war.

But all this is an impossible dream that has never had the slightest chance of coming true. Europe has had to manage as best it can, each country with its own banks and its own stock exchange of greater or lesser capacity. It is thanks to the Americans that one can now detect the faint lines of a single financial network, superimposed on the map. The enormous balance-of-payment debts that they have run up with the rest of the world have provided a pool of unspent dollars, the Eurodollar market, that serves many countries at once. (The world's confidence in the United States has let these dollar claims remain uncashed. The confidence was badly shaken in 1968, as the debts mounted and dollar-holders lost their nerve and went in for gold instead). With no individual capital market able to cope, Eurodollar loans can be floated instead. And as American industry began to move into Europe, often financing itself out of this Eurodollar market, the American banks came too, an invasion of salesmen and technicians, bringing new techniques and a boundless belief in themselves.

Like so many American business men, they look young even when they aren't; frequently they not only look it, but are. At the beginning of 1968, Chase Manhattan's London branches were being run by a vice president of thirty-eight, its Paris branch by one of thirty-five. The oldest European vice-president was in Belgium; he was forty-four. At that time, Chase employed something over 800 people at its principal branches in London, Germany and Paris (it also had offices in Madrid, Rome and Geneva, and affiliated banks in Belgium and Holland). Only sixty-six of these were 'officers' as opposed to 'staff', and only twenty-four of the officers were Americans. All the U.S. banks in all their manifestations—branches, representative offices, affiliates—probably employ no more than 200 American officers in Europe. It just seems like more.

An article in *Fortune* in the waiting room (Morgan Guaranty, Brussels) has a sentence heavily underlined: *The central feature of our life today is change.* They believe in being explicit. Asked about his intentions in the Paris branch of another bank, an official opens his diary and extracts a folded sheet of paper, on which he has noted down points from a speech by Sir Paul Chambers, then chairman of Britain's I.C.I. He reads aloud: 'To delegate responsibility and tolerate errors among subordinates within reason and without inquest.' He hasn't answered the question, but he refolds the paper and snaps the diary shut as though he has. An English banker would be embarrassed to be caught rattling off such an explicit statement, but the American doesn't have this kind of inhibition. It's like the open-plan arrangement of officers' desks in one large room which American banks favour. The executive vice-president hurries past the visitor, sitting on the black leather sofa in the waiting area, and says, 'I've got New York on the line. I'll be with you in just two seconds.' A European banker would close the door, but there aren't any doors here to close. The visitor sits and listens. It's a bad line. The conversation is about money being transferred to them for the account of a Mrs H——, initial unclear. 'Is that Zee as in Zebra? Oh, Vee as in Victoria.' The vice-president is flattening his ear with the telephone.

'You're sure it's dollars?' he says. 'You're sure? The reason I'm so insistent is that last week they called from New York and there was the most awful mix-up over francs and dollars.' The conversation ends, the banker smiles; he is perfectly at ease.

Among Europeans, their manner combines assurance with deference. They know that local bankers are at best touchy, at worst hostile. They talk about the importance of behaving well. 'We want to be good corporate citizens of the countries we're in. It's a good platitude and sometimes we pay lip service to it, but I think it's true,' said a Morgan Guaranty man in London. They like to have been somewhere a long time, which is the case with a few branches of the larger banks. Morgan Guaranty has been in the City since 1897. 'We've been in London long enough to own a freehold. I like to state that. I don't think it gives us any more take-home pay but it makes us feel better.'

Though it's only in the last ten or fifteen years that they have made a real impact, not all the U.S. banks are newcomers. Of the twenty or so American banks now in London, five have been there since before the Second World War, besides Morgan Guaranty. But the Continent had few American bankers until less than ten years ago. In 1961 there were still only six branches of U.S. banks in Europe outside London; now there are more than thirty. The self-assured transatlantic banker is still a comparatively new figure in Europe.

What is surprising isn't that the bankers have streamed into Europe but that they took so long about it. The reasons go back to an American tradition of insularity, which (for example) prevented foreign banks from opening branches in New York until as late as 1961. Even now, only a handful of States admit foreign banks. Long after the dollar had outstripped sterling as the world's leading currency,

New York failed to develop as an international centre in the same way as London; today New York remains more restrictive than the City, which might have been left far behind as a world centre if the Americans had behaved differently.[1]

In the end, circumstances dragged them into world banking. Countries everywhere looked to the United States for finance, and New York banks lent heavily after about 1960. So many foreign borrowers went to New York that in 1964 the U.S. Government virtually stopped all such borrowing there by means of bond-issues. The borrowers then concentrated on getting the money from banks, and for the first time, the big American banks found themselves deep in the international lending business. This, too, was curbed later on, but by now the Manhattan bankers had seen new horizons.

They went to Europe, partly to service the American companies that were setting up there, partly to enlarge the business of lending to foreign borrowers. It was a natural progression. The first international centre for raising money had been London; then it had been New York, until the scale of American spending overseas, including military costs in the Far East, forced the U.S. Government to clamp down. Borrowers turned in desperation to the unspent dollars that were circulating outside America, thus creating the Eurodollar market, and American banks realised that by operating in Europe, they could have a share of it. It was, after all, their own currency that was providing the raw material. They could, and did, borrow dollars in Europe and send them back to America when funds were short there.

All these were positive reasons for going abroad. There was also the negative reason that American banks are confined by law to a small area—at most a single State, and usually less. To expand in what Europeans would regard as a normal fashion, with chains of branch offices, is difficult or impossible in their own country: they must go overseas. The Bank of America is the largest in the world because it happens to be in California, which is large, rich and allows

[1] Another disadvantage isn't the fault of the Americans—the time element, which means that London, Frankfurt and the rest have been trading for hours before New York starts work. European time is five or six hours ahead of New York's. When Wall Street opens for the day, it's already the middle of the afternoon in Europe. This fact alone is probably enough to prevent New York from becoming a money centre for the whole world.

banks to have State-wide branches. Founded in 1904 by an Italian vegetable merchant in San Francisco, it now has deposits of $21 billion and nearly 1,000 branches in California, with another sixty-three outside the United States. Chase Manhattan and First National City Bank, the other two comparable giants, are both confined to New York City. Both have opened many overseas branches, and First National City (often called 'Citibank') has the record in Europe, with branches in London, Paris, Berlin, Frankfurt, Hamburg, Athens, Geneva, Zurich, Milan, Rome, Dublin, Brussels, Antwerp and Amsterdam. Morgan Guaranty Trust Co. of New York, which specialises in company clients and doesn't cater for small personal accounts, has a long history in Europe. It is established in Britain, France, Germany, Belgium and Italy, and has a minority interest in a Dutch bank. Two other New York banks which have been in Europe long enough to be familiar names are Manufacturers Hanover and Bankers Trust, which both opened in London in 1922.

But some of the others were unknown on the Continent except to the *cognoscenti* until recently. Names like Crocker-Citizens National Bank of San Francisco, United California Bank of Los Angeles and Mellon National Bank & Trust Co. of Pittsburgh are now part of the scene; medium-sized by American standards, these three (and others besides) are big fish in Europe. The smallest of them, Mellon National Bank, is larger than, for instance, Germany's Dresdner Bank, Italy's Banco di Roma or the Swiss Bank Corporation. Other American banks, yet to move out of their local strait-jacket and set up shop in Europe, believe in letting their names be known by advertising there. The British business man flipping through his copy of the *Economist* will eventually get to the National Bank of Detroit or the Northern Trust Co. of Chicago.

It's not surprising that the older generation of bankers in Europe is rather nervous about the future. They see themselves being colonised—the most extreme remark I heard was made, predictably enough, by a Swiss, one of his country's senior bankers, who delivered a blast at the Americans for daring to open *branches* in Europe instead of behaving like good old-fashioned Europeans, and being satisfied with correspondent relationships. 'It's the same story everywhere,' he said. 'The Americans create a little enclave. They have a club and a school and their shops and their animals. It's understandable if they do this in Africa, but why do it in Europe? It creates the feeling that there might have been in the colonies a hundred years ago. We are not colonies. Naturally, on the whole we have to accept the American presence, and we do it gladly and willingly. Not if it's overdone.'

But the Americans are innovators, and they have to be copied. The Bank of America led the way into credit cards in 1959, and their use (despite some second thoughts about the joys of the cashless society, thanks to massive abuse of the system), is spreading rapidly in Europe. Rumbustious advertising aimed at the humble citizen was first developed in America, as a means of getting at untapped money in the affluent suburbs (one famous slogan, 'You have a friend at Chase Manhattan,' is said to have brought the sour response from a rival banker, 'How starved for affection can you be?'). Europe, in turn, is now learning that you have to be nice to the middle-class customer if you want his money.

American lending techniques are being practised in a dozen European centres, accelerating the move away from the old notion that lending and borrowing were solemn rituals enacted in whispers between the banker and his client. Industry is increasingly anxious to borrow money for a few years at a time, and the Americans are skilled at arranging these medium-term loans, which they enclose in largely foolproof agreements between bank and borrower. The company gets the money after its future has been examined with a microscope. The bank will inspect the industry in general and the management of the particular company; it will want detailed financial projections, and these have to be fulfilled if the agreement is to continue. In the United States, this type of rigidly defined term-lending has already replaced much bond market borrowing because companies find it simpler and cheaper; now the Americans are doing it in Europe, mainly with American subsidiaries but occasionally with local companies. Some companies have been refused because they won't be tied by a formal loan agreement. 'I guess they feel it's a question of their integrity,' said a Chicago banker, adding charitably that European managements must find it disturbing to have their affairs so rigorously examined.

'The idea of projection in planning is alien to most companies round here,' said a Citibank man in a Benelux country. 'Or look at the German situation, which is entirely alien to thinking ahead. A company builds up a big debt to a bank and thinks, OK, next year it'll be a bit bigger—why worry? With obvious exceptions among the larger companies, projection tends to be regarded on the Continent as American gimmickry, a red-tape exercise to make the banker happy. But it isn't just fencing, as they seem to think, it's aimed at getting a genuine forecast. The loan will be for a fixed period, probably with a series of covenants which will invalidate it if they're broken. The object is to make the company think clearly and behave properly. It says, "Lend us five million," and the bank says, "OK, if you can show us your prospects." The company says, "Oh boy, it's going to be peaches and cream." The bank says, "OK, prove it."'

Another New York banker was half amused and half alarmed by the situation in Hamburg, where there are many long-established import-export houses. 'They get terribly insulted if you're not prepared to lend them more money than they've got in the business. They say, "We've been here two hundred years," and this is supposed to make them good for credit. You ask them for their cash-flow projections, and they throw you out of the office.'

So that they can evaluate an industry without having to take other people's word for it, some U.S. banks have specialists on the payroll—engineers, chemists, geologists—and the banks organise themselves by major trades and industries as well as geographically. There is usually a big petroleum and natural-gas division at head office; the bank's security for a loan to an oil company may be oil that's still in the ground, and the bank will have technologists to advise on the oilfields, and economists to advise on likely price movements. There will be specialists in chemicals and transport, aerospace and textiles.

Americans are obsessed with the need to acquire information so that decisions can be arrived at on the basis of full evidence. Many loans are straightforward, but where there's need for scrutiny, it can be alarmingly detailed. Bankers nose into balance sheets and backrooms; they visit factories and cross-examine managements, processing their information on computers, dreaming of the day when the truth about every company and every industry will be stored on tape, available at the push of a button. This makes some industrialists uneasy even in America, but in Europe it sounds like a nightmare.

Outside Britain, companies are not used to disclosing full information to stock exchange authorities, as a condition of raising capital, or to banks when borrowing money, if they can possibly help it.

Europe clings to its secretiveness over money. The concept of 'credit-worthiness,' now part of the American way of life, is still regarded with suspicion. It is not nice to inquire too closely into whether Citizen X is a fit person to have a hire-purchase contract, or whether a shopkeeper can be trusted with a month's credit. Britain accepts the new order to a limited degree. The feeling lingers that to have, say, a national register of bad debtors is taking things a bit far: is there no quiet corner where a man can be dishonest in peace? But finance companies have come to accept the need for reliable 'status information', and banks are accustomed to phrasing cautious judgments for inquirers—'the banker tries to be honest,' said a branch manager in London, 'but he will phrase the thing in such a way that only another banker will know what he's getting at. I suppose the highest endorsement we can give is to say that "this man is considered highly respectable and trustworthy". I suppose the worst we can say is that "we cannot speak for your inquiry".'

On the Continent they are more cautious still. 'I suppose,' said an official at the Banca Ambrosiano in Milan, 'we are an underdeveloped area when it comes to information. Banks are not anxious to talk about their clients. We know that in England and the United States, it is possible to ring up a banker and ask him about a client. Here, if we are asked about a company that is good, we say it is good, and if it is not good, we still say it is good.'

Americans shake their heads at such charity, arguing that the only persons and companies it protects are the crooked and the unsuccessful. 'They have about five stock phrases in Europe to describe the condition of companies,' said a Citibank vice-president. 'About the worst is a negative thing—*we have no insight into the company*—that means, I was there yesterday, and the creditors were carrying out the furniture. In the United States, if one banker asks another about a company, the first thing he does is to give a borrowing history—*we have regularly lent up to five figures unsecured without any difficulty* and so on. Or he might reply, *payment has been slow and management has not been regarded as taking an active part in the company*. That isn't regarded as proper in Europe, yet the only guy who benefits from this situation is the guy who isn't doing so well. So why should we protect the soft ones?'

The European situation is perhaps not quite what is seems, since bad business news travels fast in a small country, without the need for formal inquiries. But this small-town approach belongs to the past, and already American bankers can be heard explaining with satisfaction how they wheedled a piece of information out of a tight-lipped European by offering him another piece of information in exchange. 'He told me the usual stuff about good character and sound business and growing sales,' said an American in Hamburg, 'until I volunteered a few facts I thought he'd like to know, at which point he saw there might be something in it for him if *he* talked to *me*.'

Europeans will soon learn to accept status-inquiries—they have no option, now that the Americans make it standard practice. All these American techniques will have their effect, both on industries and on the money-men who help to finance them; there will be more information, more cold calculation, more financial technicians. Bigness will have the usual effect. Banks would be merging in Europe in any case, since the tendency throughout industry is to form larger units, but the American example drives everyone to move faster. U.S. banks not only open offices of their own but often buy their way into existing banks, and so gain control of a chain of long-established branches overnight. The Bank of America owns the Banca d'America e d'Italia in Italy, with eighty-five branches, and banks in Athens, Geneva and Madrid. Chase Manhattan has bought a share in the London-based Standard Bank, with more than a thousand branches in Africa. It has a half-share of the Banque de Commerce in Belgium, with eighteen branches, and a smaller share in the Nederlandsche Credietbank of Holland, with sixty. U.S. banks have so many participations in European money-centres that for every visible nameplate on a door there's sure to be an invisible stake somewhere else. The Americans are also well represented in the banking groups formed to operate in Eurodollars.

The attitudes of Europeans range from anger to admiration. German bankers, who would have kept all foreigners out if they could have done so after the second war, are among the angriest. A director of the Dresdner Bank conceded that Europe needed to change its approach—'When the European meets competition he thinks, "What can I do to avoid it?" When the American meets it he thinks, "What can I do to be more aggressive?"' But a moment later he was saying slyly that the customers of German banks knew which side their bread was buttered. 'It may be true that they have to pay us a little more for our services than they would pay an American bank,' he said. 'They don't mind this as long as they know that in a crisis the bank will be ready to help them. After all, we can't guarantee that if customers get credit from Citibank, and the bank asks for it back, *we'll* step in and help them.'

But it's likely that the angriest phase is over. The wave of incoming American banks was already past its peak in 1968 when the U.S. imposed restrictions on dollar investment overseas which will reduce the flow of new bankers still further. The invaders have settled in and will expand from inside Europe—servicing American subsidiaries as they grow, and taking as much local business as they can get. British banks in the City have been dismayed to see their American neighbours acquiring hundred of millions of pounds in deposits from holders of sterling. The only sterling that the Americans are guaranteed is the remittance-money being paid in by U.S. subsidiaries in Britain. Usually this is changed into dollars at once on the foreign-exchange market, and sent back to the parent company in the United States. As an oilman put it, 'The rule is, send the money home to Daddy as soon as you've earned it.' So it doesn't stay in London long enough to be of much use to the bank. But by attracting money from British companies or from holders of sterling anywhere in the world, the American branches in London can put themselves in business as lenders of sterling on the home banks' own territory. This is what hurts the natives. The same will apply in any country where, as is beginning to happen, they can attract local deposits.

The Americans are in Europe to stay, but it's too early to say how successfully the European money-men will compete with them. The formation of banks like the Barclays group in London and the Banque Nationale de Paris is part of the response, though no one seems to know exactly *how* the new European giants (or dinosaurs according to their enemies, who are bored with bigness) will compete. For British banks, a positive advantage in size is that the Americans are legally forbidden to lend more than 10 per cent of their capital and reserves to any one customer; British banks can lend up to the hilt to a single customer.

But in general the trouble is that the merchant banks and *banques d'affaires* are usually the internationally-minded ones, and they are comparatively small. The big European banks don't believe in being great adventurers outside their own country; or if they believe in it, they are still badly equipped for the task.

The Deutsche Bank, the Banca Nazionale del Lavoro, the Crédit Lyonnais and the rest are preoccupied with domestic business. Even Britain, the old adventurer, cuts a poor figure on the Continent. British banks have the resources but not the temperament—or the exchange-control freedom to spend freely abroad. Merchant banks have been busy creating new links and improving old ones with the Continent,[2] but it's a slow infiltration rather than an invasion. The clearing banks are represented by branches that are well established but rigidly confined within each country.

On paper the total of about fifty branches looks impressive, and outnumbers the American figure. But the British network has less steam behind it. More than half the branches are in France, where Barclays (France) alone has nineteen. Barclays are there by accident; in the first world war a bank called Cox's went with the Army to provide military banking facilities, and this was later taken over by Barclays. Lloyds Bank Europe, due to be part of the Barclays group, has another nine branches in France, and the Westminster five. The Riviera is particularly well served. There is a little cluster of British banks in Hamburg, where they have been established since early this century. Barclays DCO is there, and so are three of the other British overseas banks—the Chartered, Hongkong and Shanghai, and Standard. These offices do have an international flavour, since much of their business is in trade finance, or in making loans to German firms who want to borrow Eastern currencies, rather than run the risk of buying them with marks and then finding them devalued. The

[2] Kleinwort Benson in Brussels and Geneva. S. G. Warburg & Co in Frankfurt and a Warburg stake in a Zurich bank. Hill, Samuel interests in Switzerland and Spain. A Hambros subsidiary in Zurich, and interests in the Banca Privata Finanziaria of Milan and the Compagnie Privée de Banque in Paris. Samuel Montagu in Guyerzeller Zurmont of Zurich. A Schroders subsidiary in Zurich. Morgan Grenfell in Morgan & Cie. of Paris. Lazards and Rothschilds both have long-standing connections with their opposite numbers in Paris.

Chartered Bank says it handles more dollars than the Bank of England, because the sterling-area countries where it operates sell such quantities of rubber, tin and other commodities. Its Hamburg branch is busy but the bank hardly belongs in Europe in the way that Citibank does; a coloured print of its armorial bearings is framed in glass beside the inquiry desk, a reminder of the past, informing visitors that in its coat of arms, 'Britain is indicated by the familiar figure of Britannia, India by an elephant and palm tree, Australia by a golden fleece representing her prosperity through the wool industry, and China by her characteristic vessel, the junk.' Banks like this are still important, but they grew up in a different world.

Meeting British bankers on the Continent, one often catches a breath of resignation, a feeling of 'Oh, well . . .' Bankers of all nationalities are careful to play down the extent to which they solicit business in other people's countries, but the British sound as if they really mean it. The Americans are forever stopping by and visiting with—not, they will say disarmingly, to pinch someone else's business, but just to make themselves known. If the local companies are also large enough to qualify as international, then the Americans are uninhibited. 'As far as we're concerned,' said a Morgan Guaranty man in London, 'international British corporations are fair game.' Since dozens of ambitious firms in Europe are now anxious to be thought of as international, this category alone is enough to keep the Americans busy.

But the British cough and look out of the window and say gruffly that they don't behave like the Americans. The typical American banker in Europe seems to be aged about thirty-five, ex Harvard Business School, having previously served in Siam or Saudi Arabia or both. Behind him is a corps of specialists. The typical Briton is fifteen years older, and seems to belong in a suburb rather than a capital city. Perhaps I met an unfair cross-section, but several of the dozen or so branch-bankers I spoke to on the Continent were charming men with a dying fall in their voices. 'We rather regard the Americans as cowboys. Their methods are rougher . . . I've called on I.C.I. and British Petroleum, and I hope to get some of their business in time, but they say, as so many of them say, that they've had good treatment from the local banks for years, and I quite understand this.'

In one curious episode, Barclays in Belgium was outmanoeuvred by Chase Manhattan from a position it had held in a local bank for many years. This was the Banque de Commerce, of which Barclays had rather less than a half-share until 1963, when it sold its holding to Belgium's second largest bank, the Banque de Bruxelles, in exchange for a small share of the latter. Barclays continued to use the Banque de Commerce for its operations in Belgium; its headquarters are in Antwerp, which has one of the thickest concentrations of new industry on the Continent. Antwerp overshadows Hamburg as a port, and American banks are anxious to get a foothold there. It's rather more important than the Riviera. Barclays, one might have thought, was lucky to have its long-standing interest in the Antwerp bank. But in 1965, the Banque de Bruxelles, by now in full control of the Banque de Commerce, increased the capital of the latter and offered the extra stock to Chase Manhattan, This left Barclays in what it felt was an impossible position, and eventually it moved out—as an official in London put it, 'we picked up our skirts and left'. By 1967 the Chase ads were showing smiling bankers against a background of blue skies and white spires, with the announcement that 'Now, in Belgium too, you have a friend at Chase Manhattan. New association with Banque de Commerce adds Brussels and Antwerp to the Chase world-wide banking network.' Barclays was left with a 'representative office' in Brussels.

Europe's money-men are on the defensive, most of all because they are still divided into national camps. The prospect of Europe's money-centres being run by Americans may be remote, but the possibility that in ten years' time they will have a far more commanding position than at present is real enough. Perhaps this is to be welcomed and not feared. But however Europe feels about it, the Americans have already made plain what they intend to do. As bankers and investment advisers, they are in Europe to stay. And Europe, for them, is one place, not many.

9 *How to Raise Billions*

(i) The Stock Exchanges

Of all the works of financial man, none is more splendidly elaborate than the mechanism for raising money on a stock exchange. Europe, as usual, has an unrivalled confusion of systems, side by side. Simple in theory—a company or a government raises money against the security of pieces of paper, which can then be traded in—the mechanism is designed to a different specification in every centre, with rules and customs to emphasise that it occupies a special little world of its own. Women stockbrokers are unknown; the world is male and traditional. 'We don't need skirts in here,' said one jolly broker in London, just after a members' poll had rejected a proposal to admit females to 'the floor of the house'—the dealing-area of the Exchange. 'As one wag remarked last week, women are all right in bed, but they're no use on the floor.'

Each stock exchange has its own flavour. Government influences range from powerful (France) to weak (Britain). In Belgium they have to wear lapel badges complete with photograph, so there can be no mistaking who they are, which gives them a hunted look. Every stock exchange is noisy but in Paris and Milan it sounds like a zoo. Banks may run the market, as in Germany, or share it with grumbling stockbrokers, as in Holland, or play no direct part, as in Britain. Advertising by stockbrokers is generally frowned upon, though some stock exchanges advertise themselves in a general sort of way. Frankfurt has a publicity film in which an old gentleman with a red face wants to invest 20,000 marks because it's his birthday. London tempts the young with a film starring the Koobas, a pop group.[1] Amsterdam has a film that is so old, they won't show it.

Bearer shares are popular everywhere on the Continent, in some places more than others. They make tax-dodging easier, and, although more trouble to look after than 'registered' shares on the British and American pattern, where the certificate itself is worthless, they give the owners something bright and material to keep in the bank or under the bed. Belgium has nothing else; only a few German companies issue registered shares; France has both; shares in Italy are usually registered but bonds are in bearer form.

Not all stockbrokers are rich, but enough of them are affluent to make a seat on a stock exchange, when a man is in business on his own account, desirable; a well-established broker, looking after the investments of wealthy families, can make a comfortable living without exerting himself. No one competes for places as they do in the United States, where the rewards are so ample that a seat on the New York Stock Exchange was sold not long ago for nearly half a million dollars[2]—this isn't the entrance fee, which is something else again, but the supply-and-demand price that the outgoing member can obtain from one of those who are clamouring to get in. A seat in London can fetch a modest price when auctioned, up to a couple of thousand pounds if it's a good year for business; otherwise Europeans expect to enter a stock exchange by means that may include ballots, examinations (due to be introduced in London within a few years), guarantees of integrity and knowledge of the right people.

A broker in Milan (where they rank as public officials, nominated by the State) said that in an exceptional year like 1960, it was 'not

[1] Called *Money-go-Round*, this is a distinct improvement on an earlier and stuffier effort, still showing, called *My Word Is My Bond*. *Money-go-Round* begins with a woman having a piece of fish wrapped up in the *Financial Times*, and moves on to a fantasy in which two teenagers have the Stock Exchange and its marvels explained, with pop-art props and deafening music. Sample lyric: 'Today's stockbroker doesn't always live on a yacht in Monte Carlo/In fact he has been known to rent a council house in Harlow.' (Asked whether a stockbroker really has been known to rent a council house in Harlow, the artisan 'New Town' north of London, a Stock Exchange spokesman said 'Actually, no.')

[2] The highest price ever paid for a seat was $625,000 in February 1929, the fantasy-year, when business was booming. Eight months later came the stock market crash of 'Black Tuesday,' October 29.

uncommon' for a man to have an income of eighty or ninety million lire, say £60,000, though in a bad year it might fall to a tenth of this. In Paris a broker said that a reasonably successful member of the exchange would expect to make about £12,000 a year, before tax, plus substantial expenses which would cover things like a car, and hunting parties to entertain clients. In Paris, too, the stockbroker, known here as an *agent de change*, is officially nominated. He must pass an examination, have had practical experience of the work, and, for good measure, not be a deserter from the French Army. There's a little nepotism, of course. But times had changed, said an *agent de change*. Formerly, if an *agent* had a couple of sons, the duller one followed in his footsteps. Now they were getting quite intellectual: the brighter son followed in his footsteps instead.

The fact that some brokers are clever, diligent and knowledgeable, and that not all of them are wealthy, does little in Britain to change the popular idea of the stockbroker as a sinister plutocrat with a long cigar. The Americans are more at home with investments and in general are less envious of the rich. On the Continent the stock exchanges are less important in the economy, and so attract a smaller degree of attention; if a money-man is going to be abominated, it's likely to be the big fat banker rather than the big fat stockbroker. But Britain combines an important stock exchange, once the centre of the world's money-raising, with a streak of puritanism about wealth. The combination of activity and squeamishness has turned the London Stock Exchange into what must be the most thin-skinned financial institution in the world, sensitive to insult and desperately anxious to show how good and useful and well-behaved it is. I once wrote a television script in which I spoke of 'the smell of money' at the Stock Exchange. A few minutes before recording the commentary in the studio, a telephone call came from a senior official of the television company, who had been approached by a still more senior official, personally connected with the Stock Exchange. Official 1 had asked official 2 to ask me if I could possibly modify the script a little, and make it the *odour* of money instead of the *smell;* that would have been more acceptable.

Europe's assortment of stock exchanges has been written about at enormous length in the past fifteen years, not directly but in the abstract terms of 'Europe's capital market.' There is no such thing as a European capital market, which is why so much is written about it. Each capital market is self-contained and run as part of a national money-system, its efficiency varying from place to place almost as much as the idiosyncracies of the stock exchanges—which are the mechanism of the markets—vary. As Europe feels its way towards unity, the need to harmonize financial institutions looms up as one of the nastiest obstacles that has to be overcome. At the same time, the condition of capital markets on the Continent, in a period when industry's need of money is growing, has directed attention to their weaknesses. Books, articles, speeches, reports and surveys all come to roughly the same conclusion, that what is needed is for every stock exchange to improve itself along generally agreed lines, gradually removing impediments to mutual trading, so that efficiency and unity will arrive together. This happy ending may be achieved one day, but there are few signs of it at present.

London is in a special category, with a stock exchange (supported by a chain of provincial exchanges) that is generally agreed to handle a large amount of business with satisfying efficiency, and to operate an effective capital market that is in the same class as New York's, though much smaller and rather less professional. Turnover on the London exchange in 1967 was £38 billion; gilt-edged stocks (where the Government is borrowing money from investors for a fixed period) accounted for most of this, but the equity market (representing money invested permanently in industrial and commercial companies) had a turnover of about £6 billion. New issues of securities by industry—either equity shares, which are more of a gamble, or fixed-interest stock, where the company is borrowing for a given period—have totalled £600 or £700 million a year in Britain recently. In London, Government borrowing makes up most of the total; on the New York Stock Exchange, nearly all the money is being raised for industry (in addition, New York has the American Stock Exchange, doing an enormous volume of business).

The London Stock Exchange has 3,300 members, some surviving in one- or two-man firms, but increasingly grouped in bigger partnerships. It's an enormous membership, higher than that of all the Continental exchanges and New York's put together. New York manages with about 1,300 members (it's not surprising that seats are so expensive, since the 1,300 are sharing considerably more business than in London). The largest individual memberships on the Continent are in Belgium (more than 500, all brokers) and Amsterdam (more than 400, some brokers and some nominated by banks). Milan has 130 brokers, Paris just over eighty. Zurich has fewer than thirty full members, nearly all banks and other institutions. German exchanges have a membership made up of a small number of official traders and a larger number of bank representatives; Frankfurt has about 250 altogether.[3]

Of London's 3,300 members, about 500 are technically stockjobbers—middlemen who specialise in particular kinds of security, which they deal in as principals, for their own account, instead of on behalf of clients. Stockbrokers, acting for clients, don't buy and sell direct with one another, but deal through the intermediary of jobbers. The system, which is peculiar to London, is supposed to make for flexibility, but has been running into trouble because jobbers can't command the resources they once did, in the days of lower taxes, and which they need in order to be able to 'run a book' in hundreds of securities. Some very large stockjobbing firms have now been formed.

Another sign of change in London has been the enterprise of stockbrokers in going outside Britain altogether. A few firms have set up on the Continent, in places where they think they are most likely to attract British investment business—Paris, Geneva, Brussels, Zurich, Luxembourg and—useful for expatriates—Lisbon and Malta. But the boldest move came at the end of 1967, when Cazenove, one of the largest London firms, paid $50,000 for a seat on the Pacific Coast Stock Exchange, with trading floors in Los Angeles and San Francisco. Other London brokers followed, looking, among other things, for British clients living in the United States with money to invest all over the world. The idea of a British invasion doesn't please American stockbrokers, though after their penetration of Europe they can hardly complain if somebody else does it to them.

[3] Other cities have less important exchanges. Britain has sizeable exchanges in Scotland, the North and Midlands, and some smaller ones; there is an exchange as far off the beaten track as Cork in southern Ireland. Some of the provincial stockbrokers have emerged as serious rivals to London in recent years. Germany has seven exchanges besides Frankfurt, notably Dusseldorf and Hamburg, and France has seven outside Paris. Milan does three-quarters of the stock-exchange business in Italy, but the country has nine other exchanges; if you know where to look, there are eight stockbrokers in Venice.

The European stockbroker's attitude to publicity is something else that may be changing. The New York Stock Exchange helps to organise more than a thousand lectures a year. Speakers from Merrill Lynch address more than 200,000 people annually.[4] Scores of American stockbrokers have set up European offices to cope with growing demand for U.S. securities—Merrill Lynch is in more than a dozen cities, including Cannes and Athens as well as the more obvious ones—and their advertising can be seen all over the Continent. But local stockbrokers are either forbidden to advertise or they don't want to bother—the distinction isn't always clear, but the result is the same. A Paris broker complained that until the rules were changed in 1967, he couldn't even display his name outside the office. The council of the London Stock Exchange has asked members what they think and concluded that they don't want advertising, though a strong minority is certainly in favour.

What has happened in London, and to some extent in Continental centres, is that the Stock Exchange publicises itself as an institution. London will run a newspaper ad with a girl in a flowered mini-skirt, waving balloons, soliciting new business in a rather unhopeful tone of voice—'If you don't know a stockbroker and feel it's now time to become an investor, write to the Stock Exchange . . . for a list of member firms from which to choose.' Visitors can stand in a windowed gallery and look down on the floor, pausing to hear a pretty girl describe the scene before they move on to see the Koobas. In Frankfurt, younger bankers have been prodding a reluctant old-guard into publicising the exchange. The literature for visitors isn't very inspiring:

Visitor: What is happening now? Does the sound of the bell mean that the session is about to begin?

Guide: Quite right, Sir. The session begins at 12 noon and goes on till 2 p.m.

Parties from schools, banks and women's organisations can be seen at stock exchanges, trying to understand the guide as she ex-

[4] *Time* magazine reports a combined fashion show and sales talk. 'Says the fashion commentator: "Aren't they lovely? These are opaque crepes by Hanes called Flower Pow." At which point the Merrill Lynch man interjects: "Hanes—now there's an interesting stock! Our research division gives it a good quality rating and Hanes's outlook is improved by the demand for panty hose".' Women control just over half all the stock issued in the U.S.

plains the difference between a *Kursmakler* (specialist) and a *freie Makler* (floor trader) in Frankfurt, or why it is that in Paris some shares are dealt with in comparative quiet around a velvet-topped enclosure, the *corbeille*, while others involve standing in a mass of bodies in front of blackboards and dealing *a la criée*, which means howling at the top of your voice. Visitors to some exchanges can circulate among the dealers, suitably accompanied, and get close enough to feel the hot breath and sharp elbows. One sees the point of keeping visitors isolated in a nice little glass gallery, as in London; too much exposure to the bellowing and sprinting might alarm potential investors. (In Paris, the banker who was showing me around spoke to a colleague, then put his lips to my ear and shouted, 'He says you can understand much more when you're in the *middle* of the crowd.' It was all hands and elbows, like a rush-hour train on the Métro, without stations. As we were going we passed a man with his head bandaged. 'I wouldn't be surprised if someone threw him down the stairs,' said the banker).

Advertising and publicity have a large potential audience in Europe of people who could be investors but aren't. The United States has twenty-two million direct investors. France has about 750,000. Italy, according to one report, makes do with 300,000. Even Britain has only 2,500,000. But the real shortage of investors on the Continent is of those who provide the money indirectly, by contributing to private pension funds and life assurance schemes. Britain has an estimated 22,500,000. Their contributions pour in week by week, and investment managers with wide powers put the money into the stock market. These funds and companies, together with unit trusts and investment trusts, are coming to predominate in Britain and the United States.

Dr Segré once pointed out in a speech that 'Efforts to interest, in the securities market, a public for which the world of finance often begins and ends at the doorstep of the local savings bank, can perhaps be successful in the long run. It is quite clear, however, that they could only affect a fraction of total savings, which will always be channelled towards the market by financial institutions. Here is the crux of the problem; the lion's share in this intermediation between savers and the markets in Europe still belongs, to a much larger extent than in the United Kingdom or in the United States, to savings banks and commercial banks (not to mention the postal savings system), while insurance companies, pension funds, investment trusts and other intermediaries oriented towards the long-term capital market still play in many countries a relatively modest role.'

The Continent is short of institutions. Governments run social-security schemes of their own, and the money that does go into private insurance must often be invested in a restricted range of securities. Holland, and Germany to a lesser extent, are the only Common Market countries where insurance-company money is important in the British and American way.

Inflation and wars have blunted the investment habit; countries have been ruined too often; weak stock markets owe something to the mentality that keeps a couple of billion pounds worth of gold hoarded by private owners on the Continent. People save more than they do in the United States, but they put their money into real estate, leave it in banks or lend it to the government and to official agencies against bonds. Governments decide where the money shall go—in a general sense they decide this everywhere, but on the Continent the supply of money for industry is more directly controlled. The stock exchanges are hamstrung. The capitalist machinery clanks away—all that shouting and rushing about is caused by excitement at the thought of making money and anguish at the thought of losing it—but it doesn't run freely. The cost of issuing shares and bonds is high. Governments may decide which issues they will approve, and make tax concessions that give official borrowing an advantage. The best places in the queue are usually pre-empted by official and semi-official borrowers. Coupled with this top-heaviness is a general lack of interest in stock-exchange investment. The tradition is missing and so is the necessary range of specialist banks and brokers. Germany's capital market is comparatively free as far as the Government is concerned, but it's a restricted market—run by a handful of banks, unattractive to investors, and not used by industry to the full.

Many Continentals deny that their capital markets are as bad as this, and they can always produce impressive figures for savings per head, or even for the total issue of securities; what they fail to show is how the savings are then allocated between private industry, nationalised power and transport, house-building and so on. Something that no one can even pretend to deny is that the poor state of company information on the Continent is bad for investment, enabling managements to conceal figures that investors want to know, or *should* want to know. Investment analysis is still rare by U.S. standards. Germany's national association has 136 analyst members, which is fewer than Merrill Lynch have in New York.

Ironically, the State has more direct control over stock exchanges on the Continent than in Britain and the U.S., and a number of governments could presumably press for more information if they wanted to. In France, Italy, Belgium, Germany and Switzerland, the authorities have a close interest in the daily running of stock exchanges.[5] Only Holland has an exchange which is entirely run by a private association, and even here, the Ministry of Finance theoretically has the last word.

The world's leading exchanges, New York and London, are both privately-run. New York has its Board of Governors, with a salaried President. London has its Stock Exchange Council, with an unpaid Chairman. The idea of putting the London exchange under Government control was rejected by a royal commission a century ago, since when the place has survived slumps, share-pushers, dud companies, bankruptcies and other dismal happenings without any serious attempt being made to nationalise it. It is, in fact, even less regulated than stock exchanges in the United States, where the official Securities and Exchange Commission has brooded over the markets since 1933. The S.E.C., with a qualified staff of about 1,000, demands detailed disclosures when a new issue of securities is made, and administers several Acts designed to stop false information and unfair trading. Stock Exchange scandals are not prevented—a series of spectacular episodes, some involving infiltration by the Mafia into a firm of brokers, exploded noisily throughout 1967—but at least the system includes an effective weapon to use against rogues. The stock exchanges are powerful private organisations but they are balanced by powerful federal authorities.

[5] In *France* an Exchange Committee, with the Governor of the Bank of France as chairman, is responsible to the Ministry of Finance. *Italian* exchanges are run by a committee nominated by the Ministry of the Treasury, with inspectors. In *Germany* the exchanges are responsible to the regional governments. In *Belgium* a Government commission supervises exchanges. Exchanges in *Switzerland* are closely supervised by the cantonal authorities.

In London a British-type compromise has left the Stock Exchange to regulate itself. It has done so for the last twenty years with a nervous eye on radical politicians who might interfere; a series of increasingly stringent Companies Acts lays down the basic principles, and the exchange enforces good standards of behaviour and disclosure among companies that want a quotation. Continental exchanges are less concerned with the companies whose shares they trade in—though one country, Belgium, does have a body that's comparable to the S.E.C. This is the Commission Bancaire, set up (like the S.E.C.) after the troubles of the 1930s; all Belgian companies wanting to raise money on the capital market must tell the commission everything it wants to know; but unlike the S.E.C., the commission treats the information as private.

Seen from the outside, it's possible for men from Wall Street or even the City to see the scattering of disconnected Continental exchanges as anachronisms in a developing Europe. Perhaps they are, but they can't be expected to feel it themselves. The fact that a single block of shares worth $20 million has been traded in at New York intrigues them in Milan without making them want to give up hope. In a good year all the Italian exchanges put together have a turnover of about $2 billion, equivalent to about one week's trading on the New York exchange alone. Paris does rather better, with $5 billion. They are small fish beside New York or even London, but each is a national market with its own sharp sense of identity.

What the Eurocrats Want

A unified capital market is the most important forseeable step on the road to a Europe that will have one overall money-policy, not six (or seven, if Britain is included). But even to hint at this raises questions of sovereignty. As a result, the Treaty of Rome, which set up the Common Market in 1958, refers in the relevant article (No. 67) only to the movement of funds between member countries. It says that:

> Member States shall, in the course of the transitional period and to the extent necessary for the proper functioning of the Common Market, progressively abolish as between themselves restrictions on the movement of capital belonging to persons resident in Member States and also any discriminatory treatment based on the nationa-

lity or place of residence of the parties or on the place in which such capital is invested.

Since 1958, exchange-control has been abolished between the Six for 'personal' investment. The Dutchman can buy German shares; the Frenchman can invest in Italy; the Belgian can buy property in France. Any of them can buy U.S. securities if he wishes. No British person can legally do this sort of thing without paying a crippling premium of about one-third the amount of the transaction, and one of the British arguments against Britain entering the E.E.C. has been that as soon as she was in, British investors might start throwing money into Europe, as they would then be allowed to do, and that it would be difficult to stop some of it finding its way into American securities.

Capital movements within the Common Market are free by British standards. But in a full-blown European capital market, a borrower will be able to go wherever he likes to raise his money. A French textile firm might use the Frankfurt Stock Exchange; a Dutch car manufacturer might go to Milan. So far this has not happened much. Governments are afraid of losing control over their own economies if they let in too many foreign borrowers. An escape clause in one E.E.C. directive allows exchange-control by any member of the Six if it finds that freedom over capital movement is an 'obstacle to the realisation of economic objectives.'

Dr Segré once remarked that in the age of Telex, many governments go on taking a coffee-house view of their capital markets. He said it at a conference, not in the Segré Report, which is a circumspect document, wrapping up every criticism in long grey paragraphs that almost but not quite remove the sting. In public all E.E.C. spokesmen are careful to say that the report commits no one. When it came out at the end of 1966 it was deliberately under-publicised because of mutterings from Bonn and Paris. The Germans objected that it criticised their capital market and the dominant part played by the banks; the French objected partly because the report remarked on the way the French Government regulated the stock market to favour its own issues, partly because it recommended a loosening of exchange control that the French were already planning, and announced soon after. (A nice instance of how touchy nations can be about money. 'Debré [the French Finance Minister] was unhappy because we were advocating measures he intended to take,' said a member of the Segré group. 'He hated the idea that he was being put in the position of appearing to do things at the suggestion of the Commission.')

Not only are governments nervous about having their private policies interfered with, but they fear, probably with good reason, that if each separate capital market loses its identity, the all-Europe market that emerges will favour one city and one stock exchange. This would be a nasty knock for the prestige of all the others. The natural place for centralised money-raising would seem (to those who work in it) to be the City, but this is hardly going to raise a cheer in Paris, or even in Frankfurt. At the moment the Continent has nothing to fear, because Britain is too poor to allow foreign borrowing there. But a Britain that was strong enough (or sufficiently propped up by the other Six) to get into the Common Market would immediately become part of the same capital-movement system; and money-men in the City can already be seen, in unbuttoned moments, rubbing their hands with glee at the thought of channelling European stock-exchange business through London.

This, too, is looking well into the future. Capital markets are still divided, and the Eurocrats are still wondering how to set about achieving some of the aims that the Segré Report sets out in 382 pages of small print. This spells out what needs to be done—harmonise tax policies, encourage institutional investors, generally brighten up equity markets—and leaves no one in any doubt that the reason industry in one country doesn't try to raise money in another isn't simply that governments prevent it. The Germans, flush with money, have encouraged others to raise capital there, and in some years foreigners have done so to the extent of several hundred million dollars. In general, though, Europe-wide borrowing is on a small scale; and the reason is primarily that it's awkward, uncertain, poorly organised, and encounters the basic weaknesses of each individual market. Germany invites foreign borrowers to use her capital market, but many of them think it's an inadequate outlet for their shares. The essentially political business of bringing the markets together is inseparable from the essentially technical business of improving them all at the same time.

The commission issues encouraging directives, and a body called the International Federation of Stock Exchanges is nibbling at the question of agreeing common standards. London jollies everyone along with its usual tact. 'The basic concept is to establish a common ethic,' says a member of the Stock Exchange Council, flower glowing in his buttonhole. 'We've had a considerable effect on the French attitude. The Spanish say we've been *most* helpful.' However, each stock exchange continues to go its own way, and a solution has begun to emerge from events rather than discussions. A new type of international capital market has appeared. This is the Eurobond market, which was unheard of ten years ago, but is now flourishing and apparently indispensable: novel, large, well-organised and faintly mysterious. It has no marble-floored stock exchange, busy with brokers and touched with glamour or notoriety, but exists, like the foreign-exchange market, as a presence in many places at once. Outsiders are often intrigued by the fact that it exists at all, but light-hearted attempts to explain what it does are quickly strangled by technicalities. Yet the changes are making important financial history, partly by accident and partly by intention. Eurobonds reflect the new fluidity of money throughout the world; if they didn't exist, it might be necessary to invent them.

10 *How to Raise Billions*

(ii) The Magical Eurobond

Before 1914 there was an 'international capital market' in the sense that borrowers could go to London and other European centres to raise money. This is how the first railways and public utilities were financed in many countries, among them the United States. For years before 1914, £200 million a year was going out of London, most of it into foreign bond-issues on the stock exchange. It was never the same after the first world war, and since the second, Britain's reduced circumstances have virtually excluded her from the foreign capital-raising business, though Commonwealth countries can still make issues through London.

The world badly needed a benefactor after 1945, and the United States was the only possible one. Nearly $13 billion came to Europe as Marshall Aid, and further amounts were raised through New York, borrowed by European governments which issued bonds there. The dollar shortage lasted so long that when it ended, few people realised it at first. But by the early 1960s, U.S. spending around the world—whether on aid, war, industrial investment or tourism—had risen to the point where it outran American earnings. A humbler country might have introduced exchange control; the Americans couldn't risk undermining confidence in the dollar, and so used indirect measures to reduce overseas spending. One way was to cut down foreign borrowing in New York—not by forbidding it, which would have been an open declaration of weakness, but by introducing, in

1964, the interest equalisation tax, which allowed Americans to go on buying foreign securities, but penalised them with a tax when they did. Sharp operators later found ways of evading it, but the tax effectively stopped new issues of foreign securities.

This seemed fair to those American Treasury officials who saw Europe as a prosperous nephew, continuing to scrounge from his rich but hard-working old uncle. The irony of this view, which soon became apparent, was that most of the money that Europe was borrowing in New York turned out to be its own. When the City of Oslo went to the market, the New York investment banks that handled the bonds were likely to sell the majority of them to Europeans, or at least non-United States, dollar-holders. They might be converting their local currencies into dollars in order to buy the bonds; or they might have earned or borrowed the dollars themselves. Europe lacked the financial machinery on a Continental scale that would have allowed dollar borrowers to make contact with dollar lenders, and so it all had to happen in New York.

Some Europeans had seen what was happening even before the interest equalisation tax. Dr Abs at the Deutsche Bank was one of them, but most of the interest, and the action, came initially from London. 'We had always been interested in this market,' said a director of S. G. Warburg, 'and we discovered that if we secured large amounts of the bonds from New York, we could distribute them to other banks and brokers on the Continent. It was a ludicrous situation. We began to notice that when the bonds were traded later on, they weren't traded in New York—their Stock Exchange ticker would be registering the sale of one bond a day or something. So taking our cue from the official American attitude, which was to ask why the hell Europe couldn't organise its own capital market, we asked the American authorities if they would mind if we arranged a sort of offshore operation. They said they didn't mind at all, though they couldn't guarantee that there wouldn't be a howl from Wall Street. And of course, there was.'

Wall Street hated the thought of losing the business but for the moment could do nothing about it. In London, the Bank of England and the Stock Exchange gave permission for the market to deal in the dollar bonds—they had to be quoted somewhere, if only to give some guarantee of respectability. In July 1963, Warburgs headed a group of banks that offered bonds worth $15 million on behalf of Autostrade, the Italian State highways authority. This was the real beginning of the market.

Long-term European borrowers, without a Continental capital market of their own, realised that quantities of dollars were available on the doorstep. Short-term borrowers had already realised this, and the Eurodollar market was taking shape. This supply of money now came to be tapped by long-term borrowers as well. It wasn't only the pool of dollars that created the Eurobond market. All the major European currencies (apart from sterling) are freely convertible, so that investors might be obtaining the dollars in exchange for their own marks or francs, as they had been able to do for years. The important thing was that a reliable system for organising loans in a common currency now came into being. It was the idea that mattered.

At first the securities were called 'Euro-dollar bonds', later shortened to 'Eurobonds.' This is a catch-phrase, not a legal term; Eurobonds are simply dollar bonds in bearer form, issued by whoever is doing the borrowing, usually in units of $1,000, and aimed at non-American buyers. They pay a good rate of interest, currently 6 or 7 per cent, and it arrives without a withholding tax being deducted, which makes it an ideal security for tax-dodging.

For a year or two, the market was used mainly by State and municipal borrowers. Then in 1965, American industry overseas, which was under the same save-dollars pressure that had produced the equalisation tax, turned to it. Instead of sending out dollars from the United States, which was now officially frowned upon, why not borrow the dollars in Europe to finance their foreign expansion? Mobil Oil was the first to do so, and dozens of the biggest firms in America have followed, using Luxembourg subsidiaries at first, and 'Delaware' subsidiaries later on.

To begin with the amounts borrowed were small—$10 million was a lot in the early days. But the companies grew hungrier, the investors had bottomless pockets, and soon twenty and thirty million dollars was normal, with some issues of seventy or eighty million. This is still small beside the capacity of New York, where up to $400 or $500 million can be borrowed at one swoop—a breathtaking amount by European standards. But the Eurobond market has continually upset predictions. In 1967 it raised $1,900 million, of which $527 went to American subsidiaries and $1,100 to European borrowers, which by this time included many industrial companies as well as governments. Citroën cars and British Petroleum, Olivetti and Shell Petroleum, joined the Honeywell computers and the Pepsi-Colas from America. This removed some but not all of the sting from complaints that Eurobonds were a means of financing American firms at European expense.

To some Europeans, especially chauvinistic ones like the French, the idea of American industrialists wanting to borrow locally in order to finance their economic invasion adds insult to injury. This is to see Americans as intruders, whose high-powered presence will relegate European industry to a second-class role; the dangers exist, but whether or not Europe's worst fears are justified is irrelevant as far as the Eurobond market is concerned, since it is beyond anyone's power to regulate it. It would take a concerted decision by at least half a dozen governments, each of which would have to tell its banks and stock exchanges what not to do.

If an American company wants to use the market, and the investors have the dollars, then nothing will stop the two connecting. Investors put their money where it's safe, and nothing could look safer than the great American corporations. Whether they are Belgian investment trusts, Italian financiers, Arabian oil sheikhs or beef barons in the Argentine, they are international money-men who are acutely aware of the nuances of safety. The rate of interest for a loan to Finland has to be slightly above average because Russia is next door; it's the far edge of fraternal Europe, so that bankers think vaguely of spies and rocket-bases, and add another quarter per cent interest to tempt the wary. 'For example,' said a Dutchman, 'Austrian loans are always a tiny bit slow because the country is a fraction tainted politically. There's a history of unrest and political troubles. Also it's like Finland, it's near the Russians. You may remember there was an Austrian Government loan and a loan by an American firm, National Biscuits, at almost the same time, for twenty million dollars in each case. The Nabisco rate was six and a half per cent but the Austrian rate was six and three-quarters.'

It seems rather rude to a sovereign State to be assessed as a worse risk than a biscuit manufacturer, but an oil sheikh with a million dollars to invest won't be swayed by such thoughts.[1] He might even remember that the first European bank to collapse in the 1930 crisis that swept the Continent was Austrian—the Oesterreichischen Creditanstalt.

Safe, blossoming prosperity is what attracts money, which is why there are few Eurobond borrowers from less developed parts of the world. If the large international investors had fewer attractive outlets for their money, they might be willing to put more of it into underdeveloped areas. Nineteenth-century investors had a smaller range of investments to choose from, and money that went to build a railway across some distant prairie might have gone into a biscuit company in a big city if one had been available. The last great banking crisis in London was the threatened collapse of Barings, the merchant bankers, in 1890, after they had over-reached themselves with investments in the Argentine. The City came to their rescue, after a week in which the directors of the Bank of England carried 'the horrible secret in their breasts,' as the *Bankers' Magazine* put it at the time. The point is that in those days it was perfectly in order to invest large sums in countries where things could go wrong—in this case an unwise issue of shares on behalf of the Buenos Aires Drainage and Waterworks Co. was at the root of the debacle. Today, unfortunately for underdeveloped nations, the oilman's royalties and the shipowner's profits can find a safe resting place in the City of Oslo or Pepsi-Cola. (The underdeveloped nations' habit of nationalising everything in sight hasn't helped; thus Belgium's Société Générale de Belgique lost its copper empire in the Congo, and is busy making up

[1] The prospectus for this issue, in 1967, included a statement by the Austrian Finance Minister, anxious to allay all fears. 'After the occupation of Austria by Germany in 1938,' it said, 'the German authorities refused to recognise liability in respect of the external debt of Austria, and the service of such debt ceased. In 1952 a conference was held in Rome . . . Austria proposed, and the representatives of the creditors approved, arrangements for the resumption of the service of Austria's pre-war external debt. Austria has since fulfilled the terms of these arrangements and has also paid punctually all amounts due on foreign indebtedness incurred since 1945.' That seems reasonable. Austria is a safe little country where tourists go to ski and eat cream cakes, with seven and a quarter million people and a gross national product of $1,290 per head. But the bankers smile indulgently and add one-quarter per cent to the interest. The price of a stormy history, in this case, is the $50,000 or so a year more than National Biscuits that the Austrian Government must pay for its money.

for it by, among other things, developing a glass-cement-petrochemicals empire—in Canada).

All investors need to be realists; Eurobond investors have a choice of options that enables them to be realistic in the nicest possible way. Various technical devices have been introduced to make the bonds attractive, and competition among borrowers keeps interest rates high.

Founder-members like Warburgs and Deutsche Bank are still there, but have been joined by many more. Wall Street's investment bankers, after the initial jolt to their business, have entered the market in strength, and now lead well over half the Eurobond syndicates. Some of them have offices in Europe—White, Weld in London, Zurich and Paris, First Boston Corporation in London. A great cloud of banks and stockbrokers fills the air whenever a Eurobond issue is being made. Underwriting and placing has become big business.

Underwriters (in issues of all securities, not only Eurobonds) agree to take the shares or bonds before selling them elsewhere, so guaranteeing that the issue will succeed. They are well paid for it, and new-issue underwriting is much sought after; the risks are usually small and well spread. Eurobond underwriting has become a multinational affair in which about 200 banks and firms of brokers jostle for prestige and profits, their behaviour a mixture of polite smiles and sharp elbows. It is a 'placement market', in which no effort is made to sell the bonds to the public in the first instance: the professionals take them up, then feed them out to buyers. A Eurobond syndicate may contain 90 or 100 names, and the lists of underwriters published in fat oblong advertisements called 'tombstones' name the financial establishment of Europe, plus successful hangers-on, with many American names as well. The bonds have already been sold to the underwriters and their friends by the time the ad appears. It's published as 'a matter of record,' providing everyone with some desirable publicity.

A typical list might include eight or nine London merchant bankers —Warburg, Morgan Grenfell, Hambros, Hill, Samuel and so on— plus one or two rich City stockbroking firms, possibly Cazenove and Strauss, Turnbull. Italy is usually well represented, with the big banks like Banca Commerciale Italiana and Banca Nazionale del Lavoro, and often a sprinkling of smaller ones. Ancient banks in Naples and Turin come in for a slice of the business.

Germany's all-purpose banks like the Deutsche and the Dresdner are rarely absent, and the French deposit banks, after a slow start, have joined in successfully. The Banque de Paris et des Pays-Bas pops up as a matter of course, usually accompanied by Paribas Corporation, its New York firm, and there is a hard core of similar investment-type bankers—Banque Lambert in Brussels, Piersons and Mees & Hope in Amsterdam, German banks like Trinkaus and Berenberg, Gossler.

The Deltec Banking Corporation, which often appears, is registered in the low-tax Bahamas, and is part of Deltec Panamerica, registered in low-tax Panama, a finance group active in South America; its shareholders include Warburg of London, the Bank of London and South America, the Deutsche Bank, the Belgian Société Générale de Banque and the French Banque de l'Indochine. The Rothschilds may appear in Eurobond syndicates as N. M. Rothschild in London, Banque Rothschild in France and the uncompromisingly titled La Compagnie Financière, which belongs to one of the French Rothschilds, Edmond. Lazards may appear three times, with the suffix Brothers in London, Frères et Cie in Paris and Freres & Co. in New York. Banks with interests in Luxembourg have their share, especially the Kredietbank, which may appear twice, once in Belgium as Kredietbank N.V. and once as its subsidiary, Kredietbank S.A. Luxembourgeoise. Austrians and Scandinavians provide a few names. American investment banks and stockbrokers may provide as many as thirty or forty.

Interesting absentees include the British deposit banks, which so far have no stomach for this kind of business, and, in many cases, Swiss banks. These claim to place more bonds than any other European group, but in the early days of the market there were internal tax and policy objections in Switzerland to their joining the syndicates. These were later modified, but the Swiss Bank Corporation, the Groupement des Banquiers Privés Genevois and the rest don't appear as often as they might.

A tombstone ad is arranged by the managers, whose names come first. An official of British Petroleum, which raised $24 million by a Eurobond issue in 1966, said wearily, 'You know how the schoolmen used to argue in the Middle Ages over how many angels could stand on the head of a pin? That's nothing to the arguments over how each block of names has to be arranged.' A director of White, Weld says that organising a tombstone is 'a science in itself.' Men agonise over it as theatrical agents agonise over the billing for star names. If the managers are out of alphabetical order it means that the first name has a larger share. Next comes the biggest block, the 'major bracket', which is strictly alphabetical, but may give way to a 'minor bracket' which goes back to the start of the alphabet. The Americans usually come next in a 'special bracket,' and they, too, may go from A to Z and then back to A again, once or even twice, to indicate that the first group has a larger share than the second. Banks have sulked and refused to take part in syndicates because they thought their place in the tombstone unworthy, or they have agreed to take part but declined to let their names appear in print.

Vanity apart, banks are only too anxious to get their names in the tombstone and their hands on the money. Most banking fees are kept as quiet as possible, but the prospectus for an issue has to say who gets what. The usual fees and margins amount to 2½ per cent of the sum being raised—a million and a quarter dollars in the case of a $50 million loan. The managers get one-half per cent between them, or $250,000 in the above instance. Another half per cent is divided among the underwriters—$250,000 between, say, eighty or ninety names, averaging a few thousand dollars apiece. But a further 1½ per cent goes to the 'selling group,' the group of banks that actually places the bonds with the buyers; this will include the managers and underwriters, who collect a further share of the money, and up to 100 or so brokers and banks whose names don't appear in the prospectus or tombstone.

To organise the syndicates, bright young executives travel and meet, disperse and come together again—bankers from different countries have never seen so much of one another. The managers ensure that the issue price and rate of interest are attractive, but not too attractive. Lawyers and accountants examine the tax, exchange-control and legal aspects in all the countries where the bonds may be sold. Men gobble down sandwiches in rooms full of stale smoke and catch too many planes and think up foolproof schemes in the bath in pursuit of the managers' half per cent. A man at Rothschilds in London explained how matters had been arranged in the case of Transalpine Finance Holdings, a Luxembourg company formed to raise money to help build the thickest pipeline in Western Europe, from southern Germany to the Adriatic via Austria. They had just raised another $30 million. The trouble with pipelines, he said, was that the oil companies for whom they were built (thirteen of them in this case), while guaranteeing the loan, usually preferred not to guarantee it in a way that had to appear on their balance sheets as a 'contingent liability'. A 'throughput agreement' is the answer in such cases. 'We employed a very elegant arrangement,' said the Rothschild man, 'under which the fundamental agreement was that the oil companies undertook to put enough oil through the pipeline to enable the debt of the operating company to be met—to convince investors in Europe that the security was enough to enable them to buy the bonds. You have to pitch your terms so that their accountants won't say it's a guarantee, but also so that your investor will say, "I don't care if it's a guarantee or not, I'll buy it".' The details ran to a lot of small print in the prospectus, and the investors duly bought.

Precisely who these investors are is a secret split up and hidden away in the vaults and minds of bankers. Many of them are evading tax, and to be known as purchasers of these anonymous bearer bonds, safely buried in rock and steel under Luxembourg or distributed among the safes of a dozen banks, would be embarrassing if not disastrous. Their purchases are not reported to any authorities; no central register has their names written down. There's nothing new about people's desire to find a safe resting place for money they would rather not talk about, but the Eurobond market has a unique combination of virtues: it can absorb an endless number of private fortunes, it pays a good rate of interest, and it asks no questions. A Swiss bank account is equally safe, but the depositor gets little or no interest, and may even have to pay to have it looked after. American stock-exchange investment involves taxation difficulties and the shadow of interfering officials, however hard the Swiss banker works on his client's behalf.

It is the capacity to swallow millions of dollars at once, in a market that is perfectly legitimate yet removed from prying eyes, that makes Eurobonds so attractive. The technical standards of the market are high; the prospectuses reveal more about the borrowing companies than is usually the case on the Continent. Some of the money stolen in Britain's Great Train Robbery in 1965 was later said to have been invested in British Government securities. The robbers would have done much better to put it in Eurobonds.

Few Eurobond investors are likely to have it on their conscience: if they are dodging tax, they regard this as part of their legitimate war against officialdom, like motorists versus the police. In some cases they may not be required to pay tax at all, and so regard the tax-free interest of the Eurobond as only right and proper—'Kuwaiti rulers don't have to pay taxes,' said a man at Hill, Samuel. 'Neither do Canadian pension trusts. There are others who ought to be paying taxes but don't. There are people—God knows who they are, I don't—South American, Swiss, Arabs, Englishmen for all I know, who have accounts outside the control of their own countries. Some of them are legitimate. Some of them aren't.'

The pension funds of international companies are big subscribers. Shipowners are well represented. 'We all have a Greek tanker owner,' said a London merchant banker. 'We all have shipping income. The money accrues on the high seas, whether it's a Texas independent or a Norwegian or a Greek, and gets left in some tax-free area like the Bahamas. Then we're asked to invest it. Don't listen to the Swiss when they say they place more Eurobonds than anyone else. They don't: we do, in London.

'The bonds themselves have been left in Switzerland for the same reason they've been left in Luxembourg, because till recently if they were kept physically in London it meant paying tax when the interest coupon was cashed. You'll hear someone say at the Swiss Credit Bank, "Look at all the bonds we've got in our safe," but as often as not they're being held for the account of British banks. Half the time the Swiss are acting as domestic servants, that's all.

'London has the placing power because we've got the clients. We all have a little bit of Vatican money. We have emigrant money from the Costa Brava—the wealthy British who live abroad, which is something that's growing all the time.'

A stockbroker in London with this kind of client described them as 'people who have emigrated with a few thousand pounds, gone to live in Spain and Italy and the south of France and Portugal, and want a steady income. We've got dozens of clients like this. Ten years ago they bought American treasury bills or invested in American securities. Now they buy Eurobonds instead.' One of his clients was 'a group of trusts, whose funds, I can assure you, are greater than the resources of some central banks. They are so secretive that everything has to be done in handwriting. Their letters don't go to a typist.'

A study by the International Monetary Fund up to 1966 estimated (but couldn't prove) that three-fifths of the money was coming through Switzerland, a sixth through the Middle East, Hong Kong and the Bahamas, and another sixth through other parts of Europe, where the largest buyers were in Belgium, Holland and Italy. Money labelled Switzerland, Hong Kong and the Bahamas is being channelled there from other places. A partner in White, Weld, Mr Robert Genillard—who would know the names of many Eurobond investors—referred in a speech to 'wealthy individuals . . . not only Europeans, but also South Americans, Middle and Far Easterners who fear inflation or political risks in their own countries and want a fair return on their money combined with freedom from taxation. Therefore the Eurobond market transcends Europe and serves as a catalyst for many overseas lenders and even borrowers: the market truly stretches from Hong Kong to Zurich, via Beirut and Caracas.'

The market helps international hot money to move from insecure parts of the world to places where it's cooler. National Biscuits may be marginally safer than the Government of Austria, but either are infinitely preferable to the local savings bank in Saigon or even Brasilia. One commentator,[2] noting that 'money from less developed areas constitutes the bulk of purchases, and adds to European investments,' calls the Eurobond market 'a type of reverse-development plan.' The relentless gravity of self-interest sees to it that money slides downhill to the pleasant valleys of the prosperous.

When the bonds have been issued and sold, they can be dealt in like any security, except that few of the deals go through a stock exchange. The market is run by banks and a few stockbrokers, trading by Telex and telephone. It's an amorphous market in all ways, but it's now a permanent feature of the financial landscape: not (according to most authorities, who could of course be wrong) a substitute for the long-awaited European capital market, but supplementary to the national markets, existing around and within them. It raises about one-eighth as much as all the issues, public and private, in the Common Market

[2] Dr Sidney E. Rolfe, in 'Capital Markets in Atlantic Economic Relationships,' published by the Atlantic Institute, 1967.

countries, plus Britain and Switzerland. The new market is oddly uncontrolled, with its apologists always anxious to point out how self-disciplined it is, and how it represents the financial genius at work, inventing and adapting in response to the demands of a free market. Moralists and tax-collectors could object, but in the international money-world their voices sound rather squeaky. The flight of money from poor countries to rich ones can be deplored, but the Eurobond market didn't invent this process; it just makes it easier.

Europe has gained from having these extra funds invested there, even though some of the money is spent on plant and materials owned by American subsidiaries. By attracting money that might otherwise have gone to New York, the Eurobond market is directly benefitting Europe. A U.S. broker's survey estimates that in 1967, Europeans bought $7,000 million of American securities; two-fifths of all securities owned in Switzerland are American, with much smaller, but rapidly growing, percentages elsewhere. This is money flowing downhill from Europe to America, just as it flows downhill from the Middle East to Europe; Eurobonds are one way of keeping some of it at home.

Not all the Eurobond issues are in dollars; a few have been made in European currencies, notably the Deutsche mark. Some ingenious fellows, headed by M. Fernand Collin, chairman of Belgium's Kredietbank, have had a limited success with a device invented for the purpose; this is the Unit of Account, in which a number of issues have been made, a sort of money-equivalent which, being related to the value of gold, can protect its holders against any devaluation of a currency they happen to be involved with. Each Unit of Account is worth 0·88867088 grams of fine gold; everyone speaks kindly of them, but they are a little theoretical for money-men going about their daily business in the jungle.

In practice, the universal currency for Europe is coming to be the dollar. One set of banks runs the flourishing short-term Eurodollar market; another (which includes many from the first category) is busy with Eurobonds at the long-term end. Both these markets, but particularly the second, have provided Europe with a framework it badly needed. The markets are international, but it's Europe that has the most sophisticated financial machinery outside the United States —the clever bankers, the ingenious stockbrokers—and yet has not been able do itself justice because its markets are national and parochial. Events are slowly changing this. It may be a long time before Europe agrees on a common currency or a single capital market with one set of rules for everyone, but in the meantime the Eurobond men are doing it their way—a working model, full of possibilities.

11 The Trouble with Money

With luck, financial historians will be able to summarise the international upheavals of the 1960s in a few cheerful paragraphs, recording a hectic period of change that brought in a new world financial order, where governments co-operate successfully to defeat mistrust of one another's currencies. But our luck may be out. The record of the sixties may be just another and even crueller episode in the long-running serial of financial cops and robbers, where nobody ever wins.[1]

Though the outcome affects all countries, few have as much to win or lose as Britain. This in turn involves the rest of Europe, since by seeking admission to the Common Market, Britain is implicitly asking the other Six to help share its own financial problems.

Inasmuch as the British problem consists of earning too little, the only way to solve it (short of drastic reductions in government spending) is by earning more—raising exports or reducing imports or both. No amount of international camaradie will prevail if a country is in economic difficulties and continues to multiply its debts to other countries. But the case against the world money system is that it has a malign life of its own, and, if it can't create a crisis out

[1] A still bleaker possibility is that the world's monetary system will collapse altogether, leading to economic slumps on a massive scale as trade slows up. It's hard for a layman to reconcile the views of economists and other financial insiders, some of them crying that the end is near, others keeping cool and insisting that world technological progress is too advanced to be stopped by difficulties over money.

of nothing, can make an existing crisis worse. Sterling, being both a key part of this money system, and the currency of a country that has real economic difficulties, is thus the perfect candidate for trouble.

There are three main kinds of money that most countries will accept for the payment of international debts. Two exist only as entries in ledgers—the pound and the dollar. One is visible and tangible—gold. References to 'selling pounds' or 'being short of dollars' can be confusing because outside its own country the money has no symbolic pieces of paper (pound notes and dollar bills) to make it visible; it's 'pure' money. It is, in bankers' language, a debt: what is money to the man who receives it is a debt to the man who pays it. The principle is the same in all money affairs. In one of the classic definitions, 'Banks are institutions whose debts, usually referred to as "bank deposits," are commonly accepted in final settlement of other people's debts'.[2] But inside a country, there are banknotes and coins to be seen and handled; the symbols are taken for the real thing. Internationally (and apart from gold) there is only the *idea* of money.

An American Senator (in one of those unavoidable examples) purchases a Rolls-Royce for $19,000. At some point, his bank must 'sell dollars' and 'buy pounds', at the agreed exchange rate of about $2·40 to £1, in order to pay for the car in British money. This is a routine foreign-exchange operation, instantly swallowed up by the mass of trading in currencies, run by telephone and Telex between banks throughout the world, that forms the foreign-exchange market. By 'selling dollars' the American bank is selling part of the Senator's claim against his own country's monetary system. Whoever buys the dollars now has a $19,000 claim on the system: the debt has been transferred. By 'buying pounds' on behalf of the Senator, the American bank has purchased someone else's claim on the British money system, to the extent of £8,000. Another debt has been transferred. Since this particular debt is against the British system, it can be handed over to Rolls-Royce in the form of an £8,000 credit to their bank account in London.

These debts are the reality behind international money. The American (or the Frenchman, or the Japanese) who 'owns pounds' owns a

[2] 'Modern Banking' by R. S. Sayers.

claim against the British banking system. He can sell the claim to someone else because whoever buys it ('buys pounds') has sufficient faith in Britain's willingness and ability to honour the debt, should he demand payment—that is, spend the money in Britain. The virtue of having it lies in knowing that everyone will accept it—just as the virtue of a pound note in Britain is that, although it's only a piece of paper, people all agree to the rule that says it's worth four packets of cigarettes or twenty loaves of bread.

Until the nineteenth century, no country had generated enough faith in its credit-worthiness to let these claims-against-itself become completely acceptable as international money. Sterling supplied the credit that was needed to finance the expansion of world trade and investment because it was backed by the promises of a rich, powerful nation. It was international money that could be used as required, safe in the knowledge that the debt it represented would be honoured by the British system. This primacy has passed to the dollar. The United States is now the rich, powerful nation whose promises are good enough to induce people to employ claims-against-America as their international money.

Sterling is used as well because the world has been in the habit of using it for more than a century, but faith in it has dwindled. To own pounds is to own debts incurred by the British system. It is precisely the fear that Britain—whose commercial strength has declined steadily over the years—would not be able to meet the debts, in the terms in which they were incurred, that is a major cause of the chronic weakness of sterling. In time of crisis, sterling becomes unsaleable at the official price; the foreign-exchange market can find no buyers for pounds, because of acute fears that the debts are not going to be repaid in full. Buyers would be found at a lower price, but Western governments are obliged, by agreements made after the second world war through the International Monetary Fund, to keep their exchange rates within one per cent of the agreed level or 'parity.' Once the price falls to the lower edge of the limit, someone must intervene to stop it falling further. In the case of sterling that someone can only be the British Government, acting through the Bank of England, which in turn acts through the everyday mechanism of the foreign-exchange market.

The pounds are being offered on the market but no one is buying.

The owner could turn them into British goods and services but doesn't want to. He wants an alternative currency, usually dollars. Since no one else will supply them, the Bank of England must. The Bank takes the pounds and hands out dollars in exchange. This is what drains away the official foreign-currency reserves—the pool of claims against other countries, expressed mainly in dollars, which has been built up over the years by the Bank of England. For nearly twenty years after 1949, the British Government said the pound was worth 2·8 dollars, give or take a fraction. Whenever there was an acute lack of confidence in Britain's solvency, owners of pounds were saying to Britain, in effect: Prove it. The strain of proving it finally became too great in 1967, when Britain devalued the pound by 14 per cent, which meant that anyone who owned sterling lost one-seventh of its foreign-currency value after the night of Saturday November 18. Britain's basic failure to earn more foreign-exchange by exports, overlaid by waves of nervous (and sometimes speculative) selling by owners of sterling, made it finally impossible to go on meeting the debts in the terms in which they were incurred. The pound was declared to be worth 2·4 dollars, give or take a fraction.

This rule of the financial game is permitted when a country is really in the soup. In Britain's case the agony was dragged out by pride and bitterness and nostalgia for the old days, and the length of the process helped to make sterling even shakier than it might have been if the technical considerations had not been overlaid by sentimental ones. Finally the situation was horribly mismanaged by the British authorities just before November 18, when rumours of impending disaster brought a week in which the world rushed to sell its pounds, and the Bank of England, forced to buy them in, had huge quantities of dollars drained away from it, up until the last moment. In the *Economist's* phrase, it was a 'botched, panic-stricken flight from an overwhelmed parity.'

Widely-expressed fears that mistrust of pounds would now become mistrust of dollars were soon realised after November, 1967. If the dollar was the ultimate form of international money, it would be safe simply because no alternative existed. Unfortunately there is still the alternative of gold, the mad metal, which has been used for so long throughout the world, and has acquired such magical associations, that everyone trusts it, knowing that it will always be accepted by everyone else. Gold is still the foundation on which the structure rests. From 1934 the United States guaranteed this gold standard by agreeing to buy or sell from or to central banks at a price of $35 a fine ounce, plus or minus handling charges. The owner of dollars could always exchange them for gold.

For years after the end of the second war, the world outside the United States was short of dollars. But by 1960, American spending overseas was distributing them throughout the world at a prodigious rate. America, like Britain, had a balance of payments problem because it was spending more foreign-exchange than it was earning, But unlike Britain, it was not a question of importing too much and exporting too little. Even allowing for military costs in Vietnam and elsewhere, the Americans had a surplus on current spending in 1967 of about $2,000 million. What turned the surplus into an overall deficit was capital spending—American money invested abroad, buying up chemical companies in Germany, building oil refineries in Britain, opening banks in Japan.

The British problem stemmed from weakness, the American problem from prosperity; dollars invested abroad are storing up treasures for the future in the form of foreign-exchange income for the United States. But the short-term effect has been to put billions of dollars into world circulation. Insofar as these dollars have been left uncashed, as claims against America, they have been a godsend to the world money system. There have been enough of them to supply the raw material for an international short-term money-market (Eurodollars) and an international long-term capital market (Eurobonds). This is all to the good, especially since a major preoccupation of economists and finance ministers for years has been a fear that there is, or soon may be, a shortage of international money. But although dollars are attractive, the fact that so many are held outside the U.S. —around $30,000 million by the end of 1967, growing all the time— has made some of the holders uneasy. Is it right? More important, is it safe? Not being certain, the holders exchange their dollars for gold.

This gradual shift from invisible claims to visible metal had reduced America's gold stocks from $23,000 million in 1957 to $13,000 million at the time of Britain's 1967 devaluation—a billion dollars worth of gold every year.

After sterling was devalued, undermining confidence in the world's monetary arrangements, the shift into gold accelerated; the Americans lost a billion dollars worth within two or three months, and still more in the next wave of selling, early the following year, so that by the spring their stocks were down to little more than $10 billion. Hundreds of tons a week were moved around, stretching the capacity of airlines to fly it and foundries to melt and remould it. Some of the gold was being hoarded as a precaution, both by central banks (usually those of small, nervous countries in Africa or South America) and individuals. Much of it was being bought as a straight speculation, in the hope that the United States would raise the price it paid for gold. The speculators were rebuffed, at least for the moment, in March 1968, when central bankers agreed to sell gold only to one another, and so prevent any more of it getting into private hands. This meant a two-tier price, with the 'official' price fixed at $35 an ounce, leaving the speculators and hoarders to do what they liked among themselves.

Arguments about raising the price of gold have been perennial in world money circles. With its value fixed in 1934, at present prices there is too little of it to finance world trade. This doesn't matter if sterling and dollars are used to do most of the financing instead. But even a comparatively small movement away from dollars and into gold is enough to cause alarm, since the world's stocks of gold are inadequate; if the holders of dollars and sterling all tried to change their claims into gold, they wouldn't be able to. The rational course, as it seems to many people, is to move away from gold altogether. If any extra form of international money is needed, it is argued, a new currency should be created. The International Monetary Fund has proposed to call it, or them, by the uninspiring name of 'Special Drawing Rights,' or SDRs, which would be an international currency created out of thin air, distributed to member countries in proportion to their I.M.F. contributions. There would be more money in circulation; everyone would benefit.

This optimistic theory is not shared by all, notably the French, who insist that a gold standard is the only realistic one, and change most of their dollars into gold as a practical demonstration of their contempt for invisible currencies. They aren't the only ones who like to have plenty of gold underground. Two-thirds of the British foreign-exchange reserves are in gold; so are over half Germany's much larger reserves. Sweden and Norway, with respectively one-fifth and one-thirty-fifth in gold, are among the few highly developed countries to rely almost exclusively on invisible money. But the French position has been dramatised by their prosperity, which has given them so much foreign exchange to turn into metal. With the third largest reserves in the world (after the U.S. and West Germany), most of them accumulated in recent years, France has exchanged three-quarters of them for gold worth more than $5,000 million (private hoards in France may hold as much again). The French go further, and insist on keeping all their gold physically in Paris, instead of leaving some of it earmarked as theirs in American safe-keeping, which is common practice.[3] The French solution means sticking to gold and making it more effective by increasing its value—say, doubling it, so that one fine ounce would be worth $70. This can be represented as French craftiness or French wisdom, the truth probably being that it's a bit of both.

The French justify themselves by saying that the world's monetary system is in need of reform, and that a return to the 'discipline of gold,' revalued to a realistic price, is the answer. Gold may be only yellow metal, but it has to be mined expensively—South Africa and Russia can do it economically only because they are both countries with very cheap labour; gold can't just be summoned up from nowhere. The French complain that by relying on invisible money, the world enables the U.S. (and Britain, to a lesser extent) to get away with debts that it never has to meet. The debts may be useful as money, but carried to such lengths they give the U.S. an unfair advantage over everyone else.

Political motives are denied. But there's little doubt that France would like to damage the U.S. by forcing it to increase the price of gold. No one is very clear as to what happens then, except that in one sense the dollar would be devalued, since gold is the standard against which everything is measured. Gold would be more powerful

[3] The vaults are under the marble halls and patrolling soldiers of the Banque de France, where an official described them as being 'twenty-five metres deep, built with their own kitchens and services so that two hundred people could live down there for weeks on end.' He added without apparent irony that it was 'a bit like the Maginot Line.'

than ever, which would be fortunate for those who have a lot of it, like the French. They are old lovers of gold; it suits their temperament, which is nervous and proud at the same time, to put their faith in its traditional glories.

The French have led the outcry against paper money as a substitute for gold, but the crisis of confidence goes deeper. The act of devaluing the pound in 1967 was the signal for widespread fears that the money system was in trouble, combined with widespread hopes that the solution to the trouble would be revalued gold. It was worth buying, both as a hedge against chaos and a speculation. This is what caused the galloping gold sales, with huge daily orders going through the London gold market. Many of them came through Swiss banks, acting for their nameless international clients, with informed guesswork putting Middle Eastern oil sheikhs high on the list of leading buyers. Companies as well as individuals were stocking up, and, at the other extreme, so were the world's poor. Even more gold than usual was smuggled into India. Some of it was joining its ancestors under the bed and up the chimney in Continental countries. Whoever the buyers were, the violence of their response dismayed the economists, central bankers and finance officials who have been co-operating to take the wrinkles out of the money system.

The co-operation, chiefly involving Western Europe and the United States, is designed to keep currencies out of trouble by a complicated network of aid that is never fully revealed at the time. There is a confusing array of organisations, often overlapping. The International Monetary Fund, set up after the second world war as an agency of the United Nations, provides a pool of credit, contributed by members, and is the chief talking-shop of Western finance. Its headquarters are in Washington. Years of discussion about 'international liquidity' (the amount and nature of available money) have resulted in the I.M.F.'s plan for Special Drawing Rights as a paper currency for countries to use among themselves. A sub-section of the I.M.F., the 'Group of Ten,' comprises the leading European nations, including Britain, plus the U.S., Canada and Japan; Switzerland isn't a member of the I.M.F. but contributes to the Group of Ten funds. The same countries wearing different hats appear in the Organisation for Economic Co-operation and Development, which is descended from the body set up to administer Marshall Aid in Europe; the most newsworthy part of O.E.C.D. is its 'Working Party 3', which meets in Paris, has access to much private information about member countries, and is useful for inquiries-in-depth into the state of their economies.

The Group of Ten is the 'Paris Club', not to be confused with the 'Basle Club', perhaps the most important part of the network for mutual aid (though not for long-term planning, which comes under the I.M.F.). The Basle Club is the focus for Europe's central bankers, who meet there once a month under the aegis of yet another institution, the Bank for International Settlements. This was set up in 1930, ostensibly to sort out the tangle of German reparations, and it has developed into a quasi-commercial bank whose clients are mainly central banks.

Central banks in the West are in an odd position. They are responsible to the State, but some have a large measure of freedom; they are technicians in the baffling business of international money (as it seems to many politicians) and their special knowledge entitles them to make policy as well as interpret it. 'Governments come and go,' says Sir George Bolton, 'but central bankers are there for forty years.' In day-to-day affairs they are the key operators in the foreign-exchange market, intervening to influence the price of their own and other people's currencies. They are the agents of their governments but they are also bankers doing business with other bankers.

This area where the central banks make contact with the everyday money-system is always a delicate one. The Bank of England, working in the foreign-exchange market through its own dealers, is customarily referred to as 'She'—'Things were rather quiet and then She came in as a buyer.' The Bank is connected to all the foreign-exchange brokers in London by direct lines, which it pays for itself, thus emphasising that these lines of communication belong to It. Central banks must be sharp and canny operators but they also need to stand on their dignity, and this is why they find the Bank for International Settlements so useful, since it gives them a channel into the world's gold and money markets, and between one another, which they can use without the knowledge of anyone except the B.I.S. —including fellow members.

Central banks own most of the shares in the B.I.S. and provide many of the small staff of just over 200, which has miraculously stayed almost the same size since 1930. Britain, West Germany, France, Italy, Belgium, Holland, Switzerland and Sweden are the major shareholders, but every country in Europe except Russia and Spain has a stake—including the East European States and even Albania, a cosmopolitanism that reflects the Bank's origins in the old pre-Communist Europe. The United States isn't a member, but the Federal Reserve System sends a team to the monthly meetings of central bankers from the eight main shareholding countries, and so do Canada and Japan.

In effect the B.I.S. is run as a co-operative, by and on behalf of central banks, the rule being that it mustn't do anything that goes against the monetary policies of its members. They (and international bodies such as the O.E.C.D.) deposit money with it and use it for trading in the gold and foreign-exchange markets; most of the Russian gold that comes into the West is bought by the B.I.S. It can lend money to central banks but not to governments, a fine distinction that shows how much central bankers value their independence. 'It's terribly easy to deal with us,' said an official. 'No committees—just a telephone call. There's complete secrecy. Central Bank A may not want to know that it's dealing with Central Bank B, but they can both deal with us, running their balances up and down without anyone being the wiser.'

The senior management of the bank is a deliberate mixture of nationalities, working in a solid building opposite the railway station in Basle; it used to be an hotel, and still has a certain faded atmosphere, with palms in pots and a lot of metalwork. Officials seem to enjoy knowing that the slightly seedy exterior conceals a hard-headed bankers' bank.[4] The B.I.S. assets include more than a billion dollars in gold bars and coins, but it has no vaults to keep them in; about half is in the United States, the rest divided between Switzerland and the Bank of England. It likes to think of itself as a sophisticated place, taking a cool view of money, knowing all the gossip, sending its managers on frequent trips around the Continent.

[4] Visitors are bemused by its unpretentiousness, tucked away in the neat Basle setting of trams and delicatessen. *Time* magazine says the bank is between a tourist agency and a watch shop. The *Sunday Times* found it between a tea shop and a hairdresser. I thought it was between a jeweller's and a sweet shop. It must be the way everything merges into the quiet grey background of old Europe.

But more important are the journeys that the bankers make to Basle. Apart from the war, these monthly meetings have gone on since the B.I.S. began, though in the 1930s there was little real co-operation between central banks. During the war most of the central banks from occupied countries had representatives-in-exile installed in rooms at the Bank of England, which may have helped to encourage co-operation when the war was over. The climate that produced the I.M.F. and a sense of alliance became noticeable at Basle in 1961, when the central bankers, meeting at one of their regular sessions, acted to stop a wave of speculation that was upsetting the foreign-exchange markets. The German Deutsche mark had been revalued—raised in price in relation to other currencies—and holders of sterling were selling out and buying up other Continental currencies in the hope that they, too, would be revalued. The bankers at Basle announced that there would be no more revaluations and that they were co-operating in the foreign-exchange markets. The Swiss claim to have been the leaders in this. The Swiss franc was an obvious candidate for revaluation, and in a single week, nearly $300 million was withdrawn from London and placed in Switzerland. The Swiss National Bank immediately offset this by depositing $200 million with the Bank of England, and organised short-term credit arrangements that became the pattern for central-bank aid in the future. It's difficult to tell who exactly was doing what; but somebody was certainly doing something. In effect, the bankers were saying from then on that wild selling and buying movements that could endanger currencies, to the point where countries might be forced into some drastic action like devaluation, would be choked off by the central banks, which would intervene with their own resources to keep the market stable.

The central banker is in a strong psychological position for this sort of thing, since he works in an atmosphere of carefully cultivated dignity and reserve; he is set a little apart, and draws authority from this. Almost invariably, central banks are in buildings that look like palaces or fortresses, guarded by a mixture of attendants in comic-opera uniforms and soldiers with guns. There are secrets in the files and gold in the vaults; visitors drop their voices and listen to the footsteps echoing. At the Bank of England, heavy with chandeliers and antique furniture that's kept in good repair by the Bank's own workshop, pink-coated attendants greet one another solemnly as they pass in the corridors. A lorry of armed troops arrives at a back entrance after tea; they stand on the pavement, stamping their boots while the City crowds hurry past, before marching in with their officer. At the Bank of France, a huge building that looks even less hospitable than the Bank of England from the outside, the attendants wear blue uniforms with silver badges, like something from a child's bus-conductor set; even the fire notices are engraved in polished brass. The Governor, his two deputies and nine senior managers live in free apartments. The Bank of Italy in Rome is magnificent, with tall corridors and chambers hung with paintings. Holland's central bank in Amsterdam has the same overpowering air; the attendants wear priest-like uniforms; the marble glitters and to smoke is forbidden.

The central banks have all cultivated a similar *persona*, which proved useful when they began to present their united front. Using Basle as a convenient regular meeting-place, and often with the B.I.S. itself as a clearing house, the central bankers embarked on a regular programme of mutual aid. The basic instrument was the 'currency swap,' at its simplest an arrangement between two countries under which each hands over a specified amount of its own currency to the other for a fixed period, usually a few months. This enables a country with a weak currency to temporarily obtain a strong one. A maximum figure is agreed in advance, then drawn on as necessary; by the end of 1967 the Federal Reserve Bank of New York had arrangements with central banks and the B.I.S. to swap $6,700 if requested. Most of the Basle Club members had substantial reciprocal arrangements with one another.

Considering the generally slow progress towards European unity, the Continent's central bankers acted smartly. Bankers move faster than politicians. The most active co-operators come predictably from the countries where central banks are least under Government control, Germany and Italy. In Germany the Bundesbank is strong because there are bitter memories of the way its predecessor, the Reichsbank, was manipulated by the Nazis. The law says it has to support the Government's general economic policy, but only when this is consistent with safeguarding the currency. Dr Otmar Emminger, the No. 2 at the Bundesbank, points out that 'this has its origin in the experience of the German people. They have had two major inflations in their lifetime, and they know that a government can misuse a central bank for its own purposes.' Far from being regarded as a branch of the Government, the Bundesbank seems to be thought of in Germany as a guardian of the middle-class savers. Instead of being aloof it has gone out of its way to explain itself—'As a counterpart to our independence,' says Emminger, 'we feel that we must explain our actions to the public at large. So we have acted in contradiction to the old British tradition that a central bank doesn't have to justify its behaviour.'

The Bank of England remains reticent; though it has lowered a veil or two, it is still not a giver of Press conferences and a source of informal background information in the way the Bundesbank is. But this is hardly a sign of strength. When, for example, Bank Rate is raised in Britain, protocol lays down that the announcement shall be made by the Bank with the approval of the Chancellor of the Exchequer, the British equivalent of a Finance Minister, thus emphasising that the Bank can't act on its own. In Germany the Government could delay such an increase but not prevent it.

The Bundesbank's independence, combined with Germany's prosperity, has given its officials an authority among central bankers that would have been inconceivable in 1945. Dr Emminger, who is its overseas specialist, believes in co-operation in general and helping the pound in particular. An affable Bavarian Catholic who was previously in Government service and later with the O.E.C.D., he wrote his doctorate thesis on British monetary policy, and, fortunately for Britain, has maintained a benign interest in sterling.

Emminger is one of the small band of innovating central bankers; another is the Governor of the Bank of Italy, Dr Guido Carli, who is more independent than might be expected in a country where the State owns so much of the banking system. According to the rules the Governor has to implement the decisions of an 'inter-ministerial committee for credit and saving'; but a strong personality like Carli, in a country like Italy where governments are not particularly stable, has more freedom than appears on paper. At one time the economic adviser to I.R.I., the State group of holding companies and banks, Carli, like Emminger, has had experience of international organisations—in his case, posts with the I.M.F. and the now defunct

European Payments Union. His reputation in Europe is high, and he can make political capital out of this: the threat of resignation is always a useful weapon.

Carli became Governor in 1961, and two years later faced a financial crisis. Italy's balance of payments was in the red, and there was talk of devaluation. A 'credit squeeze' was applied by Carli and the Government to reduce home demand for goods and encourage Italian firms to export more. The British have had so many credit squeezes, none of which appears to have had the desired effect, that they are astonished to be told that the method actually works. Whether or not it was simple cause-and-effect, Italy soon found itself with too much foreign exchange instead of too little. Carli persuaded the Government to allow Italians to buy foreign securities freely, and Italy became a major provider of funds for the Eurobond market. This is why Italian banks suddenly appeared in strength as managers and underwriters of Eurobond issues. All this was good for the country's image, especially since a few years before, Italy had been an impecunious borrower, a sort of poor relation down in the south of Europe. Carli's star brightened accordingly.

An intellectual who has been quoted as saying that 'the first quality of a central banker is to be cold-blooded,' his contributions to the monetary debate include ideas as to how other countries might help Britain with its problem of 'sterling balances' (described later on). *The Times* has praised Carli as a 'monetary diplomat,' and the City is as ready to acknowledge the efforts of both Italy and Germany to do something about the pound (and monetary reform in general) as it is to condemn the French for bloody-mindedness.

The French participate in the inter-bank arrangements, but only to a limited extent. Their withdrawal from the so-called 'gold pool,' another Basle-centred arrangement for supplying gold to the London market when demand is heavy, made a small but undeniable contribution to the world crisis that began in late 1967. (The pool ceased to exist altogether when central banks stopped selling gold to anyone but other central banks in March 1968). No problem of conflict between central bank and Government arises because the Bank of France, nationalised in 1946, is virtually an extension of the Ministry of Finance. Paradoxically, there is less informal contact at the top than there would be in London. A senior Bank of France official said that whereas in London one would expect Governor and Chancellor to have lunch together and explore one another's views in an amicable setting, in Paris the Governor and Finance Minister were not so close: 'When he goes from his office to see the Minister, it is more of a démarche—more of a business'.

This keeping of a distance doesn't mean that the Bank is left to go its own way, but rather that it is assumed to be so bound up with the State that the maintenance of a careful balance between separate but interconnected powers, typical of the London way of doing things, doesn't arise. The close community of *inspecteurs des finances*, who change jobs but not allegiance as they move between posts in the Treasury, the Bank, the nationalised deposit banks and a range of State credit institutions, tends to draw them all together and make them into departments of one huge Ministry of Money.

Altogether the French have spoilt the charming picture of a bankers' co-operative working for a brave new monetary world. In part their motives are narrowly political, an expression of national pride and egoism, but they are also reluctant to help sustain a system with which they genuinely disagree. They didn't try very hard when the pound was in trouble in November 1967, and, although sterling was ripe for devaluation in any case, the rumours, snide remarks and cold comfort that came out of Paris left a bad taste, at a time when the bankers' co-operative was visible failing to cope.

The trouble with mutual aid is that when one of the currencies being aided has to be devalued, it begins to look like an international calamity rather than a technical adjustment. Shortly before the 1967 devaluation a Bank of England official, emphasising the need for strong nerves and clever dealers, said to me, 'If the authorities in various countries are joining together in defence of a certain line, i.e. that the pound will bloody well not be devalued, then you have to pull out all the stops—and we do.' Remarks like that are a poor prelude to devaluation a few months later.

Again, the atmosphere of secrecy in which central bankers organise their swaps and credits is a two-edged weapon that hurts the bankers as soon as people begin to suspect that behind the secrecy, the wise men are biting their nails. Straight loans are announced as they are made; in November 1967, outstanding British borrowings included \$1,400 million from the International Monetary Fund, \$250 million from the Bank for International Settlements, and $105 million from the three leading Swiss banks—who did the wicked-gnome image a lot of good by lending the money the previous month, though the gesture brought hoots of wounded pride from the City at the sight of Her Majesty's Government accepting, 'with appreciation', a loan from commercial banks. These massive borrowings are known about in detail. The short-term agreements between the central bankers are in a different category. The general pattern of credits is known, but details of who is drawing what amounts at any given time emerge only later—sometimes much later.

The Basle credits available before devaluation were known to be worth $1,000 million, and another $1,350 million could be taken in swaps with the U.S. Federal Reserve Bank. Other swaps and short-term borrowings were not announced at all; but even where they had been made public, the extent to which the Bank of England was drawing on them was kept secret. The Bank official just quoted justified the practice by saying, 'It's always preferable to keep the enemy guessing about the size of your forces. A general doesn't get on the loud-hailer on the eve of the attack.' He admitted that this wasn't the only reason: 'Sometimes a central bank wants it to be known that it is making a bigger contribution. At other times it doesn't want it to be known that it is making a smaller contribution.'

A number of central bankers, including Dr Emminger of the Bundesbank, favour a more open policy. Oddly enough, deals between central banks can be kept secret in a way that Government borrowing can't. The parties can plead the banker's privilege of silence—as Dr Emminger points out, 'It's a business deal, so either party to the deal can veto publicity'.

When sterling was finally devalued, an impression that the mysterious magic of the central bankers had been defeated by bigger and better spells was unavoidable. Economists and politicians kept repeating that devaluation had been needed to give the pound its true value in relation to other currencies, but phrases like 'defeat' and 'humiliation' reflected the widespread feeling that sterling had been propped up for years by loans and swaps, only to collapse in the end. It looked like a defeat for Britain, and some of the defeat rubbed off on those who had done the propping up. This sharpened the feeling that the financial community was not altogether in control, and contributed to the panic-stricken escape from dollars into gold that followed. From devaluation onwards, the central bankers' reputation for collective omniscience, built up so carefully over the previous decade, suffered badly. Speculators were out to make pickings from an increase in the price of gold; bankers and business men everywhere were anxious not to lose their shirts if the monetary system deteriorated to a point of general no-confidence. The central bankers, hurrying from jets or pausing to make brief statements, remained as tight-lipped as ever, but one couldn't help wondering whether, in private, their jaws were beginning to tremble.

As for the actual weaknesses of sterling which had caused so much trouble, to Britain and to everyone else, these continued after devaluation, to the accompaniment of desperate assurances that all would soon be well. Underlying the weakness is the economic malaise that has prevented the British economy from expanding as it might have done, and kept the cost of imports uncomfortably higher than the income from exports. But the economic troubles, whose remedy is in Britain's hands, have been aggravated by more technical troubles that are less controllable. Sterling is still, with the dollar, one of the two currencies in commercial use throughout the world. These claims-against-Britain are held in great quantity by companies, banks and individuals, all of whom are continually buying and selling pounds as they need them for international business. Often the pounds are bought so that they can be invested in the London money market. Not less than £15,000 million is in circulation to finance world trade alone. The existence of so much moveable sterling means that even a modest tendency to hold fewer pounds and more of something else (dollars, marks, francs, gold) can mean heavy selling of sterling that depresses the price, forcing the Bank of England to intervene and spend some of its hoard of dollars to buy the unwanted pounds.

The movements of a world currency like sterling are intricate and depend on the mood of people who can hardly be expected to have an abstract concern with the health of a currency; like factory workers at a time of national wage restraint, they may pay lip-service to high principles but are really interested in saving themselves. To talk to a foreign-exchange dealer in the middle of a crisis is to realise how basic it all is—men are using the technicalities of the market to make as much money as they can. The dealers, whose attitudes can do a lot to influence the clients they are acting for, are quick-witted men who live on their nerves, working in a small international community of a few hundred people. 'The man at the other end likes to be recognised immediately,' said a foreign-exchange broker in London. 'You say, "Hello, Bob, Hello, Charles," You don't mumble in your beard. It's often a question of personality. If you talk on the telephone in a high-pitched voice, it's likely that you won't get the business of someone with a lower voice. They think, who's this juvenile? Each person wants to be treated as an individual. Some want to be advised. If you try to advise others, they say, "What the hell do *you* know?"'

Each deal is a matter of protecting money and adding to it if possible. 'Let's say I own a million dollars in Switzerland. I sell it for £400,000 or so and invest it in London for one month at eight per cent with a local authority, via a bank and a local-authority broker. After a month, if I want the money back, I sell the sterling and get the dollars again.'

In this operation, the British reserves benefit to the extent of a million dollars for as long as the investor chooses to leave his claim against the British banking system uncashed—that is, as long as he leaves the pounds in London. This is hot money, going wherever it's most profitable, a movement that is sometimes reported as though it's not quite proper. But the money belongs to foreigners who are entitled to do what they like with it. The London money market is glad enough to have it; the City banks and brokers are paid commissions for handling it; when it flies away again it isn't immoral, only unfortunate.

It's impossible to define where hedging ends and speculation begins. The holder of sterling—whether he holds it for trading or to deposit in London—may cover himself against any future fall in the value of his pounds by 'selling forward': agreeing a price at which someone (usually the Bank of England in time of crisis) guarantees to buy it back again in three months' time. This forward dealing cost the Bank of England a fortune when it had to honour its commitments after devaluation, and later the Bank began refusing to make forward contracts (which meant that the price of 'forward sterling' was left to find its true level on the open market, and fell alarmingly, reflecting once again the lack of confidence in its future). No doubt some of the forward dealing at the end of 1967 was speculative, but most of it was probably hedging against devaluation rather than gambling that it was going to happen. The London *Sunday Times*, reporting a survey of major companies in New York, said that there was 'only one flat denial, from Standard Oil of New Jersey, of extensive hedging operations in the six months before devaluation. Most other firms admitted that hedging had been part of "our normal day-to-day financial activities for months." Two firms, Singer and Joy Manufacturing, hoped to profit from hedging deals.'

One of the clearest summaries of what speculation doesn't mean was given by the Prime Minister, Harold Wilson, speaking in the House of Commons in the summer of 1966, when there had just been a run on the pound. Mr Wilson, who is an economist by training, gave a rather different account to the one he produced to help justify devaluation the following year. Then, on the day after devaluation, television audiences heard him complain about 'the present tide of foreign speculation against the pound.' Later that week he used television again to talk about 'the power of speculators at home and abroad.' But in 1966, in Parliament, he said that 'we should perhaps eliminate from our thoughts the somewhat naïve caricature that what has been going on is a machination of some bearded troglodytes deep below ground [the Gnomes] speculating in foreign currencies for private gain. Of course, there is a speculative element based on the hope of private gain. But in fact—and our detailed analysis of what happened a year ago bears this out [that was the 1965 crisis]—I would distinguish two main elements in the monetary movements. In the first place, we have the large international companies with substantial trade in and with this country which, in periods of doubt, are tempted to reduce their holdings of sterling for purely precautionary reasons—precautionary, not speculative. . . . But even more important . . . the external trade of the United Kingdom alone—quite apart from the rest of the sterling area— is on a massive scale. Our imports in the past year were just under £6,000 million and our exports were just over £5,000 million. But we have to take account of the transactions of the sterling area as well. If payment for all sterling area imports from the rest of the world for just one week were made one week early this could cost our reserves over £150 million immediately. Of course, there can be an element of speculation in this, but to be realistic I think that the precautionary motive rather than the hope of speculative gain must be the motive we have got to attribute to these transactions.'

Whatever the motives of buyers and sellers, the fact that sterling is a currency in such wide use, mistrust of Britain's capacity to support it, and uncertainty about the future of the world monetary system, combined to cause the chronic and apparently endless tribulations of the pound.

An additional burden on sterling is that not only is it used as a currency for world business, but it is (again, in company with the dollar) a 'reserve currency,' in which some countries (both their governments and their private sectors) keep a proportion of their reserves, depositing the money in London, usually with banks or in British Government securities. This 'reserve' function is generally the first to be mentioned when people talk of sterling's international position, though it's the money in everyday commercial use rather than the money left more or less permanently in London that has caused most of the pound's troubles. To be a reserve currency sounds rather grand; it adds to Britain's prestige that other countries should treat her as a banker.

A proportion of the balances come from non-sterling countries, but most of them are from inside the Sterling Area.[5] The area isn't finite, and it is slowly falling apart; it came into being in the 1930s, was officially defined in 1940 as a wartime measure, and has continued since the war as a group of countries which pool their earnings of non-sterling currencies in London. In its capacity as banker, Britain is known to hold over £3,000 million from sterling area countries—foreign currencies worth that amount have been changed into pounds and deposited in London. Further large but unknown sums are invested in shares and other assets. Something under half the total is private money as opposed to official deposits. Since the Sterling Area countries are all busy making their own place in the world, the balances in London are always liable to be taken away for political and economic reasons. A country may drift away, as Australia seems

[5] It includes Australia, New Zealand, Malaysia, Singapore, Hong Kong, India, Pakistan, Ceylon, South Africa, various African States, and Arab oil States such as Kuwait and Libya.

to be doing, because it is establishing its own currency for international use (in this case, the Australian dollar). As Britain withdraws its forces from the Far East, places like Hong Kong and Malaysia may decide to keep more of their reserves in dollars as they see the links with Britain weakening. The oil-producing Arab countries are a perpetual headache because their enormous balances are at the mercy of the rulers and rich men of small, volatile States, who might decide to reduce them for purely political reasons. One country alone, Kuwait in the Persian Gulf, is known to have £350 million officially invested in London, and is thought to have not less than another £600 million privately invested. This is nearly a billion pounds, controlled by the Government of a country with a population of half a million, and by a handful of Kuwaiti's citizens—fewer than 20 families own nine-tenths of the country's private foreign investment.

During the Arab-Israeli war in 1967, Arab oil States reacted against what they saw as Western imperialism with various expression of rage which included taking some of their money away from London. Most of it seems to have gone to Switzerland, whose banks promptly reinvested it in London. No great damage was done, but the episode underlined the dangers of relying too heavily on the members of what used to be thought of hopefully as a sort of near-British club.

Governments, companies and individuals hold sterling, whether as reserves or for trading, because it suits them to. Sentiment and habit may play a tiny part; but London's high interest rates, and the fact that pounds are in continual daily use, are the only reasons that matter. Britain makes a convenient bank. The bank has considerable advantages, which include the machinery of the City; it has equally considerable defects, which are partly the fault of Britain, partly the fault of the system.

These defects are relevant to Britain's attempts to enter the Common Market. The six E.E.C. countries worry that sterling's troubles might be catching. One can also detect an undercurrent of irritation on the Continent at the way the British perpetually moan about the 'burdens' of sterling, while keeping quiet about its advantages—in prestige, resources and commissions earned by the channelling of so much business through London. 'It is always nice to have the assets without the liabilities,' wrote an honest City banker in the

Bankers' magazine, 'but having had the money and the resources which that represents, it is not too reasonable to complain about the debt. By and large, as anyone in the banking business knows, it is a good thing to have deposits, and provided one makes proper use of the resources they represent it is a profitable thing. Britain has, in fact, gained from having had the use of the resources, and from the use of sterling as a reserve and trading currency.'

By the end of 1967, anxiety over sterling had become the most potent objection to British entry into the E.E.C. A long report by the E.E.C. Commission in October that year was generally favourable to Britain, apart from the chapter which dealt with sterling. This was cool and critical, and led to angry complaints in London that it had been written by the awful French. The French commissioner, M. Raymond Barré, was mainly responsible for the chapter, but the grumbling in Whitehall missed the point: what the chapter said was true. 'The grave doubts about sterling in the Commission's report are entirely justified,' wrote a British economist, Professor Alan Day.

The solution, it was widely agreed, would be for Britain to end its balance-of-payments deficit. But as well as criticising the British economy, the report pointed to the danger to which sterling was exposed by being a reserve and trading currency. It appeared to be saying that this put Britain at a serious disadvantage, but its precise meaning was clouded by the Civil Service language, and also, one suspects, by a general uncertainty as to how any country can stop its currency from being an international one, even if this is what it desires. No Government decreed that sterling should be a world currency, as Mr James Callaghan used to point out when he was Chancellor of the Exchequer: it just happened. And the No. 2 at the I.M.F., Mr Frank A. Southard, once said that 'it has never been quite clear to me just how a country whose currency is a reserve currency would set about abolishing its role.' It might be possible eventually to merge sterling and its embarrassing balances into a new common currency for use within the E.E.C.; but no one seriously thinks there is any chance of such a currency being adopted for many years to come.

The troubled career and complicated destiny of sterling are sufficient to give the French and any other opponents of British entry into the Common Market ample excuse for barring the door. Much of the wrangling to come in Brussels, Paris and London will centre on the pound and its place in tomorrow's Europe, and this in turn will be bound up with what happens to the world's money system. Sterling's troubles belong to Britain in particular, but everyone else is entitled to a share.

Sources

Interviews provided most of the material for this book. Banks, stock exchanges, etc, supplied quantities of literature about themselves in particular and their countries' systems in general. Other sources: English-language journals such as the London *Economist*, *Banker* and *Financial Times*, and the American *Fortune* and *Business Week*.

Books:

Comparative Banking. Edited by H. W. Auburn. Macmillan London.

Banks of the World. By Roger Orsingher. Macmillan, London.

Eight European Central Banks. Published under the auspices of the Bank for International Settlements, Basle.

The Rothschilds. By Frederic Morton. Penguin Books, London.

The Merchant Bankers. By Joseph Wechsberg. Weidenfeld & Nicholson, London.

The Development of a European Capital Market. Report of a group of experts appointed by the E.E.C. Commission. Published by the Commission in Brussels.

The European Capital Market. (Report of a two-day conference). Federal Trust for Education and Research, London.

Capital Markets in Atlantic Economic Relationships. By Dr Sidney E. Rolfe. Published by the Atlantic Institute, Paris.

The Principal Stock Exchanges of the World. International Economic Publishers, Washington.

The City in the World Economy. By W. M. Clarke. Published by the Institute of Economic Affairs, London.

How the City Works. By Oscar R. Hobson. Published by the News Chronicle, London.

The Corporation of London. Oxford University Press.

Committee on the Working of the [*British*] *Monetary System* (the Radcliffe Report), Cmnd 827. Published by the Stationery Office.

Proceedings of the Bank Rate Tribunal. Published by the Stationery Office.

In the Red. The Struggle for Sterling 64/66. By Henry Brandon. Deutsch, London.

Montagu Norman. By Andrew Boyle. Cassell, London.

The City. By Paul Ferris. Pelican Books, London.

The Gnomes of Zurich. By T. R. Fehrenbach. Leslie Frewin, London.

The Banking System of Switzerland. By Hans J. Bär, in collaboration with Ernst Rüesch. Published by Zurich Buchdruckerei Schulthess.

Zurich as a Center of Finance. By F. E. Aschinger. Published by Neue Zürcher Zeitung, Zurich.

French Banking Structure and Credit Policy. By J. S. G. Wilson. Harvard University Press.

Gold or Credit? By Francis Cassell. Pall Mall Press, London, for the Federal Trust for Education and Research.

Money International. By Fred Hirsch. Allen Lane the Penguin Press, London.

Inside Europe Today. By John Gunther. Hamish Hamilton, London.

Modern Banking. By R. S. Sayers. Clarendon Press, Oxford.

Index